ANDY
SE...

...e Mask

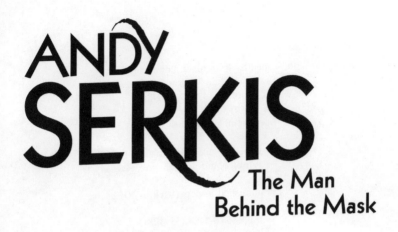

ANDY SERKIS
The Man Behind the Mask

JUSTIN LEWIS

JOHN BLAKE

Published by John Blake Publishing Ltd,
3 Bramber Court, 2 Bramber Road,
London W14 9PB, England

www.johnblakepublishing.co.uk

www.facebook.com/Johnblakepub facebook
twitter.com/johnblakepub twitter

First published in paperback in 2012

ISBN: 978-1-84358-408-7

British Library Cataloguing-in-Publication Data:

A catalogue record for this book is available from the British Library.

Design by www.envydesign.co.uk

Printed in Great Britain by CPI Group (UK) Ltd

1 3 5 7 9 10 8 6 4 2

Papers used by John Blake Publishing are natural, recyclable products made
from wood grown in sustainable forests. The manufacturing processes
conform to the environmental regulations of the country of origin.

Every attempt has been made to contact the relevant
copyright-holders, but some were unobtainable. We would
be grateful if the appropriate people could contact us.

CONTENTS

INTRODUCTION

When *The Two Towers*, the second film in Peter Jackson's lavish epic screen trilogy of J. R. R. Tolkien's *The Lord of the Rings*, became a worldwide box-office sensation at Christmas 2002, the big mystery surrounded the grotesque, crawling and emaciated figure of Gollum. Because he had been developed via computer-generated imagery (CGI), it was assumed that the man who was playing the role of Gollum had merely donated a voice for him, as someone might do for any kind of animated character. In fact, Andy Serkis had played every aspect of Gollum – physical, emotional and psychological – and his physical movements and facial expressions were converted digitally into a specially created version of the character. But just who was the man behind the mask of Gollum? Who *was* Andy Serkis?

Perhaps one of the many reasons why Serkis's Gollum made such an impression was that the actor was not a star name, and so few who saw the films had any preconceptions about him. He had been a versatile professional actor since 1985, constantly in demand with stage roles all over Britain. His virtuosic level of physical acting had made some theatre critics single him out of a cast by name, but, despite landing roles on TV and in films, it took the Tolkien trilogy to bring his name to millions.

The Lord of the Rings made Andy Serkis an internationally renowned actor, and he has remained loyal to Peter Jackson's film work, having collaborated with him again on *King Kong* and, more recently, once more as Gollum in the forthcoming multi-instalment adaptation of Tolkien's *The Hobbit*. Meanwhile, his work with CGI has also been seen in *Rise of the Planet of the Apes* and *The Adventures of Tintin: The Secret of the Unicorn*. But elsewhere he has continued to wear a variety of masks for other characters, too, both real and fictional figures, from Albert Einstein to Bill Sikes, culminating in his award-winning and high-profile interpretation of Ian Dury in *Sex & Drugs & Rock & Roll*.

What Serkis brings to each and every part is a commitment, a determination to research the heart, soul and mind of whichever part he has been assigned – and then reporting back his findings to the audience. He also displays a generosity to his fellow actors and collaborators. He regards acting as sharing the limelight with the audience rather than monopolising his performance space.

In this book, we will follow Andy Serkis through his life and career to date. We will discover how his ambition to be an artist as a youth was overtaken by a raging passion for the stage. We will separately investigate his work for theatre and television, two strands that would intertwine from 1989 onwards, and then introduce a third strand: his first few years in film. Over three chapters, we will dive into Middle-earth and discover how he tied together all of this experience when helping Peter Jackson reinvent Gollum for the screen, before doing the same as Kong in 2004–5. Next, we will explore his thoughts and feelings about portraying villainy and evil on stage and screen, and discover that his highly praised screen performance as Ian Dury was by no means the only time he played a figure who had actually lived. And, finally, we will find out more about his accomplishments as a director, and examine some of his current and future projects. Along the way, we'll also glimpse into his home life with his family and the woman who has been his partner and wife for more than 20 years: fellow actor Lorraine Ashbourne.

No matter who he portrays – ape, pop icon, killer or Gollum – there's always a little bit of Andy Serkis behind the masks of the wide range of figures he has played. 'You can always see yourself,' he told the *Guardian* in November 2010. 'People tell me they can see elements of my personality. It's subtle – timing, eye movement and gestures – but it's there if you look closely.'

CHAPTER 1

RUISLIP, BAGHDAD, LANCASTER

Long regarded as reliable, resourceful and adventurous, Andy Serkis has always been interested in the power of stage and screen acting as 'a transformative experience', seeing how drama can transcend entertainment and actually change people's lives. He has often spoken about acting being a service to the community and a responsibility, which may explain why stardom has – albeit belatedly – found him. As we will see, at no point in his career has he consciously pursued celebrity. 'Working for others is something my parents instilled in us,' Andy said in 2010. 'There was a strong sense of the importance of helping other people.' And Clement and Lylie Serkis's separate but tireless career paths had set a clear example of service and responsibility to their three daughters and two younger sons.

English-born Lylie taught children with special needs, but continued to raise all five of her offspring almost single-handedly. Clement, whose surname had been shortened from Serkissian, was of Armenian descent and worked as a doctor in Iraq throughout the time that Andy and his siblings were growing up. Clement had already qualified as a gynaecologist when he first met his future wife; she was recovering in Baghdad after contracting tuberculosis back in England. Following the couple's marriage, Clement continued to live and work in Iraq, while Lylie and their children would relocate to Ruislip Manor in Middlesex, 13 miles northwest of central London.

Clement and Lylie's fourth child, Andrew, was born on 20 April 1964. In that same year, Clement was one of four medics who co-founded a private hospital in Baghdad called Ibn Sina. The founders had expressed grave concern that the city, despite its size and population, had no hospital with sufficiently modern equipment and facilities. Although it had been founded for the benefit of the ruling class, Clement and his three co-founders fervently believed that Ibn Sina should provide free treatment for anyone in need, regardless of their race, religion or social status.

Until the mid-1970s, the Serkis children would see their father only during school holidays. They would travel to the Iraqi capital of Baghdad, where they would be reunited with him and other relatives. Clement's absence from home life in Ruislip could make Andy a tense youngster.

The boy's unruly nature would mellow with maturity, but would be accompanied by a resigned sense of sadness about his absentee father. 'I always mourn the fact I never got to know my father, or spent time with him,' he told *The Times* in 2009, as Clement was entering his 90th year. To relate to him now was 'unfathomable. It's like, Where do you begin? So much has gone on. So much.' Yet this regret was tempered by an admiration for his father's belief in justice, supporting those people who needed it. 'Times weren't easy for him in Baghdad,' Andy told the *Guardian*, 'but he carried on going there because he believed in what he was doing.'

The childhood trips to the Middle East were certainly enlightening, and would help to give Andy and his siblings a sense of acceptance and flexibility about different countries and cultures that were very different from west London. These journeys, coupled with being brought up by his mother alone, also made Andy start to relate to the idea of being an outsider in society, something that he would explore a great deal in many of his stage and screen roles, from Gollum to Ian Brady. 'We were outsiders,' he said, 'and I've always sympathised with those who feel excluded, probably as a result of this.'

From the age of 11, Andy attended St Benedict's, a Roman Catholic school in the west London district of Ealing. The school's other former pupils have included the biographer and critic Peter Ackroyd, the former Conservative MP and Hong Kong governor Chris (later Lord) Patten, who was appointed chairman of the BBC Trust in 2011, and the comedian Julian Clary. Clary was already entering St Benedict's sixth form when Serkis enrolled at the school in the autumn of 1975. Although it was strictly a boys-only school at that point, some girls were admitted to its sixth form by the end of the 1970s. Serkis remembers 'lots of gangs and lots of fights', but was not on the receiving end of bullying. He did, however, gain a nickname: perhaps inevitably, 'Billy Smarts', after the famous Billy Smart's Circus, whose spectacular shows were a mainstay of festive television at the time.

Andy's passions during his formative years were diverse. He spent his pocket money on model kits, was a lover of cricket (the Australian wicketkeeper Rodney Marsh was a hero) and, before becoming an accomplished saxophonist, he learned to play the clarinet. The first record he ever bought, when he was about eight, was Acker Bilk's clarinet instrumental, 'Stranger on the Shore', which was already around 10 years old at the time. He would become a fan of jazz later on, but the musical soundtrack to his boyhood was heavily influenced by the contents of his older sisters' collections – the soft rock of Fleetwood Mac, Supertramp and Steely Dan. Then, when he was 14, he would first hear the music of Ian Dury, the man he would later portray to great acclaim on the big screen in *Sex & Drugs & Rock & Roll*. He was travelling on a coach for a school trip when he heard 'Hit Me With Your Rhythm Stick'. 'You could hear this voice that wasn't saying anything that you've ever heard before, something that was exotic and magic and weird, and yet dangerous and thrilling.'

Summer visits by the Serkis family to Baghdad – and other places too, including Damascus, Beirut and the ruins of Babylon – had ceased by 1978. Four years earlier, Ibn Sina had been converted into a military hospital by Saddam Hussein. It was now considered too dangerous an environment for their holidays. 'Things began to get dodgy, and we couldn't travel out there any longer,' remembered Andy 30 years later. It would be some time before his dad returned to home turf, though: after being imprisoned briefly by the Saddam regime, Clement did not permanently relocate to the UK till 1990 (the year before Operation Desert Storm), by which time Andy was in his mid-20s. Clement's sister was still resident in Iraq in 2007, when Andy explained to *Wired* magazine, 'People forget that there are still people there who are not radicalised in any particular direction, trying to live normal lives in a very difficult situation.'

At around the age of 14, then, Andy Serkis may have no longer been able to have exciting trips to other continents, but a sense of adventure had been planted in his mind and body, and he needed to continue that thirst for new challenges. It was at this point that an interest in climbing became apparent. Before long, the interest became a passion. With a few friends, he formed a mountaineering club at St Benedict's, and soon they had progressed from hill walking to trekking and eventually to proper climbing. By then, his love for the activity was so entrenched that it helped him decide where he would further his education. Lancaster University in the North of England was on the doorstep of the Lake District, home to the highest peaks in England.

Lancaster University also boasted a highly esteemed visual-arts course. Andy was a budding artist even when young, deeply obsessed with painting and drawing. It was 'one thing that really took a grip on me', and, even when his mother had tried to convince him that he needed to get a proper job, he felt certain that art was the path for him. But he wasn't sure how one became a professional artist. By the age of 16, he was aware that edging into the world of design and graphics might help maximise his chances, and so he applied for a visual-arts course at Lancaster.

Serkis's independent spirit had formed. As time

progressed, he seemed less and less likely to follow a safe, if secure, career. He was driven by instinct and desire. Years later, he would summarise this as, 'I'm only really good at things I want to do and I'm hopeless at putting any effort into things I don't want to do.' His understandably cautious mother and father hoped he might knuckle down for something reliable as a career. Lylie figured he might join the army or become a surveyor. Clement may have hoped – so Andy thought – that he might have opted for anything 'apart from becoming an actor, really...he worried that it was precarious, that the art world was a precarious living.'

Andy Serkis arrived at Lancaster University in the autumn of 1982. He was intent on concentrating solely on visual arts – that course encompassed sculpture, painting and graphic design – but he was also obliged to plump for a second option. Reluctant to do so at first, he eventually chose theatre studies, as he became aware that that department was a strong one there: the university campus had its own theatre, the Nuffield Studio Theatre. 'You could get involved in productions, and you could design them, or go more in a direction of stage management. All sorts of areas around theatre, not just acting. They had production meetings and you'd do the whole thing properly, and you'd have a budget.'

Any spare time left over for Serkis was spent either hill walking alone in the wilderness of the Lakes, or participating in broadcasts for the student radio station, Radio Bailrigg. The service was one of the earliest student radio stations in Britain, having been launched in 1969, and over the years its airwaves have also featured regular contributions from future broadcasting giants such as James May (now of television's *Top Gear*) and Richard Allinson, DJ for Capital Radio in London and, latterly, BBC Radio 2.

There was plenty of nightlife on the Lancaster campus. The University Union Great Hall would welcome many high-profile rock acts in the next couple of years, among them Echo & the Bunnymen, Elvis Costello, U2, the Smiths, Julian Cope and even Tina Turner. A newly opened venue, the Sugar House, staged cabaret from many exponents of the 'alternative comedy' boom from the London circuit: Alexei Sayle, Rik Mayall, and the National Theatre of Brent (Patrick Barlow and Jim Broadbent). Nearby, on Moor Lane, there was also the Dukes Playhouse, which would showcase productions ranging from Bertolt Brecht's *The Threepenny Opera* to (in January 1984) the world premiere of a play called *The Life of Einstein*.

It was theatre that became Serkis's obsession. Combining visual arts with theatre studies meant that he was set-designing for productions at the Nuffield Studio Theatre. He became involved at an opportune moment. Prior to the 1982–3 academic year, the theatre had been predominantly staging musical events. Only now was a greater emphasis being placed on drama and revue. The Theatre Studies department staged a wide range of productions from classical theatre to contemporary works, and they were often bold and left-field in their choices.

Before long, Andy Serkis became a lighting designer as well as a set designer at the Nuffield Studio, but incidental performing roles came up too from time to time: minor appearances in Shakespeare's *Henry IV Part I* in early 1983 and a new play by Tony Marchant called *The Lucky Ones*. He was fascinated by the theatre, and not just by those who performed, either. Years later, he recalled how, while still an undergraduate, he had been enthralled to visit a London production of the musical *Little Shop of Horrors*. Every aspect of the production interested him, down to wondering how the brickwork on the sets for the 'little shop' had been painted. Theatre was an inviting new world, an exciting destination to escape to, just like the Baghdads and Damascuses he had visited as a child.

Actually *working* in theatre was a different proposition from watching it, though, obviously. The demystification started in his first term at Lancaster, and it was a slightly disappointing discovery to find that, for instance, no one painted the reverse sides of the sets. 'I just thought that these things were real, from watching things as a kid. "What's on the other side of this wall? Oh, you can see the plywood." It's a bit of a shame, really.'

A life-changing moment for Andy Serkis came in his third term at Lancaster, in the summer of 1983, when he was cast in the lead role of a confrontational play. *Gotcha* was penned by the playwright Barrie Keeffe in the mid-1970s, and told the story of a disaffected pupil at school (known as 'The Kid') who, on the final day of term, holds his chemistry teacher hostage. 'He has this packet of 20 cigarettes and he's holding them over the petrol tank of a motorbike and basically launches a tirade at this teacher. I thought it was so powerful,' remembered Serkis. But he was already familiar with the play, anyway, from a TV showing six years earlier. He had seen it on television just days before his 13th birthday in April 1977, when a production of it – starring

Phil Davis as The Kid – had been shown as part of the BBC's long-running *Play for Today* strand.

Gotcha had also been performed in Lancaster a few months earlier when a visiting theatre company staged it at the city's Dukes Playhouse. It is not known if Serkis saw it there, but there's no doubt that, when he was cast as The Kid, he felt totally liberated to immerse himself in the persona of someone else. He instinctively recognised a lost soul in The Kid, 'factory fodder...who was going to be undervalued for the rest of his life. I could tell people about it.' When he communicated the role at the university theatre in Lancaster, he knew that he couldn't sit behind a drawing board for the rest of his life. 'When I played that role, that was it. I knew this is what I wanted to do at the age of 19,' he said. He felt so comfortable in connecting with such a powerful character that he thought, 'I'll have some more of that.' Of course, he wanted to prance about onstage, but it was also 'a real calling'.

So it was, in the balmy summer of 1983 – the close of his first academic year at Lancaster University – that Andy Serkis decided to drop visual arts and change course. Fortunately, Lancaster had a module system whereby a student could build a degree (called an Independent Studies Degree) from lots of seemingly disparate subjects. 'I drew elements from the arts. I still did little bit of set designing. I concentrated on areas like Stanislavski and Brecht and theatre history, and then some practical stuff like mime and dance.' His artistic background would serve him well in acting, too, when it came to spatial awareness: being able to relate to different environments, and understanding what one's relationship is within that space.

Serkis was full of trepidation, though, as to how to convince his parents that he was doing the right thing. They, who would have preferred their firstborn son to embrace a career as a lawyer – 'something solid and professional' – had been uneasy enough that he had planned to be a painter. For him now to reject art in favour of acting would, for a short time, horrify them. 'There was this resounding silence down the telephone,' he told *The Times*'s Hugo Rifkind in 2010.

But both Clement and Lylie had carved out successful careers – in medicine and education – in contexts that can be unpredictable and that require flexibility and sensitivity. Both of their professions have required them to react to occurrences that are unfamiliar at times. That familiarity with the unfamiliar had been mirrored in Serkis's travels back and forth from the Middle East during his earlier years, which would lay the foundations for the unpredictability of acting. 'It was having a childhood filled with journeys and new experiences that prepared me for it. It was putting yourself onto a path and not quite knowing where you were going to end up, that was at the root of my life.'

CHAPTER 2

THE INVESTIGATOR: SERKIS AND STAGE WORK

Having abandoned visual arts as his university degree in favour of his second option, theatre studies, Andy Serkis now knew that he wanted to be an actor. He remained a member of the company at the Nuffield Studio Theatre, but the democratic nature of the department meant that productions were not star vehicles; they were for a group of performers who all held equal weight. 'I'm really glad that I went that way, and didn't go to drama school,' Serkis later said of his time at Lancaster. Understanding the collaborative nature of theatre would help years later when he was confronted by the challenge of playing roles like Gollum and Kong. Serkis would always relish working with those behind the scenes. 'I've been more open to that than, perhaps, some other actors who might not have wanted to get involved in it.'

Working on stage would teach Serkis stamina of all kinds:

physical, psychological, emotional. It also helped him focus his mind and concentrate. 'You don't learn that concentration on a film set, but to play a role through two or three hours of a night, every night, and to prove it and to constantly evolve it over a period of a run...It is like you do get your emotional ballast from doing theatre.' Serkis would come to apply this same focus for his later, substantial career in television and film.

Serkis would occasionally land a mention when the local press showed up to review one of the department's many productions. One particularly positive notice came in January 1984, when he was cast as the villainous Iago in William Shakespeare's *Othello*, under the direction of department tutor Keith Sturgess. A critic from the local newspaper, the *Lancaster Guardian*, wrote of Serkis, 'A fine performance. If he had any first-night nerves, these were certainly not detectable.' Serkis would revisit the part of Iago nearly 20 years later at Manchester's Royal Exchange Theatre for what remains, at the time of writing, his last major acting role for the stage.

From time to time, opportunities at other major roles abounded. In May 1985, almost exactly two years after *Gotcha*, Serkis found himself in another schoolroom play, this time Nigel Williams's *Class Enemy*. Set in inner-city London, it followed six teenage boys, one of whom (Serkis, whose character was nicknamed 'Iron') used a mixture of charisma and cruelty to squeeze a five-minute 'lesson' out of each of his peers.

Class Enemy was one of Serkis's last outings as a student actor. During that summer of 1985, he graduated from Lancaster University, and – as luck would have it – found himself in gainful employment almost straight away. He had been advised to seek a postgraduate place at a drama school or college, but, happily, his good fortune had secured him his first professional acting job. Because of the links between the university and the city's Dukes Playhouse theatre, he had spent a good deal of his final academic year there, building sets and working behind the scenes. In this way, he got to know Jonathan Petherbridge, who in 1984 had been appointed the Dukes' artistic director.

Petherbridge gave Serkis his break, and took him on as part of the theatre's repertory company. He could not have worked as a professional actor in the UK without an Equity card and, at that time, only two Equity cards per year were given out by each rep theatre. 'They were gold dust,' said Serkis. 'It was a closed shop at the time – you could not work as an actor unless you had an Equity card.' Serkis was, in his words, 'over the moon' at securing his Equity card, but, by his own admission, he was so naïve about how the theatre business worked for actors that he was to have a momentary panic on his first day of rehearsal at the Dukes. 'I was so green, I turned up, and there was an actor standing outside. He said, "Can I see your Equity card, please?" ' On telling him that it had not arrived in the post, the more experienced actor refused him entry. Momentarily crushed, Serkis soon found, to his relief, that it was a wind-up.

Over a period of about two years, then, from July 1985, Serkis would work consistently (though not exclusively) at the Dukes. His first role there was in a production of *Privates on Parade*. It was a musical set around the exploits of a military concert party of British soldiers in Singapore and Malaysia during the Malayan Emergency of the late

1940s. The cast was put through its paces by a former drill instructor with the Scots Guards. Twenty years later, just as Serkis was opening in *King Kong* all around the world, the Dukes' archivist Bernard Gladstone remembered in the *Lancashire Evening Post* just how keen Serkis had been to get involved in everything. 'Whether it was a musical, a panto or a serious play, he wanted to be in it. He was always full of life, and always keen to play oddball characters.'

'We had strong work ethics and practices,' Serkis has said of his time in rep in Lancaster, 'and you had to get this amount of subsistence. I remember getting the regional Equity deputy to come down to us. I was quite militant, saying, "We're not going to do this, unless we get our proper money."' It was a stance worth taking in Serkis's view, shared by countless others in the arts, because of the sharp cuts to regional theatre funding under Margaret Thatcher's three terms as prime minister. But, all the same, 'the whole thing just got demoralised and every actor had to do more work for less'. On the other hand, did it mean that it was worth making actors hungrier to make their mark, in order to find out that they *really* wanted to act? Anyone whose heart wasn't quite in it would soon find out. 'People who really wanted to do it found a way there,' admitted Serkis. 'By hook or by crook, they worked out their contracts. People really, really went for it, because they believed that that's what they wanted to do.'

Serkis's time in rep under Petherbridge would be an invaluable apprenticeship. He later said of his artistic director, 'His philosophy really affected me for a long time, in terms of how the theatre related to the community, and his whole attitude towards theatre being about storytelling, and the power of changing a local community with theatre. I carried that ethos for a long time.' The communal nature of the Playhouse's environment extended to some of the actors helping with musical content on some productions, and jazz lover Serkis would enhance several productions with his saxophone playing.

Some of Petherbridge's workshops were inspired by the work of the Brazilian theatre director Augusto Boal, who founded the Theatre of the Oppressed. One of Boal's techniques was to visit South American communities and encourage the people, who were not professional actors or playwrights, to devise their own plays based on their own experiences and difficulties. 'They'd literally workshop what their common problems were for wherever they lived,' said Serkis. 'If it was oppression by the police, it would be that.' Any production like this would be sufficiently open for any member of an audience watching the play to become part of it, to take over the role of the protagonist and influence the direction of the story. But Boal also believed that the way to act was to research, and bring back evidence to feed into a role. 'The job is to bring back the evidence,' explained Serkis. 'Go out, research it as thoroughly as possible, inhabit it, bring it back, and get it to the audience.'

It was quite a principle, one that pushed an actor to be responsible and communicative, the very antithesis of self-indulgence. Only by investigating a part as thoroughly as possible could an actor hope to access the full persona of a character, and then be able to convey their findings to their fellow performers, a director and an audience. Serkis was eager to conduct this level of research, although, in retrospect, he had to admit to an occasional part that failed to fire him up in the right way. He regarded Shakespeare's *The Winter's Tale* at the Dukes in October 1985 as one of his misfires. On the whole, it was well received, and the presentation was novel: the Dukes auditorium was converted so that the audience was on the move throughout, following the cast of 11 around the arena; the actors also functioned as ushers, musicians and guides for the audiences, who were themselves unofficially cast as onlookers to the action that unfolded. One newspaper review recommended that any paying customers should bring 'sensible shoes and a cushion'.

Serkis found his own reading of Prince Florizel somewhat lacking: if the job of acting is to investigate a character and report back to the audience, he felt he had floundered during *The Winter's Tale*'s four-week run. 'I found nothing of any interest to show anybody,' he confessed in 2003. 'It's only in hindsight that you realise that you've completely fucked up, basically. It's just a sense of feeling totally unrooted, and that's because you've not found something to connect with.'

Even so, if Serkis felt that he fell short on one play at the Dukes, there would be another one along within a few weeks or – at most – a month. Repertory theatre work required any actor to be versatile and flexible, and Serkis would find himself during 1986 and 1987 appearing in everything from pantomimes to Agatha Christie mysteries, and from musicals to specially commissioned works by local writers. 'They all required different skills, playing different age ranges, completely different parts of society.'

Still only in his early twenties, Serkis was battling to establish an identity for himself, both as a young man and as a stage performer. He was obliged to imagine experiences that had not happened to him. What might it be like to play a man apprehensive about his impending marriage to a neurotic fiancée? He could explore such thoughts and feelings when cast as thirtysomething Paul in the Stephen Sondheim musical *Company*. Similarly, how might he react if his own career prospects in acting were compromised by a physical injury? A part as an ageing thespian in Ronald Harwood's *The Dresser* provided food for thought. How would he contrast his performances as two different newspaper editors in the same play (as he would in Howard Brenton and David Hare's satire on the news media, *Pravda*)? Onstage and off, Andy Serkis was growing up fast.

Such was the diverse nature of the Dukes' productions that the lack of typecasting encouraged actors like Serkis to attempt lots of working methods rather than rely on one single approach to performance. Serkis, for his part, found it unhelpful to have his mind crammed with the spectres of his previous characters, and would try his hardest to stay in the moment with any part: 'I just tend to stick to the relevant – the world that we're creating, wherever the director's leading you.'

After performing in more than a dozen different plays at the Dukes Playhouse, Andy Serkis took his leave of Lancaster in 1987. He had been mostly resident there for nearly five years, and through university and rep theatre had already learnt so much. 'My enjoyment of acting comes from inhabiting other characters,' he would later say. 'To be able to do that so regularly, and to be performing one and then rehearsing another…It was just a joy, really.' It was a wealth of useful material he would call upon in his future career.

Performing with touring theatre companies would bring

some fresh practical challenges. While it would be fun to visit a new town every week, the accommodation would often be cramped. 'Of course, you're doing it for no money, and you're doing it all yourself – that's enjoyable, at that level, when you're that age.' For a man in his twenties, it was another stage in a career adventure. 'They were great days, because they were formative years. It was the stuff you really believed in – and I'm not saying I don't believe in stuff now, because I do – but it was just fuelled by that youthful enthusiasm.'

Serkis's Lancaster swansong (in July 1987) was as Lysander in the Shakespeare comedy *A Midsummer Night's Dream*, but it was staged outdoors, at the city's 40-acre Williamson Park. A few years later, Jonathan Petherbridge explained to the *Independent* why the park was an ideal space for works by the Bard. 'The audience feel they're going through the same experience as the young lovers. You have to plan it carefully, though, to keep the structure clear. And few writers apart from Shakespeare have broad enough shoulders to take outdoor productions.'

Serkis and the director would reunite in the future, most notably in 1990, on another open-air project: Bertolt Brecht's *The Threepenny Opera*. By the summer of that year, Petherbridge was running the London Bubble Tent, whose speciality lay in organising plays in parks in and around London. The Bubble Tent's priority was to entertain, but hopefully not in a superficial fashion. 'Half our audience doesn't go to see any other theatre,' the director told the *Independent*. 'People come because it's colourful. In the evening, the tent has a wonderful atmosphere – and if it rains you feel like boy scouts.'

Serkis had made his London stage debut in November 1987 in Nigel Gearing's *Berlin Days, Hollywood Nights* (where he would share the limelight with another rising star, the comic improvisational actor and singer Josie Lawrence), but it was the following spring that he became involved in the most ambitious and gruelling project of his career up to that point: a two-part, seven-hour epic tragedy at the Lyric Theatre in Hammersmith, west London.

Faust – based on a German legend – was a cross between a play and a long poem, which had been written in the early nineteenth century by the German author Johann Wolfgang von Goethe. A sprawling circus of a production that blended folklore, philosophy, romance, theology and broad humour, its sheer spectacle and length meant that no one had attempted to stage it in Britain thus far in the twentieth century. Few had even tried to bring it to life in its German homeland. Under the guidance of opera director David Freeman, the cast of 12 actors (led by Simon Callow in the title role) and one musician had their work cut out, with multiple roles for some of the company: Serkis would play eight different roles across the duology. A great deal of physical stamina and agility was additionally required of the players, who had to tackle, among other things, ropes, nets and ladders.

Faust is a figure who cannot be satisfied. He is driven by a frenzied curiosity towards a sense of contentment that both attracts and repels him. He is a chameleon of a character who, by turns, is a knight and a civil engineer, and in one review was likened to enigmatic figures both real and fictional, from Howard Hughes to Peer Gynt and Orson Welles's Citizen Kane.

Faust's three-month residency at the Lyric began in April 1988. Parts I and II ran on alternate nights of the week, but each Saturday brought a killer double bill. Simon Callow would begin each Part I as a 70-year-old Faust delivering a 40-minute speech, before being rejuvenated as a man in his mid-twenties, then coursing to the ripe old age of 120. He described the experience as like 'climbing a mountain every day', and explained to the *New York Times* that the complex personae of his role required him to overcome 'an unbelievable series of hurdles', from the plaintive despair of his opening soliloquy to the many shifts in voice, posture and attitude that made the ageing process of the part believable to an audience. 'What I'm always striving for is a state of jazz, where things could always be different even when they're not.'

Callow believed that, in order to tackle a multifaceted part like this, it was necessary to be ahead of the text and be at one with Faust's thought processes of the character. Having painstakingly memorised his many lines, he felt it appropriate to half-forget them, so that he could retain some spontaneity for each performance, and remain receptive to whatever else was happening around him. 'What characterises great actors is their ability to enter into the thought processes of the character,' he said. It was the sort of commitment – investigating and researching a character – that Andy Serkis was already starting to appreciate.

The boldness of *Faust* was a partial response to an uncertain, worrying period for the Lyric. It had not been long since it had narrowly escaped closure. For its artistic director, Peter James, it was a throwing-down of the gauntlet. If the Lyric was to exist, it would be through taking a risk with something like *Faust*. 'Everyone walked tall after that and thought, Two fingers to the world – we've done something good.'

It is striking how many similarities a production like *Faust* shares with a project like the *Lord of the Rings* cinematic trilogy over a decade later: hard to realise convincingly as a spectacle, an epic length, a central complex character who requires great shifts of tone, and, perhaps above all else, a production that demanded that all involved should take risks. Reviewers for *Faust* did not call it flawless by any means, but most felt that it was well worth trying for the dazzling heights it did achieve, and despite any shortcomings that came about during the journey. Actors, directors, theatre companies, filmmakers – all must take risks from time to time.

Inspired by how investigating a character could make that character more real, Andy Serkis would reach greater heights on the London stage from the early 1990s. He aimed to explore method acting more and more, hoping to gain as much detail and authenticity as possible. But occasionally he was in danger of identifying too closely with a creation, and losing himself, for the sake of nailing a part. 'I kind of nearly sent myself insane playing one role,' he said much later. That role was of Dogboy, in *Hush*, a play by the British dramatist April de Angelis, which was staged at London's Royal Court theatre in August and September 1992.

In *Hush*, Rosa (Dervla Kirwan) is trying to come to terms with her mother's suicide the previous year, but discovers that she is pregnant after sleeping with a schizophrenic, homeless man on the beach. When the man finds that his dog has died, he suffers a breakdown, and in his anguish absorbs the canine's spirit. He comes to be known as Dogboy, and shows up at Rosa's family home on all-fours, naked and caked in mud, a creature summed up by a critic in *The Stage* as 'a sort of modern refugee from the cruel world of *King Lear*'. His invasion of Rosa's family home has a major effect on their relatively comfortable existence.

As the despairing Dogboy, Serkis does not utter a decipherable word. His way of communicating is through barks, yelps and growls, and he is symptomatic of all that cannot be contained or tamed. 'We are not supposed to like or dislike him,' observed the *Independent on Sunday*. 'That is who he is.' Dogboy acts as an uncomfortable reminder about those on the outside of society, and their often desperate need to be heard and helped. 'What do you do about people who don't quite fit?' asked the *Financial Times* critic. 'Throw them out, try to be nice to them, or send them to the social security?'

The critics were unanimous that Andy Serkis had excelled himself in the most courageous way as Dogboy, prepared to be naked and primal on stage for two and a half hours. Many years later, Serkis singled out *Hush* as the best possible preparation for Gollum in *The Lord of the Rings*, who also spent countless hours crouched on all-fours. Dogboy prepared him for the challenge of embodying someone with such extreme physical and psychological behaviour.

In order to understand the character of Dogboy and his motivations, though, Serkis spent several weeks living rough on the streets. It was an early example of the lengths he would go to in order to be as true as possible to a role. He would become near-evangelical about his belief in acting, in how he regarded it as his chosen path in life, and the closest thing he had to a religious belief. He had long ago renounced the Catholicism of his childhood. 'Once you become an actor, you can't adhere to these things,' he told *The Times* in 2006. 'Acting doesn't allow for absolutism. The questions you're asked are too big to adhere to one belief system, and, whether that weakens you or not, I don't know. I suppose sometimes I do wish I had the resolve of one belief system as a guiding measure.'

The totality of Serkis's commitment – which he described as 'an all-consuming quest' – reached some kind of limitation during his preparation to become Dogboy. 'I found that a hard role to shake off,' he said in 2008 to the *Sunday Telegraph*. 'It really messed with my head.' Exploring Dogboy would, inevitably, become harrowing and dispiriting in an almost uncontrollable and even unhealthy way, 'just getting deeply depressed about the hopelessness of the character and the world he lived in. I suppose I got consumed by the role, but they do always affect me. Can't not.' That sort of extreme research would be diluted once family life intervened during Serkis's thirties. 'It does alter drastically when you have children because you have to come home as a sane human being.'

After the hard-won triumph of *Hush*, Andy Serkis became a regular attraction in Royal Court offerings. A radical and irreverent adaptation of Shakespeare's *King Lear*, with Tom Wilkinson in the title role, opened there in January 1993. This version of Lear was set in the Edwardian era, where the Fool (Serkis) is portrayed as a transvestite, wearing a satin frock, bouffant hair-do (later removed to reveal a shaven head) and a padded bra. The reasoning behind this was to show that, with no sign of a queen in the play, the king is unable to relate to real women and so must confide in the comic jester figure of the Fool.

The sight of a Fool in drag, flitting from falsetto to no-nonsense south London gruffness, and strumming a ukulele to accompany his own original compositions, was a reworking too far for some pundits. Serkis was variously described as a 'fashion accessory' (London *Evening Standard*), looking like Angela Lansbury (*Sunday Express*), looking like Charley's Aunt (*Daily Express*), and resembling 'something between Dame Hilda Bracket and a tougher, punked-up Julian Clary' (*Independent*). The last of these critics was at least an admiring one, arguing that this Fool-ish portrayal was less about lazy shock tactics than a comment about Lear's misogyny and distrust of women in general.

The decision to play the Fool as a Victorian music-hall drag artist (the closest thing to womanhood in Lear's eyes) was, indeed, carefully considered by Serkis and director Max Stafford-Clark during rehearsals. Serkis carried out thorough research into music-hall turns of the late nineteenth and early twentieth centuries, examining their respective performing styles. 'I sort of created my own act, if you like, and then brought that back into the play.' He also penned some songs – for voice and ukulele – inspired by the period's music-hall oeuvre, and which were garnished with Shakespeare's original words. However, while the original play does not record the fate of the Fool (he simply disappears around two-thirds of the way through), in this production, Serkis's incarnation of him is shown to be the victim of a hanging.

Assisted by some television exposure (see Chapter 4), by the early 1990s Serkis's stage roles, in both London and the provinces, had been steadily growing in stature, from incidental to supporting – and to starring ones. And critics on national papers were starting to take notice of him. Take, for instance, his contribution to the musical comedy *Sugar*, staged at the West Yorkshire Playhouse in Leeds at Christmas 1990. Some performers might have been tempted, if appearing in a musical comedy based on the screenplay of *Some Like it Hot*, simply to watch Billy Wilder's classic film and do little more than mimic the relevant actor. To the relief of the *Observer*'s Michael Coveney, Andy Serkis had not just copied Jack Lemmon as Jerry/Daphne. 'Serkis does not attempt to squeeze out Lemmon,' he wrote early in January 1991, 'but recycles him to match his own juice. This is a wise and cunning ploy. He respects the audience's memory of the film while asserting his own right to bounce off it.'

Since Coveney's appraisal, Serkis has been praised on many other occasions for how he has breathed new life into an established character from a much-revered text, be it Shakespeare, Dickens or Tolkien. How did he manage to do that, time and again? He did not watch other actors playing that part. 'If I'm going to do something that's been done before, I won't watch that actor's performance,' he told American reporter Paula Nechak in 2004. 'I'd end up being influenced. I'd feel disempowered, so I try and stay away from other people's ideas.'

What doubtless kept Serkis's mind fresh during the 1990s

was a range of stage projects as broad as those he had been assigned in student drama and repertory theatre days in Lancaster. Drawing on his growing lexicon of imaginative acting techniques and styles, he was every bit as likely to commit to a new play as a classic.

He certainly excelled in *Punchbag*, a newly written comic play for 1993 by *Red Dwarf*'s Robert Llewellyn. It was set in a self-defence class for women, and Serkis donned padded armour to play Peter, a tortured soul whose function is to withstand assaults from members of the class, only to wind up smitten with one of his attackers. On one level, Peter looked absurd, 'like a Gladiator crossed with a Transformer toy' in the words of London's *Evening Standard*. Then again, his marvellous portrayal of sexual frustration and torment for what he was being denied moved the *Guardian*'s Michael Billington to describe him as 'a frog-eyed bundle of unfulfilled lust'. It was not the last time that Serkis would have to be in tip-top physical form, or tackle someone consumed by their own envy and self-disgust.

Plenty of acclaim, then, when it came to singling out Andy Serkis in individual productions. And yet, while each of these had its critical supporters, each had its detractors, too. What will help any performer's reputation, though, is a play or film that is unanimously hailed as a contemporary classic, and, during one summer in the mid-1990s, one such play hit the London stage with considerable force. It also was one of the defining plays of its time, which placed the importance of the ensemble cast above any of its individual players.

Mojo, the first play to be written by 26-year-old Jez Butterworth, was a black comedy – sparky, tense and threatening. Its critical reception was such that it packed out the Royal Court night after night during the scorching summer of 1995. 'That was just a buzz,' remembered Serkis of the sensation it caused, 'going out and playing in front of full houses, knowing that the audience was getting it.'

The play is set in a club in late 1950s Soho. The owner of Ezra's Atlantic club in Dean Street faces a bid from one of his mobster rivals for the headlining act, teenage rock'n'roller Silver Johnny (Hans Matheson). It is not long before Silver Johnny is abducted and his owner is attacked, and then his son, manager and entourage await a further call. With lots of fast, bragging dialogue competing for space among all the cast, Serkis (as Potts) was half of a wisecracking, frequently amusing, sharp-suited double-act with Matt Bardock (as Sweets). Their vaudevillian bantering was just part of an orchestra of voices, each fighting to make itself heard – the sort of lively, noisy barrage of talking that requires careful attention from any audience.

What Butterworth and *Mojo* seemed to achieve, with extraordinary self-assurance, was to refresh and overhaul the stale and overcrowded genre of east London gangster drama. 'A comedy with the psychotic pace of an Alexei Sayle sketch but the verbal precision of Beckett,' commented the *Mail on Sunday*'s admiring critic. With a cast also featuring Tom Hollander and Aiden Gillen, *Mojo* would win several awards, including the 1995 George Devine Award, and led to the funding and shooting of a cinematic version, which also involved Serkis, and which we'll come to in Chapter 5.

Serkis regarded *Mojo* as a highlight of his stage career. Another credit he remains particularly proud of is *Hurlyburly* by the American playwright David Rabe. It was written in 1984, and the cast of its Broadway run had included Harvey Keitel, Sigourney Weaver, William Hurt and – a long time before *Sex and the City* made her a worldwide star – Cynthia Nixon. But it also took 13 years for *Hurlyburly* to be staged on British soil.

As well as Serkis, the cast over the two London runs included future James Bond Daniel Craig, Kelly Macdonald (who had made a remarkable big-screen debut in *Trainspotting* the previous year), Mark Benton, Jenny Seagrove and a young David Tennant. The play is a study of a group of cynical figures in Hollywood culture. All are rootless beings. Serkis played Phil, a troubled ex-con with a seething contempt for the opposite sex. Phil yearns for a big movie break, and badgers an amoral, unscrupulous casting director called Eddie (Rupert Graves), but he cannot control his short fuse and unpredictable, explosive rages. Critics such as the *Guardian*'s Michael Billington were struck by Serkis's 'terrifying sense of uncertainty that manifests itself in acts of random violence. You quiver with apprehension when he holds his baby in his arms.'

Serkis was inspired by *Hurlyburly*'s American-born director, Wilson Milam, to feel free onstage, and to feel relaxed with the part's intensity. It was impossible to phone in a character like Phil. 'Phil was just a dream part, really. Every performance felt like an improvisation.' Not least the opening night. Shortly after 10pm on 24 March 1997, the announcement of a bomb scare meant that everyone at the Old Vic theatre in south London had to be evacuated from the building. So the maiden night of the run climaxed in a small park opposite the venue, with the cast forced to raise their voices above the heckling of the nearby road traffic. There was an implicit understanding that this was an unusual but spontaneous performance of the play, and, when one actor momentarily forgot their next line, an audience member handed them a copy of the script.

Responding to new challenges all the time had become second nature to Andy Serkis. Over many years of stage work, it was rare for him to spend longer than a three-month spell in a stage play, which lengthened the odds on his performing on autopilot. In any case, he recognised that the way to maintain an interest in a role is to address and appreciate the audience. For Serkis, a theatrical audience is forever unpredictable. 'I never see them as passive,' he said. 'They're a living, breathing organism.' Nor was an audience a single entity, but a cluster of individuals, all with their own unique personalities. 'As a young actor, you tend to judge them as a mass. "Oh, they're a bit 'this' tonight", or "Hmmm, they were very quiet." As you get older, you realise audiences are made up of lots of different people.'

This is a Chair, a curio of a stage project from 1997 written by Caryl Churchill, went so far as to reverse the power balance between audience members and stage performers. The staging placed the audience of 60 on the Royal Court stage, with the actors (including Timothy Spall, Lennie James and Linus Roache, as well as Serkis) perched on the front stalls of the auditorium, ready to perform a series of sketches. Each item was preceded by music and a title caption (e.g. 'Hong Kong', 'The Northern Ireland Peace Process') that seemed to bear no relation to the deliberately mundane and everyday scenes that followed.

Serkis didn't just learn from audiences, of course. He had been watching fellow actors and directors, absorbing and assimilating their methods over the years. 'As an actor, you're drawing from lots of different directors all the way down the line. So you do work as a magpie, and you pick up lots of different ways and apply them to whatever's appropriate.' Reluctant to take a shortcut in locating a character, he nevertheless was becoming aware of how his own mind worked in relation to a part. As a result, he was less likely to become trapped in the dead end of a character.

Andy Serkis's many years of stage work were the making of him. They would make him an independent spirit as an actor, bring a powerful energy to his screen output, and make him think carefully about how to inhabit a character's body and soul, and not render them superficial. They would make him sympathetic towards audiences. They would even change his life on a personal level: he would meet his future wife through stage work too.

CHAPTER 3
LORRAINE

When Andy Serkis met fellow actor Lorraine Ashbourne in the last days of the 1980s, it was unlikely that either of them thought for a moment that they would become a couple, marry, have three children, and still be together more than 20 years later – especially in the entertainment business, where there are often unwelcome whispers about the security of celebrity marriages. But, then, neither Serkis nor Ashbourne behaves like a celebrity in the first place. Both are principled, hard-working and acclaimed actors who don't tend to give interviews unless it is to discuss their work. Just occasionally, though, both have offered an insight into their lives together away from acting.

They first met at Manchester's Royal Exchange Theatre in December 1989, when they were cast in the same play. Both were familiar with the venue in different ways. Ashbourne had worked as an usherette there some years earlier. Serkis had trodden its boards in 1988 in a tense and radical interpretation of Shakespeare's *Macbeth*. It was performed as a play within a play: a group of concentration-camp prisoners, all with cropped hair and dressed in striped pyjamas, are forced to mount their own production of the Shakespeare play. With no other costumes or sets to refer to, it became a play for voices, as performed by a nervous company who were in fear not of negative reviews, but of their own lives at the hands of the Nazis.

'It's an incredible theatre, an indoor round space,' Serkis said of the Royal Exchange, which, despite seating a maximum of 750 people, felt like a very intimate venue, because it was in the round. 'You can really sense every single, individual member of the audience – especially with Shakespeare. It worked perfectly in there. I could relate to the audience, too. I was very much feeding off of who they were.'

At the turn of the 1990s, then, Andy and Lorraine opened at this same venue in *She Stoops to Conquer*. Written by Oliver Goldsmith in 1773, the play was a 'comedy of manners', in which characters carefully endeavour to maintain the utmost politeness and etiquette, despite the disasters that unfold around them. It was intended to provide theatregoers with an alternative to the many pantomimes dominating Manchester's other theatres over the Christmas period but, despite its unseasonal flavour, it sold out its entire seven-week run before setting off on a national tour.

Sharing a stage with a cast that at various points included a Yorkshire terrier and a Border collie, Serkis played Tony Lumpkin, an impish playboy with a liking for practical jokes. His mother, Mrs Hardcastle, was portrayed by Una Stubbs, perhaps best known for her long-running role as Rita, daughter of bigot Alf Garnett, in the TV sitcoms *Till Death Us Do Part* and *In Sickness and in Health*. In fact, *She Stoops to Conquer* was not the first time that Stubbs and Serkis had explored the mother–son dynamic: earlier, in 1989, they had done so on television in the BBC comedy series, *Morris Minor's Marvellous Motors* (see Chapter 4).

Lorraine played Mr Hardcastle's lascivious daughter Kate in *She Stoops to Conquer*, so, as she and Andy were playing, essentially, siblings, there would be no sexually charged encounters onstage between them. Was there love at first sight between the pair backstage, though? Seemingly not, as Ashbourne would recall a decade later. 'There was no spark between us at all. I wouldn't say I disliked him. I just didn't get to know him.'

Relations between the pair were very different just over a year later when they shared the stage in another Royal Exchange production. *Your Home in the West* was an angry, gutsy new work by Rod Wooden, set on a rundown estate in the West End of Newcastle upon Tyne. Ashbourne played Jean Robson, a woman trapped in a vicious circle of prostitution and with a daughter likely to follow her into the same line of work. As Jean's Irish boyfriend Sean, Serkis was a club performer with ambition: one scene found him accompanying himself on the guitar as he sang the song 'Your Little Grey Home in the West'.

Your Home in the West was sombre fare all in all, but had it been at all light-hearted, it would have stifled audience empathy for the characters' unhappiness, and been little more than a contemptuous cartoon. And it didn't seem the most obvious environment for romantic relations to flourish between them, but flourish they most certainly soon would. Their personal relationship grew out of a professional need to explore their roles in the play. 'We actually decided to meet in character,' Andy recalled 20 years later. 'So we met up at this pub at the back of the station and began talking.' Though, as he admitted, 'I think subconsciously it was just a way of getting off with one another.'

'Meeting Andy wasn't a life-changing experience,' Lorraine emphasised in retrospect. 'Our relationship developed gradually. We would do a play together, then not see each other for a few months, then work together again. We just became closer and closer.'

Lorraine Ashbourne is three years Andy Serkis's senior. She was born in 1961 in Manchester, and trained at the Webber-Douglas Academy drama school in London, where her contemporaries included Ross Kemp, later Grant Mitchell in *EastEnders* and the star in the ITV action series, *Ultimate Force*. While at Webber-Douglas, she was told by one teacher that she faced a difficult time as a professional actor. 'I was told that I wouldn't be commercially viable until I was past my twenties, which for a woman of 21 was a pretty terrifying prospect.'

She would prove that teacher wrong. Gaining her Equity card by singing in clubs, in 1985 she made her professional stage debut in *Steaming*, a play by Nell Dunn set behind the white tiles of a Turkish baths. Further roles followed in everything from farces to pantomimes to musicals. The late 1980s found her graduating to film work: Terence Davies's *Distant Voices, Still Lives* (a series of vignettes about working-class Britain in the 1940s and 1950s), and then, in 1989, *Resurrected*. There were guest spots, too, on television, including cameos in *The Bill*, *London's Burning* and *Casualty*. The nature of long-running TV dramas about the three emergency services – police, fire, ambulance – with essentially a standalone story meant that there were many vacancies for young actors to portray suspects, eyewitnesses and victims of accidents or their relatives. In turn, those same actors were trying to gain a foothold in small-screen work. We'll see in Chapter 4 how such TV guest spots would also help Andy Serkis.

During the 1990s, both Lorraine and Andy became used to the mad whirl of trying to maintain a relationship while separately having to attend film or television location shoots, or stage work. From time to time, their professional commitments would coincide and they would be in the same geographical area. Very occasionally, they would end up in the same play – Steven Berkoff's *Decadence* or an English translation of the Hungarian musical *Doctor Heart*, in which Serkis starred as a physicist who discovers a way of turning dreams into reality. The two of them had an especially close relationship with the Royal Exchange, usually working on productions with the director Braham Murray.

Time spent apart was made up for with trips away. Holidays were crucial for the couple, from their first break in 1991, when they travelled out to the mountains over the border from Chamonix in Italy. Another subsequent journey abroad saw the pair jump into a Volkswagen camper van and drive from their home in Hackney, east London, to the island of Sicily. The pair would take some adventurous holidays around the globe during the

1990s, from backpacking in Vietnam and Thailand, to paragliding, to scuba-diving, and ice-climbing on glacial peaks. 'I got into ice-climbing through Andy and we've been to the Alps, places like that,' recalled Lorraine. 'It's not as dangerous as it seems. I did lose my nerve once and couldn't move for about half an hour, but I forced myself to get going again, by which time the mist had come in and we had to camp on the mountain for the night thousands of feet up.'

By the late 1990s, after a string of stage successes and supporting roles in films such as *Jack and Sarah* (with Richard E. Grant) and *Fever Pitch* (with Colin Firth), Lorraine Ashbourne was a mainstay of two peak-time BBC drama series: the Manchester-based police series *City Central* and Kay Mellor's *Playing the Field*, about an all-female football team. Just as both became recommissioned for second series during 1998, she discovered that she and Andy were to become parents for the first time, but it was only very shortly before the baby was due that she took time off from hectic shooting schedules.

It just so happened that Geraldine Powell, whom she played in *Playing the Field*, would herself give birth at the start of its second series. Geraldine's fictional birth scene was filmed only two months before Lorraine's real one, and it was an interesting dress rehearsal. 'Filming the birth scene was amazing because I knew I was going to have go through it for real two months later. If anything, I felt more responsibility for making it look as genuine as possible.' But, with Lorraine seven months pregnant in real life, midwives were standing by just in case. 'I was actually quite far gone when we filmed the scene. I was told not to push too hard but to show it more in my face than down below.' So how did her real-life partner feel about the pretend birth? Lorraine believed that, for Andy, who was used to making acting an authentic, intense experience, the fictional delivery was perhaps slightly traumatic. With a giggle, she told the *Mirror*, 'I think those scenes were more disturbing for him than if I was doing a love scene.'

There was tension when it came to the real-life birth of Lorraine and Andy's daughter in October 1998. Defying the fears of doctors, Lorraine opted to bring Ruby into the world in a birthing pool in the kitchen of the family home she shared in London with Andy. To begin with, she wanted Andy to join her in the pool, and so set about looking for the largest one she could find. 'But, when it came to the day,' she told the *Daily Mail*, 'I decided I wasn't going to share it with anyone.'

Surrounded by candlelight, Lorraine lay in the birthing pool for many hours – 16, maybe 20 in all – with a team of three midwives, who at one point were granted the surreal sight of watching tapes of Lorraine's TV labour from *Playing the Field*. A supportive Andy was next to her throughout. 'He was my emotional rock,' she said. 'I must have squeezed his hand for about 12 hours as he willed me to be patient and strong. The idea that men are useless at birth because they don't know what to do certainly didn't apply to Andy – he wanted to be involved right from the outset.' Having attended a course on mind over matter, Lorraine endured the ordeal – 'a wonderful and hideous experience all at once' – with no pain relief, and recommended birthing pools for all expectant mothers. 'It's not that you don't feel pain, because you do, but you learn to cope with it. I was physically sick at one stage and feeling awful, but the water soothed me.'

Even after Ruby was born, Lorraine was back at work within little more than a month, with near-sleepless nights and 6am alarm calls for long days of filming. 'I thought I'd have no problems coping,' she told the *Mirror* when the child was still only a few months old, 'but I definitely underestimated how difficult it was all going to be.' Help was at hand, thanks to fellow cast members and production staff on *City Central* who converted a storage cabin into a comfortable, beautifully decorated nursery. 'All the rest of the cast helped and they filled it with soft toys,' said Lorraine. 'It's known as Ruby's room. It really was so nice of them.' But most important to Lorraine was her family (who hailed from Manchester, anyway) and, of course, Andy, whose working schedule on various film and TV projects enabled him to be flexible with visits up North.

Parenthood for the couple did force them to rethink their passion for activity holidays. Ice-climbing in the Alps would be less easy, even though they had adored seeing French families there crossing hazardous glaciers with all their offspring in tow. Lorraine reflected in 2000, 'I thought that was so fantastic that I determined that's what my children would do too. I could picture them with their crampons on and their ice axes at the ready, all raring to go climbing with us. But, now that I have Ruby, I realise that it was all a bit of a romantic vision.' At least when Ruby was a little older, and she was joined by younger siblings Sonny (in 2000) and (in 2004) Louis, Andy and Lorraine started to introduce them – in a more modest way – to the joys of the mountains, even if it was just a spot of gentle hill-walking or a journey on a cable car.

Even Andy was starting to slow down a little with his climbing. His spirit of adventure was still there well into his thirties – his climbing conquests included the Matterhorn and even the Eiffel Tower – but, as he would tell the *Sunday Times* in 2005, he began to feel, as the years flew by, that he couldn't quite take the risks of old. 'It's harder now the kids have come along. I did notice, when I was climbing in New Zealand as we were just about to have our second child, feeling I didn't quite have the edge I once had – just not being willing to take that little extra risk.'

So, with a new baby, such excitement would have to be put on hold for the time being. 'Now we're hoping we can balance work so someone is always there for Ruby. I think that's important,' said Lorraine to the *Mirror*. When the question of marriage between them was mentioned, she would not dismiss the idea. 'We haven't made a conscious decision, it's just that we haven't had the time,' she told the *Daily Mail* in 1999. 'If I thought it would affect Ruby, I would get married tomorrow. But I think that if you can demonstrate to a child how much you love each other, then that is more important than being married.'

A year after Ruby was born, Lorraine was keen to have more children. 'Family is the most important thing to me now. You hear some actresses say they had better not get pregnant as they've signed for so-and-so series, but I don't see things that way. If anything, being pregnant has made me more ambitious than I was before. Andy has been working with a couple of actresses who are pregnant and are very worried about losing their ambition, but I've told them they shouldn't worry at all. Acting is not just about my ego and my vanity any more.' Lorraine would always stress what a great source of support her boyfriend was. 'He's a wonderful dad and very much an equal partner when it comes to childcare,' she said in 2000.

Attempts were made to incorporate Ruby into Lorraine's onscreen work. 'I thought it would be so easy to have her with us, even at work,' she told one newspaper. 'So, when there was a party scene for my screen son in *Playing the Field*, I got my mum and dad and Ruby in as extras. But it just didn't work. Whenever she spotted me, she would shout, "Mama, mama", and as I am obviously not playing her mum we had to stop.'

An alternative plan was hatched. Andy had an idea to sneak his infant daughter into a closing scene of the film *Five Seconds to Spare*, a screen adaptation of Jonathan Coe's thriller novel *The Dwarves of Death*. 'She was brilliant during all the rehearsals,' sighed her mother affectionately. 'Then, when it came to the take, she became fascinated by the sound boom. They had to cut the whole scene.' Ruby's screen debut, for now, would be delayed, although when she was 10 she and her siblings would feature as extras at a birthday party scene for the Ian Dury biopic, *Sex & Drugs & Rock & Roll*.

Combining the filming of two major, fast-paced television drama series with motherhood was, inevitably, very draining for Lorraine. As she finished a third run of *Playing the Field*, and a second one of *City Central*, she was looking forward to some time at home with her small daughter in the spring of 2000. Unfortunately, this coincided with the very point where Andy Serkis had to journey to the other end of the world, to begin the arduous work on *The Lord of the Rings*. One paper quoted Lorraine as saying, shortly before Andy's departure, 'We hate being apart, so I've asked him to get me a part as a goblin or an elf.'

The couple's second child, Sonny, was born in June 2000. A few months later she told *The Stage*, 'Ruby adores her new little brother, even if at times she can be a wee bit rough with him. But watching them together is a treat for Andy and I. We love having them around.'

Later that year, Lorraine travelled to New Zealand with both children to join Andy, now hard at work on the adaptation of Tolkien's epic trilogy. 'I thought that it was about time that we all had some quality time together as a family,' she said, 'and, with Andy being away for so long and the children so young, it seemed appropriate to pack our bags, put the house in the hands of some friends who will take any messages, feed the cats and open the mail, and take off.' By the time her appearance as Sue Cratchit in *A Christmas Carol* was broadcast on ITV during the festive season of 2000 – for which she was reunited with Ross Kemp from her student days at Webber-Douglas – she was temporarily living in South Island with Andy and the children.

But it had now been a decade since Andy and Lorraine had worked together professionally. In the autumn of 2001, just a few months before *The Lord of the Rings*' first instalment (*The Fellowship of the Ring*) opened around the world, they collaborated on *Snake*, a short film written and directed by Andy. A dark comedy about the National Health Service, it concerned Matt (Rupert Graves), a young medical student frazzled with exhaustion, who carries out backstreet operations in order to help fund himself and hopefully qualify as a surgeon. When a man called Maurice (Bev Willis) tells him that his wife is in urgent need of a kidney transplant, he arranges a meeting with sex worker 'Jennifer' (played by Ashbourne) in a hotel room near King's Cross in London. Matt intends to drug Jennifer, then remove her kidney and sell it to Maurice (who is hiding in the hotel bathroom) for £2,000. But, while Matt's plan seems watertight on paper, it turns out to be a disastrous one for him from the moment that Jennifer arrives at the hotel.

In order for the small cast and crew to make *Snake*, Serkis set up a temporary office in Soho with producer Paul Viragh, who would later pen the screenplay of the Ian Dury biopic *Sex & Drugs & Rock & Roll*. It was later premiered at a film festival in New Zealand in 2002. Andy and Lorraine have since co-written a feature film screenplay together under the title *Frankly My Dear*, while Andy has co-directed *Ride* (a short film for Lorraine to star in).

By the end of 2001, Andy and Lorraine had been together for a decade. They had intended to get married for some time, but they did not want to delay it any longer, and wanted to start 2002 with a wedding ceremony of some kind. 'I'd always wanted us to get married on top of a mountain,' Andy remembered. 'So we went to the Lake District, where we'd spent our early courting days. Unfortunately, we were all hit by a stomach bug and spent every day in a hotel room, while it rained relentlessly outside.'

An alternative day was named. On 22 July 2002, Andy and Lorraine became husband and wife. Their love of holidaying in Italy meant they felt there was only one suitable location for them to tie the knot. They married at a twelfth-century church just outside the Italian city of Florence. The ceremony was followed by a reception at a castle near Fiesole, overlooking Tuscany. More than a hundred guests were in attendance. The celebrations went on for several days, but work commitments for the newlyweds meant that the 'honeymoon', such as it was, took place in the by-now very familiar confines of the Royal Exchange Theatre's rehearsal rooms. They were about to open there in a new production of Shakespeare's *Othello*, which reunited them with director Braham Murray. Lorraine was to play Emilia, while Andy was to tackle Iago (his first attempt at the part since his days as a student).

Serkis's diary was bulging by this point. After weekdays in Manchester with Lorraine rehearsing Shakespeare, there was no letup at weekends, when he would zoom down to Pinewood Studios for long hours recording dialogue for Gollum in the postproduction marathons of *The Lord of the Rings*. Then, just as *Othello* was about to premiere, he happened to injure his lower back. He managed to struggle through almost its entire two-month run, thanks to painkillers, but it only served to postpone the inevitable. During one matinée, after 40 *Othello*s, he passed out on stage in front of an audience of 750 people. The play's director had to go on instead. Serkis could barely move for three weeks, but was helped back to recovery by an acupuncturist and physiotherapist, meaning that he would be able to attend the New York premiere in December 2002 of *The Two Towers* – perhaps the most anticipated screen performance he had given so far.

Family life has relaxed Serkis to some extent. He now

cares about work in a different way. 'I have to work quicker, really, and I have to work more instinctively now, because I've got family, and they feed hugely into my acting.'

Since the arrival of their third child, Lorraine has often proudly accompanied her husband to his movie premieres, but her own acting career has continued apace. She remains interested in socially aware writing, and returned to the big screen in 2011 with *Oranges and Sunshine*. Directed by Jim Loach (son of Ken), and co-starring Emily Watson and Hugo Weaving, it was a sensitive investigative drama about the child migration that took place between the UK and Australia during the 1950s, and the families who were kept in the dark. Television work continues to keep her busy, most notably from writers of the calibre of Victoria Wood (the BAFTA-winning drama *Housewife, 49*) and Debbie Horsfield (BBC1's *True Dare Kiss* series in 2007), and projects from Jimmy McGovern for the BBC such as *The Street* and *Moving On*. Her husband would also grace a McGovern story in 2010, one of the crowning glories of Serkis's two varied decades of television work, which all started at the end of the 1980s.

CHAPTER 4

PUSHING THROUGH THE CAMERA: TELEVISION

In the autumn of 1988, 24-year-old Andy Serkis was at York's Theatre Royal, appearing as Bill Sikes in *Oliver!* – Lionel Bart's musical reworking of Charles Dickens's *Oliver Twist* – when he landed an early television break. Then entering its second series, *The New Statesman* was a Sunday evening sitcom vehicle for Rik Mayall as the bumptious and amoral MP, Alan B'Stard, and was one of ITV's biggest comedy hits of the time. Serkis would appear in two consecutive episodes – as a newspaper reporter for the now-defunct national title *Today* – where other guest stars included Stephen Fry and Hugh Laurie. However, it was not a high-profile screen debut for him: he is almost unrecognisable underneath a wig and spectacles; he only delivers feedlines for B'Stard; and his aggregated time onscreen over the two episodes lasts barely one minute.

Serkis's *New Statesman* episodes were recorded at

Yorkshire Television in Leeds and broadcast on 29 January and 5 February 1989. That year would also see him make minor showings in a couple of peak-time TV drama productions. Transmitted in June, *Made in Spain* was a feature-length drama based on a stage play by Tony Grounds about the wives of four conmen who have to leave Britain urgently for Spain. *Saracen*, meanwhile, which went out from September, was a new Saturday night series from the makers of *Inspector Morse* about counterterrorism and centred on a duo of SAS troubleshooters. It was in a series aimed at younger viewers, though, where Serkis would initially make his mark on television.

In April and May 1989, he was a regular supporting player in a new six-part BBC1 comedy for Saturday teatimes. Taped in Manchester, *Morris Minor's Marvellous Motors* had been spun off from the brief but startling success of the comic pop group Morris Minor and the Majors. Fronted by the songwriter and comic Tony Hawks – later to write best-selling books such as *Round Ireland with a Fridge* and *One Hit Wonderland* – the trio's Beastie Boys parody 'Stutter Rap' had been a top-five hit in the UK in 1988, and had gone on to top the charts in Australia. But follow-up singles, such as the pastiche of manufactured pop 'This is the Chorus', had not been successful.

Morris Minor's Marvellous Motors, which blended sitcom and songs, found Hawks's lead character Morris Minor attempting to juxtapose being a 'top pop star' with running a garage. Serkis played a mechanic called Sparky Plugg. The series was one of the first comedy shows broadcast by the BBC to have been made by an independent production company, namely Noel Gay Television (makers of *Red*

Dwarf), but it did not catch fire with critics or viewers and was not recommissioned for a second series. However, it was entered for the Golden Rose of Montreux that summer in the Independents category alongside the aforementioned *Red Dwarf* and Emma Thompson's queasily received solo series, *Thompson*.

The ITV children's drama series *Streetwise*, about a team of bicycle couriers, would show greater staying power. It would run for three series and a total of 27 episodes between September 1989 and June 1992, by far the largest body of TV work of Serkis's entire career. It also starred Stephen McGann (brother of Paul), Sara Sugarman (later to become a film director) and Paterson Joseph, who many years later would share a stage with Serkis and Ashbourne – in *Othello* in Manchester. On the writing team would be Matthew Graham, future creator of *Life on Mars*.

Serkis played the environmentally aware Owen in *Streetwise*, and as was already becoming typical, was conducting his own background research into what the part would entail. In this case, it meant working for a despatch company for a few days. 'I did it to get the feel of the grittiness and the pressure,' he told teenage magazine *Look-In*. 'Breathing car fumes for eight hours a day, and nipping in and out of traffic, calls for a certain type of person. The grime's bad. You get home at night and your body is just covered in black soot and grease.' Location filming on the streets of London could be hazardous. There was one near miss for Serkis when his mountain bike inexplicably jammed on Marylebone Road, and sent him sprawling under a car, which – fortunately for him – was stationary at traffic lights.

Serkis's extensive experience in theatrical work, and his

principles over how one interacts with fellow performers and the audience, has fed strongly into his output for television, and later cinema. He believed that there was a major difference between actors who had learnt their craft predominantly through the theatre and those who had largely concentrated on screen projects. There is, of course, the argument that one doesn't have to be so word perfect or pitch perfect on screen because of multiple takes and the safety net of editing. However, there is no cutting room floor for outtakes in the theatre.

But for Serkis there was a far more fundamental reason why stage actors could make more of an impression on celluloid or via the cathode-ray tube. 'I think people who have worked on stage just convey – they push through beyond the camera,' he said in 2003. 'Even if they're standing behind it, they'll work their socks off, acting with you. You work with people who are just really more interested in acting to the corner of the matte box, because their eye line's better at the camera, and then you work with people who play the scenes with you properly. For me, it's really what happens between people that's interesting.'

For people to address the camera angle rather than the other actors is to miss the point of acting, Serkis believed. 'It's going to make the shot look ridiculous if they're not. You know when an actor is giving their 100 per cent, because you've given your 100 per cent to them, and you know when people are just kind of coasting it because they've done their shot. Theatre actors are used to giving that amount of reciprocal energy on stage.'

That said, Serkis has emphasised his enthusiasm for television and film shoots, which demand a shorter, more heightened sort of concentration than the type required for stage performances. 'There is an enormous amount of satisfaction of working off instinct and the moment as well, rather than the long run of a play.' And so, from 1989 onwards, Andy Serkis found himself moving effortlessly from stage to screen and back again, using different skills and stretching different acting muscles with every job.

Bar serials, the last television series to feature Andy Serkis as a prominent cast member was *Finney*, a series broadcast by ITV in the autumn of 1994. A six-part thriller made by Zenith (already showered with plaudits for *Inspector Morse* and the gritty children's serial *Byker Grove*), *Finney*'s origins lay in the cinema. It had begun life as the film *Stormy Monday* seven years earlier, in which Sting had starred as the owner of a jazz club in Newcastle, who also had one foot in the city's criminal underworld. *Stormy Monday*'s producer, Nigel Stafford-Clark, had the bright idea to imagine the lead character's past exploits, but to set the story in the present day.

Steven Finney (David Morrissey, who learnt to play the double bass especially for the part) turns his back on his family's criminal reputation in favour of pursuing his musical career down in London, but he is compelled to return to Newcastle on learning that his father has been murdered. Now he ploughs his energy into trying to protect the family empire from being snatched by the rival clan the Simpsons. Then it is discovered that Finney Senior has left all his worldly goods to Steven's sister Lena (Melanie Hill), which sends the shunned and vulnerable younger sibling Tom (Serkis) into a downward and resentful spiral of gambling and self-destruction. Even as his elder brother offers support, Tom takes increasingly desperate action, and finally all is revealed in a shocking twist.

An elaborate study of family loyalties, *Finney* had the misfortune to be scheduled opposite the BBC's *Crocodile Shoes* starring Jimmy Nail – another drama with a Newcastle flavour (even though *Finney* had in fact mostly been filmed in Glasgow). But it was well received on the whole: critics praised the series for its sharp dialogue and ability to produce something fresh from a genre that all too often takes refuge in the clichéd rather than in the surprising. As Tom, Serkis had been given his meatiest TV role so far, and he was grateful to the writer and director David Hayman, with whom he would work again in 1995 on the film *The Near Room*. 'I've always been inspired by him as an actor and director and a human being,' he said many years later of Hayman. 'He is a real guiding light.'

Despite the warm reception given to *Finney*, Serkis's forte on television from now on, anticipating the impact he would later make on celluloid, seemed to be in the mini-series. The characters he would portray were often so intense that they would soon have to be watered down if shoehorned into a regular serial or long-running series, which may be why we have never seen him in a soap like *EastEnders* or *Coronation Street*.

Eventually, Serkis would darken a pair of serialisations of Charles Dickens novels (novels that, fittingly, originally appeared in episodic form in the nineteenth century). *Oliver Twist*, written when Dickens was only in his mid-twenties, was boldly adapted for ITV in 1999 (as four one-hour instalments) by Alan Bleasdale. Liverpool-born Bleasdale, one of the most original television writers of the 1980s and

1990s, had developed his own brand of award-winning contemporary serial drama such as *The Monocled Mutineer*, *G.B.H.* and *Jake's Progress*. Bleasdale's interpretation of *Twist* would be radical, not even introducing Oliver until the serial's second hour, but examining the boy's family background first.

Serkis would play the same part he had portrayed in York's Theatre Royal in 1988: Bill Sikes. Sikes is a terrifying, menacing presence, a thief and housebreaker who can be violent, to the point of viciously murdering his lover Nancy (Emily Woof) when he believes that she has betrayed him. Nancy has been a force for good in an intimidating society, and takes young Oliver under her wing when he enters the shady world of criminality. 'Everyone is frightened of Bill Sikes,' said Bleasdale, 'and I wanted to hold on to that presence. He is undeniably brutal, but it's the manner in which the society was.' And the writer believed that he had a few redeeming features. After one robbery, for which Oliver is in attendance, Sikes rescues the boy. 'Sikes could have left Oliver for dead, but he picks him up and runs with him as far as he can. It's not me that's written that: it's Dickens.'

In 2008, Serkis played another Dickens bad guy – the charming but cold and calculating French opportunist Rigaud – in Andrew Davies's reworking for the BBC of *Little Dorrit*, and thoroughly enjoyed discovering his murky depths. 'He's full of contradictory qualities,' Serkis told the BBC. 'Yes, he's a murderer, a blackmailer and a thoroughly nasty piece of work. At the same time, he is also very attractive and has a thing for the ladies. He's an upwardly mobile underdog.'

Little Dorrit, like almost any Dickens adaptation, would have a vast repertory company. It would co-star, among many others, Freema Agyeman, fresh out of *Doctor Who*, Ruth Jones (co-writer and co-star of the comedy series *Gavin and Stacey*), Mackenzie Crook (Gareth in *The Office*), Amanda Redman (*Waterloo Road*, *New Tricks*) and Eve Myles (*Torchwood*). There was a great sense of team spirit on the production, Serkis felt. 'It's like being back in a theatre company. Everyone comes in on different days, so you never know who's going to be in the trailer next to you.' But *Little Dorrit* had rarely been adapted for TV. Andrew Davies had a theory as to why this should be. 'Commissioners tend to go for the usual suspects with Dickens...*Oliver Twist*, *David Copperfield*, *Great Expectations*...' he said. 'But this is a tremendous opportunity to take a novel that not many people have read and introduce it to them.'

For Davies, it was important that Dickens's literature should be inclusive to all strata of society, 'from aristocrats to beggars to militaristic villains, and manages to intertwine their lives with each other'. So how would he sum up Rigaud? 'He's a big character, very dark but also quite dynamic,' he commented, but the larger-than-life stature and intimidating presence of Rigaud was at odds with Serkis's slight build and average height of 5 feet 8 inches.

This caused difficulties when Serkis had to play a scene in which Rigaud bullies Matthew Macfadyen's character of Arthur. Macfadyen, at six foot three, towered over Serkis, who was sporting a rakish earring and false nose. 'I have to be quite threatening to him and it just looked ridiculous,' said Serkis. 'No matter what the acting was like, you just couldn't get around the sheer difference in size. We had to make him sit. He had to sort of stumble back into a chair.' The only other way to beef up Rigaud was to puff up his costume. 'He kind of invades the space when he arrives in a room.' Once again, Serkis's skills for climbing were put to the test. 'My character gets to break into a house,' he told *Time Out*. 'I've actually soloed up the Matterhorn, so I loved the climb. I fell two storeys on set, but I landed on my feet.'

Facing potential critical gripes head on, Andrew Davies was aware that some would find Rigaud's wild-eyed beastliness to be a little too overpowering. 'His first words are "*Sacre bleu!*"' he laughed, 'But I thought, Why not?' He also knew that Dickens purists would question the extent to which he had strayed from the text, a common accusation with his adaptations. Some of the new ideas were in fact Serkis brainwaves. 'He kept suggesting extra bits of business for himself, like the tiny subplot in which he seduces a French landlady. That didn't appear in the original script.' The *Scotsman* paid tribute to Serkis's flamboyant portrayal. 'With eyes like a snake and a (false) beak-like nose, Serkis twitches his head around in a way that shows you Rigaud's sneaky brain at work.'

With the series being screened in twice-weekly half-hour chunks, *Dorrit* was like a period-drama equivalent of a TV soap. '*Little Dorrit* lends itself very well to this format,' believed Andrew Davies. 'You can cram an incredible number of people and incidents into a half-hour without viewers feeling they're just being given snippets.' There were also unexpectedly timely aspects to the story: as well as featuring a murder mystery and a love story (both constants in storytelling), it concerns a loss of finances for the characters. 'We've been rather lucky with that one,' murmured Davies. Production had begun on *Dorrit* before the world-changing economic downturn, which started to be reported in September 2008, mere weeks before the series began on television.

Serkis's earliest foray into the mini-series genre, though, came nearly 15 years before *Dorrit. Grushko*, starring Brian Cox, was a three-hour drama made by the BBC in association with German and Russian television, and was filmed on location in St Petersburg during the summer of 1993. It was adapted from the novel *Dead Meat* by Philip Kerr, a first-person account of a Russian detective's quest to nail the truth behind a journalist's murder. *Dead Meat* was itself based on the work of Inspector Gorbachevski, a serving chief of detectives who was working for the city's Investigating Bureau – a specialist unit that was seeking to stamp out organised crime. Gorbachevski's files of crime were eye-opening indeed, and it became clear that a huge pool of crime stories in Russia, hitherto hidden from the eyes and ears of the West, were now accessible.

The 12-week shoot on the series took place with the full support of the city's state police, but there were bigger problems with the series title. The BBC was reportedly unhappy with 'Dead Meat', then (over the following months) with 'Russian Roulette', with 'Poisoned Chalice', and with 'Dead Liberty'. Even when the title *Grushko* seemed to cause the least worry for the corporation, the drama's teething troubles weren't over. It was originally scheduled for Sunday nights, traditionally the strongest night for drama on television, but, after a few high-profile series had unexpectedly underperformed, jittery bosses moved it to a less exposed slot on Thursdays.

Philip Kerr recalled visiting the Youssupov Palace with Serkis and described him as a 'great sax player and an even better actor'. Serkis himself played Pyotr, described in write-ups as a 'Mafia thug'. The shooting of the film in St Petersburg caused a sensation: one press reporter watched in shock and wonderment as a shell-suit-wearing Pyotr raced out of a basement, triggering an apparent shootout in the street. In most other countries, the sound of gunfire might have attracted curious passers-by towards the filming to watch out of curiosity. Here, concerned bystanders shrank back at what was unfolding in front of them – even when the director shouted 'Cut'. As Serkis/Pyotr disappeared into the alarmed and puzzled crowd, it was quite obvious that many of those present had believed the events to be real, not fictional.

From time to time throughout the 1990s, Andy Serkis was reaching millions of TV viewers across Britain, practically all of whom must have been unaware of the splash he would make in the world of cinema in the early twenty-first century. Cameo roles abounded in everything from Stephen Poliakoff's three-part drama, *Shooting the Past*, to the promotional video of Neneh Cherry's 1996 top-ten hit, 'Woman'. He was kept busy with middling roles in long-running peak-time drama series and serials, from *Kavanagh QC* (starring John Thaw) to *The Darling Buds of May* with David Jason, Pam Ferris and Catherine Zeta Jones. And yes, you guessed right: he was in *The Bill*. Twice.

This steady stream of television work, plus the very

occasional move into radio drama, did not make him a star. What mattered was that he could always be relied upon to maintain a high standard in his performance, whatever each job entailed. 'It was a slow, plodding process,' he later told the *Sunday Times* about this period. 'I was working regularly, in a variety of parts. So it never bothered me that I didn't become an instant name or face.'

At least in terms of quantity, Andy Serkis's work for the medium of TV has declined sharply in the twenty-first century. As we will discover, after 2000, he would largely concentrate on film work. 'I suppose I am more compelled to work in film,' he told IGN's Filmforce in 2003, 'because of that sense of working with people who are passionate about their particular project. Television does get caught in that terrible trap, you become a bit of a functionary because it is not your vision.'

If he was going to remain part of television's world, then, perhaps it was preferable to make a contribution that was memorable, unusual and special. Aside from a one-off guest appearance in the BBC's spy drama *Spooks* in 2004 (playing a recently knighted rock legend called Riff), Serkis now mainly confined himself to single, self-contained projects: as Ian Brady in *Longford*, Albert Einstein in *Einstein and Eddington*, or as Vincent Van Gogh for a Simon Schama series about art. (All will be covered in Chapter 11.)

Serkis, who at the age of 12 had been glued to the sight of Barrie Keeffe's *Gotcha* on *Play for Today*, was arguing for the preservation of the single drama. Single plays with a theatrical pace were rare on television after the mid-1990s, with television films much more common. But *Accused* in late 2010 was one of his greatest outings for the medium.

Created by Jimmy McGovern (*Cracker*, *Hillsborough*, *The Street*), *Accused* was a series of unrelated, self-contained films for BBC1. It gave actors like Serkis the luxury of having a starring role in a continuing TV drama series with a regular audience, but without having to commit to more than one story – a hybrid of leading role and guest star.

McGovern is the ultimate example of a major contemporary writer who scorns the process of writing, preferring to be regarded as someone who tells stories. 'The only way to tell stories on TV is to convince people that what they are seeing is actually happening now and is real.' In this respect, he shared Andy Serkis's belief that drama – whether on stage, film or television – is first and foremost about storytelling.

In each *Accused* film, viewers are shown a suspect about to face sentence in a trial, and are taken back through the chain of events that brought the suspect to that point. It did not concern itself with police procedure: McGovern felt that side of crime was being explored quite enough, to the point of being overused. It wasn't so much 'Whodunit?' as 'What have they done?' The diverse storylines were powerful. One film, starring Christopher Eccleston, recounts how a plumber, who is conducting an extramarital affair with a much-younger woman, is plunged into serious debt just as his daughter's wedding is nearing. Another, featuring Mackenzie Crook as a terrifyingly sadistic corporal, is set in Afghanistan. The suspects were not habitual criminals. In the case of Liam Black, he 'just snapped': 'I didn't mean to kill anyone. Couldn't kill time. Couldn't murder a pint.'

Liam's Story, co-written by McGovern and Danny Brocklehurst, was the fourth of *Accused*'s six stories, and was broadcast on BBC1 on 6 December 2010. Liam (Serkis) is a taxi driver with a gambling addiction. He is married to Roz (Neve McIntosh), who has been battling multiple sclerosis for many years. After the couple's daughter Katy passes the entrance exam for a new school with flying colours, Liam struggles to scrape the money together to buy her a present. When he is giving an airport-bound taxi journey to a twentysomething estate agent called Emma, he is so smitten by her that he cannot help sneaking back to her home in her absence out of the country. Snooping around her living room, he steals a necklace to pass off as a present for his daughter. As he uncovers more and more about her – through private email correspondence and the contents of her iPod – and becomes her regular taxi service, his growing and corrosive obsession with her leads to disaster and tragedy.

Jodie Whittaker, who played the part of Emma, found it a privilege to work with Andy but found that their dramatic interplay had a quite specific focus, because many of their scenes took place in Liam's taxi cab. 'Many of our scenes in the cab were static, with Liam driving and Emma in the back seat, which does make performing quite challenging,' said Whittaker. 'What happens is the focus goes to their eyes. They're communicating through eye contact via his rear-view mirror.'

Liam's Story is a hugely emotive piece. Dominated by Serkis (he is scarcely off the screen for the full hour), we see how a troubled, though in many ways good, man falls further into calamity and criminality. Lorraine Ashbourne, who has herself appeared in McGovern series, spoke for many when she described McGovern as one of the most important contemporary writers in Britain. 'What he writes looks simple on the page, but, when you perform it, it really comes to life. He knows how to write about people we all care about and understand.'

As *Longford* was about to air on Channel 4 in 2006, Andy Serkis told the *Stage* newspaper that his television appearances were becoming less frequent for a quite specific reason. 'There are too many compromises in television drama, particularly in series and serials. I think it's something to do with the repetitiveness of it. I like one-off projects because they have a passion and a drive. They are their own entity – they are films, really.' By the time he said those words, to say that he was well established in cinema was an understatement. But his breakthrough in film would be no overnight success.

CHAPTER 5

THE LOW-BUDGET PRISON: EARLY FILM WORK

Serkis was nearly 30 years old when he landed his first film role in 1993. While his television work already stretched back four years, cinematic opportunities in Britain were not common. 'It was quite an elite thing to do film in this country during the eighties,' he said, 'because there just wasn't a lot of it going on.' There were exceptions – usually Merchant Ivory films or Channel 4 Television's *Film on Four* presentations – but otherwise it was slim pickings for those interested in making it in British film.

At no point did Serkis consider permanently relocating to gain celluloid glory in Hollywood. He still regarded himself, first and foremost, as a stage actor. Plus, he felt he was still learning his craft. 'I think the British mentality of that time – from my generation of actors – was you start off in theatre, and then you did your telly, and then you did film...which is exactly what I did.' It seemed a long way from what he felt happened later, where young actors might bypass stage work entirely and opt for screen parts. 'The whole kind of learning process as an actor changed from just purely it being about creating a role, to creating a business for yourself and getting a publicist...I do think I was one of the last generation of actors who did rep theatre and had the luxury of working, rehearsing one play, and performing another at the same time. That just doesn't happen any more. There just aren't those places to do that.'

Serkis's extensive experience in theatre throughout the 1980s and 1990s would be very useful in the fragmented, stop-start environment of filmmaking. 'I think, sometimes, actors on film do their performance in front of a camera, and then you do your bit, and they do their bit, and there's nothing really going on between.'

In April 1993, Serkis travelled to Denmark, where shooting was beginning under veteran Danish director Gabriel Axel on *Prince of Jutland*, a film version of the Scandinavian myth that inspired William Shakespeare to write *Hamlet*. *Prince of Jutland* takes place in sixth-century Denmark where Prince Amled (Christian Bale), the son of King Hardvendel (Tom Wilkinson), finds that his uncle Fenge (Gabriel Byrne) has murdered his father to seize the throne and the queen, Geruth (Helen Mirren).

Amled feigns madness in order to gain sympathy, but all the while, he is plotting his revenge, and persuades Geruth to play along with his plan until the moment that he can take revenge. In the meantime, he has killed an eaves-dropping henchman, an act that causes Fenge to exile Amled. Fenge sends Amled to the Duke of Lindsey (Brian Cox) in the company of two escorts (Aslak and Torsten –

Mark Williams from *The Fast Show* and Serkis) along with a stone tablet covered in instructions ordering for Amled to be killed. However, Amled cunningly alters the writing on the tablet so that the Duke kills the escorts instead.

Serkis's next feature could scarcely have been more different in tone from *Prince of Jutland*, and nor could his role – as a transvestite prostitute called Bunny. *The Near Room* was a bleak thriller, shot and completed entirely in Glasgow in the first half of 1995, and directed by David Hayman, with whom Serkis had worked on the *Finney* series for ITV the year before. The title of the film derived from a phrase uttered by boxing legend Muhammad Ali, who once described the pressure of facing George Foreman in a title fight as feeling like 'the near room, where snakes scream and alligators play trombone'. The film followed a journalist called Charlie Colquhoun (Adrian Dunbar) who must investigate the disappearance of his 16-year-old daughter Tommy (short for Thomasina), who was played by Emma Faulkner. His research means he must enter the disturbing world of teenage prostitution, and it is here he seeks Bunny for information about his estranged daughter.

Stella Does Tricks (1996) was also a film about teenage prostitution, although this story would be told from the perspective of the vulnerable but feisty Stella, played by Kelly Macdonald, who had just shot to stardom in Danny Boyle's *Trainspotting*. Glaswegian-born Stella drifts to London, where she is sucked into a prostitution ring run by a seemingly respectable but oily middle-aged man (played by James Bolam), but is resolutely determined to escape and reinvent herself. The moving screenplay was written by novelist A. L. Kennedy, who told the *Glasgow Herald*, 'She falls through this hole in the safety net. She can't get benefit so she goes to London and she just gets lost.' Serkis briefly appears in the early part of the film in the entirely unsympathetic role of a small-time thug named Fitz, whose car is blown up after he is violent to one of Stella's friends.

Stella Does Tricks was warmly received by many critics – as was *The Near Room*, in fact – but none of these first three feature films to feature Andy Serkis made much impression beyond that. Isolated showings took place at film festivals, and they had an afterlife on sell-through video, but otherwise, in terms of opening at the local Odeon, they sank without trace. The same fate awaited 1997's *Loop*, in which Serkis played stockbroker Bill, who dumps his girlfriend Rachel (Emer McCourt) when she falls pregnant, and then discovers that – in an act of revenge – she has vanished with her cherished sports car and cleared out their joint bank account. In fact, her destination is at the home of her dysfunctional family in the fenlands of Norfolk, but it is not long before Bill is on the warpath.

The novelist Jonathan Coe, author of satires like *What a Carve-Up!* and *The Rotters' Club*, was disappointed that *Loop* could not find a distributor. Writing in the *New Statesman*, he compared it favourably to the work of Michael Powell and Emil Pressburger's *Gone to Earth*, a film in which the brooding landscape is an integral part of the casting. 'Rather than bowing every time to studio-bound convention, it's important to attempt these rare, mysterious excursions into Britain's unvisited corners – as Michael Powell's failed masterpiece continues so potently to remind us.'

Ironically, *Five Seconds to Spare* – a music-biz thriller

drawn from Coe's 1990 book *The Dwarves of Death* – would be yet another title from the Andy Serkis film CV that never made it to cinemas. Nor did *The Tale of Sweety Barrett*, made in Ireland in 1998, in which an unemployed sword-swallower becomes an odd-job man who befriends a woman's young son while the boy's father (Serkis as Leo King) waits to be released from prison.

Many films made in Great Britain had a habit of either going straight to sell-through video or DVD (if you were lucky) or disappearing without trace. It could be an exasperating patience-sapping feeling, putting one's all into a film role, only to find it all sitting in a can on a shelf waiting to be distributed. 'I'd love to know where all these films we Brits make end up,' sighed Serkis. 'There must be hundreds and hundreds of British films in a low-budget prison somewhere, serving life sentences.'

For most casual movie fans, the first impression that Serkis made on celluloid is in Mike Leigh's bittersweet comedy-drama *Career Girls*, which premiered at the Cannes Film Festival in May 1997, then opened in the UK four months later. Leigh, who had established himself on television with a sequence of single plays in the 1970s and 1980s, including *Nuts in May*, *Abigail's Party* and *Grown-Ups*, had moved into cinema in the late eighties – *Meantime*, *Life is Sweet*, *Naked* and *Secrets and Lies*. In all of these projects, he would collaborate closely with a cast of actors in developing character and improvising scenes, rather than present them with a sacrosanct script on the first day of shooting.

Landing the part of Mr Evans, a disillusioned City of London trader, marked a breakthrough for Serkis, especially as he was a great admirer of Leigh's work, to the extent of contacting him by letter in the late 1980s. When Margaret Thatcher was re-elected prime minister for the third and final time in 1987, the rep actor was so 'heartbroken, absolutely devastated that she'd got in again' that he decided to write to Leigh. 'I told him I had respected him for a long time, and that he was one of the few directors with anything to say about Britain.' When the call came for *Career Girls*, which started shooting in spring 1996, Serkis was amazed to discover that Leigh had kept his passionate letter all that time. 'I was gobsmacked,' he recalled to the *Independent*'s Ryan Gilbey in 2003. 'He remembered me.'

Gilbey in turn remembered Serkis. He was the reporter who had interviewed him in 1997 on the set of the film version of *Mojo* (of which more very shortly), while *Career Girls* was waiting to be released. Serkis expressed great concern to Gilbey about how much of him might have remained in Leigh's finished film. 'That was a hard lesson to learn,' Serkis told Gilbey six years on. 'It can be tough realising that you've put in that amount of energy for one scene. But it's about the life experience you have. You don't go into a Mike Leigh film and come out the same person.'

What working with Leigh taught Serkis was how to feel rooted to an assigned role. The process would begin with the actor drawing up a list of people familiar enough to use as a starting point for a character. Having whittled it down to a shortlist, Serkis would undergo some discussions with Leigh ('It's like having a one-on-one with a therapist, really'), before a single character was isolated, which became a 'touchstone character'. From this, further, very detailed discussions would take place about that character's background and life so far, which would extend right up to the day when Leigh would start shooting on the project.

Leigh's characterisation went far beyond the shortcuts of stereotypes, and could take weeks and even months. As the part of a futures broker was developed for Serkis to play in *Career Girls*, he spent four months of 1996 in the actual job, working in the City of London. He began to live the life of the man he had helped to create, befriending his work colleagues, watching the right films, listening to the right music, and so on. For months, Serkis lived this life, and must have explored this alternative persona so profoundly that his colleagues tried to persuade him to join them – permanently. 'They said to me, "Hey, why don't you just jack the film and come work for us? You'll make more money." Before you know it, you've entered into this whole kind of way of being.' It had got to the stage where Serkis was going home to Lorraine at four in the morning. He would later blushingly recall hedonistic nights out at the Dorchester with his co-workers. He suspected, however, that the offer had little to do with how well he excelled during office hours. 'It wasn't that I was good at it,' he said. 'I think they just liked having me around.'

The preparatory months of long hours and wild parties resulted in only around 10 minutes of screen time for Serkis's Mr Evans in the final cut of *Career Girls*. He appears when Hannah (Katrin Cartlidge) and Annie (Lynda Steadman), who are two old friends from university who reunite for a weekend in London six years after their graduation, visit his apartment (overlooking the River Thames), after Hannah expresses an interest in buying a flat from him.

From Serkis's perspective, creating someone from scratch did require exhaustive research for a performance to be satisfying and believable. Actors tend to fall into two distinct categories when it comes to method acting. Serkis is undoubtedly a great believer in the practice, but there have been others, notably Dustin Hoffman, who, when making the 1976 thriller *Marathon Man*, stayed up for three nights in succession to resemble his character, who had indeed gone without sleep for three nights. Co-star Laurence Olivier is reputed to have said to him, 'Have you tried acting, dear boy?'

And it would appear Michael Caine feels the same way as Lord Olivier. When Serkis worked with Caine on the gritty gangster boxing flick *Shiner* in 2000, the younger actor could not help but be disoriented by the sight of one of the most familiar, iconic actors in British cinema. 'I'll never forget sitting in the readthrough,' he reminisced to IGN Filmforce. "Who's that person doing an impersonation of Michael Caine?" Oh – it's Michael Caine.'

Caine was playing Billy 'Shiner' Simpson, a small-time boxing promoter and gangster, with Serkis playing the smooth-talking Mel, daubed in tattoos as one of his two menacing henchmen. Watching Caine at work both on and off set was, for the younger actor, nothing short of an education. Caine's approach to the business of acting seemed almost diametrically opposed to Serkis's. Their different ways of working was starkly demonstrated when it came to the actors choosing hand props for their characters. 'My character, Mel, spent a lot of time on a mobile phone,' said Serkis, 'and I remember I spent ages choosing one. The first AD [assistant director] said, "Michael, would you like to come choose yourself a briefcase?" And Mike just came over and picked the first one up and walked away.' Was that carelessness or decades of experience at work? Serkis favoured the second option: 'Maybe that's accumulated knowledge, just cutting out the bullshit, without having to go through the agony. He's been around such a long time and you can absorb some of his work methods.'

Shiner was Serkis's second big-screen appearance said to have been inspired by a Shakespearean tragedy, though this brutal reworking of *King Lear* – relocated to the east London world of prizefighting – was some way away from *Prince of Jutland*. Having never played Lear, Caine was eager for the part of *Shiner*, whose life starts to fall apart when his son is defeated in the ring after just two rounds. 'I thought, It's the nearest I'm ever gonna get to play it, so I'm gonna do it,' he revealed to *The Times*.

The shoot brought back to Caine so many memories of his younger days. 'I'd never shot such a Cockney picture, in which every person has a Cockney accent. I've known so many characters and stories like Shiner. I've been to those boxing places.' He found the vulnerability of Shiner compelling to play, telling the *Big Issue*, 'To see someone disintegrate is, although sad, very interesting to play. And as you begin to get older you begin to fall apart yourself.'

Starring roles for Andy Serkis were elusive at this stage, but, for the man whose Gollum is just one of many figures populating a story like *The Lord of the Rings*, what mattered was being part of the cast, part of a communal experience of acting. Several films in the late 1990s cast him as a group member, rather than in a leading role. Ensemble casts require particularly careful writing, or else some of the group could find themselves marginalised.

ANDY SERKIS: THE MAN BEHIND THE MASK

Nineteen ninety-nine's *Among Giants*, a gruff, charming but slight romantic comedy from the pen of *The Full Monty*'s writer, Simon Beaufoy, was about a group of jobless mountain climbers who have just three months to paint 15 miles of electricity pylons stretching across the moors of Yorkshire. As the project's leader Ray (Pete Postlethwaite) falls in love with an Australian woman named Gerry (Rachel Griffiths) – who has joined the pylon-painting job – the other characters are sidelined somewhat. In truth, Serkis does not stand out. But then, as with *Loop*, it is the landscape of England that takes centre-stage in *Among Giants*. One reviewer amusedly noted the director's 'vertiginous shots of nude pylons', scenery that rather overwhelms any human interaction.

The group dynamic was also on show in a micro-budgeted comedy about a wedding day dominated by disaster. *The Jolly Boys' Last Stand* was actually filmed in 1998, but distributors were slow to commit, even in 2000 when one of its other leading actors, one Sacha Baron Cohen, was fast becoming one of the most acclaimed and popular rising stars in British comedy. Baron Cohen had become notorious for his alter-ego, Ali G, who trapped public figures into spoof TV interviews about current-affairs issues.

Serkis played the part of Spider, part of a group of drinking friends with something of a shared history. With little in the way of family commitments or work responsibilities, the Jolly Boys exist as a gang locked in adolescent behaviour for too long, a bunch of men who mark time by inventing juvenile games like slapping strangers with fish. On announcing that he's giving up that life of debauchery to get married, one of the group, Des (played by Milo Twomey, later of the acclaimed American TV series *Band of Brothers*), feels so rejected by his impending departure that he decides to give a personalised wedding 'present'. It is a specially made wedding video, to be made by the rest of his friends, which they intend to make so embarrassing that it will derail Spider's marriage plans. Writer-director Christopher Payne dreamt up the idea of the film as a send-up of lads' culture, telling Film4, 'We just wanted to take the mickey out of the way blokes wearing the same sweatshirts, with all the places they've been to, thinking they're so hilarious.'

Many of the young actors recruited for the film were cast based on how they coped with auditions where they had to improvise around 'squirmingly embarrassing scenes'. An ability to think on one's feet was crucial for a four-week shoot on a film that was supposed to look like discovered footage. Much of the filming had to be done on the hoof, with cast and crew working guerrilla style because they were not always secured with permits to shoot at particular locations. The cheap look of the wedding video at least pre-empted any critics who might attack the film for its paltry budget (reportedly only around £7,000). It was shot on video – partly out of sheer financial necessity – even before the likes of *Dogme* and *The Blair Witch Project* emerged from outside Britain. Payne was advised that one could not make a cinema film on video, but finally, in August 2000 – two years after it was made – it was screened at London's National Film Theatre over one week.

Some critics were impressed. The *Evening Standard*'s reviewer praised how it 'uses its zero budget to its advantage with an inventiveness that more experienced filmmakers might do well to emulate'. The *Independent on Sunday* liked it too: 'What starts as a cheery homage to laddism becomes an unexpectedly acute critique of its shortcomings.' One US newspaper *Variety*, reviewing the belated DVD release (not issued in America till 2006), gave particular attention to Serkis's versatility as Spider. 'His character is goofy enough to be a plausible leader of the Jolly Boys, yet possesses enough sensitivity to realise that there may be more to life than what he has.'

When casting the film, Payne had spotted the pre-Ali G Baron Cohen performing stand-up comedy. And he remembered Serkis from the theatrical production of *Mojo* at London's Royal Court in the summer of 1995. 'His character was a slightly smug, self-important big fish in a small pond, qualities which Spider has.' In Payne's opinion, the presence of Serkis in the cast of his film turned the project from what he called 'a soggy house of cards in a shower of disinterest to something which might happen'.

Payne was, of course, far from alone in adoring *Mojo*. The packed houses of the Royal Court, and glittering reviews, had led to a film version in 1996, for which writer/director Jez Butterworth rewrote two-thirds of the script with his brother Tom. The new version would find only two actors – Serkis as the motormouth Potts and Hans Matheson as budding teen idol Silver Johnny – reprising their roles from 1995 (Aidan Gillen would switch from the role of Skinny to that of Baby), while two previously unseen characters were introduced for the screen. One was Ezra (Ricky Tomlinson), the owner of the Atlantic Club, who is literally cut in half before too long; the other, in a cameo by playwright Harold Pinter, was Sam Ross, the boss who is muscling in on his venue, and his star.

Again spouting machine-gun banter with sidekick Sweets (now played by Martin Gwynn-Jones), Serkis's Potts switched between blustering and cringing, depending on whom he was addressing. 'We should be seeing a lot more of Andy Serkis,' recommended the *People* newspaper, 'whose slick-backed wideboy is like watching Del Boy: The Early Years.' But most reviewers, cautious about how much the film understandably looked like a stage play, were happier to celebrate the brilliance of the ensemble cast, while reluctant to single out one performer. Alexander Walker, the long-time film critic for the London *Evening Standard*, went so far as to write that it was 'the best group casting I have ever seen in a British film'. It was a statement that paid tribute to the care, precision and zest of the best stage writing, as well as the finest screenplays.

Andy Serkis felt his stage experience counted a great deal, even when performing film scripts far below the standard of *Mojo*. 'You can make bad scripts work – especially in film,' he told IGN Filmforce early in 2003. 'You're required to do a lot, believe me.' He would not say which scripts were below par, but would reiterate that he was able to draw the 'emotional ballast' and 'imagination' from his theatre days to lift weak material, which can be a creative challenge for an actor to rise to. After many years of having to project imagination out to an audience in a theatre, he found that a film set presented the stimulation to the audience for real. 'That's the one thing about graduating to working on film,' he said. 'You have all the stimulation there, for real. You're doing a lot of work on stage from your imagination – you are projecting that space out to the audience. You're doing a lot of the creating, if you like.'

And in 1999 he would secure his place in a complex, career-changing film role that would not grant him the luxury of visual stimulation. Working with a team of animators, model-makers and motion-capture (or 'mocap') specialists – as well as with a director and sometimes with actors – he would require every ounce of that 'emotional ballast', that 'imagination', and that ability to 'project that space'.

CHAPTER 6

LORD OF THE RINGS I: CROUCHING ADDICT

January 1999, in Hackney, east London. The previous day, Andy Serkis has auditioned for the part of Bill Sikes in what will become ITV's lavish remake of Charles Dickens's *Oliver Twist*, dramatised for television by the screenwriter and playwright Alan Bleasdale. He feels he underperformed at the audition, but does not yet know how he fared. Then the telephone rings. It's a call about a very different project, one that is to shift his career into a different gear, and one that – in the most unlikely fashion – will bring him stardom and international recognition.

On the other end of the line is agent Michael Duff. He tells Serkis that the casting director John Hubbard is casting British actors for Peter Jackson's big-screen trilogy of J. R. R. Tolkien's epic three-volume fantasy *The Lord of the Rings*, which is due to begin shooting in New Zealand later in the year. Duff's message has a mysterious air. 'I'm not entirely sure what they mean by this, but they want to see you for the voice for an animated character, which would probably be about three weeks' work.'

'*The voice for an animated character*.' Serkis's initial response is one of mild derision. Typical, he thinks. Aren't there any proper acting roles on offer? I mean, there must be loads of characters in it.

Over in New Zealand's capital city, Wellington, Peter Jackson had made several films, each more ambitious than the previous one, but he had been waiting for 20 years to be able to make a cinematic version of J. R. R. Tolkien's three books: *The Fellowship of the Ring*, *The Two Towers* and *The Return of the King*. Jackson had first plunged into the texts in 1978, when, as a 17-year-old photo-engraver, he faced a 12-hour train journey from Wellington to Auckland. It captured his imagination instantly, and he would for ever regard it as one of the great works of fiction. It was a favourite of many others, too – it frequently topped reader polls and had sold millions of copies even before Jackson's vision could reach the big screen. But how would he be able not only to satisfy so many readers, each of whom had their own idea of what Tolkien's imaginary world of Middle-earth looked like, but also to attract a whole new generation of people who had never sampled the books before?

A professor in Anglo-Saxon Studies at Oxford University, John Ronald Reuel Tolkien had been mapping out Middle-earth since 1917, but a moment of inspiration while he was supposed to be marking examination papers – when he started to scribble some material about a hobbit who lived in a hole in the ground – marked the start of what became

The Hobbit, published in 1937. The title character of the book is Bilbo Baggins, who embarks on a journey through dangerous terrain, and happens upon a magic ring that renders invisible anyone who wears it. *The Hobbit* was an immediate success, and Tolkien's publishers pressed him for a sequel, but it would take 12 years for him to complete his more complex and ambitious follow-up.

The Lord of the Rings begins with Baggins using the ring to become invisible at his eleventy-first birthday party, but this Ring is no toy: forged by the Dark Lord Sauron to control Middle-earth's society, it is a Ring representing evil, which would consume the spirit of any being who possesses it. The only option available to Middle-earth's society is to embark on a quest to destroy the Ring by throwing it back into the fiery chasm it originated from on Mount Doom, an act that would in turn vanquish Sauron once and for all. A Fellowship, headed by Bilbo Baggins's nephew Frodo, is formed with the intention of achieving this, while attempts are made by the wizard Gandalf to reunite and repair the spirits of Middle-earth's population. However, when the Fellowship becomes divided, Frodo must soldier on with just one loyal companion: fellow hobbit Sam Gamgee.

Yet in time Frodo and Sam will come to be accompanied on their long and dangerous journey by one more curious entity with darker, shadier motives: a hissing, spitting isolated creature called Gollum. First introduced in *The Hobbit*, when he loses the Ring to Bilbo Baggins, Gollum began life as a hobbit called Sméagol, who murdered his cousin Déagol in order to gain ownership of the Ring, and then found out about its special powers, but was sent into exile as punishment for his malicious thieving. Boiling with twisted rage, he disappears to the murky and lonely depths of Middle-earth's Misty Mountains, where his frustration and hatred consume him and render him insane. When he discovers that the corrupting Ring (which he regularly refers to sibilantly as 'My preciousss') is now being carried by Frodo – who has the noble intention of destroying it – he offers to show the duo the way to Mount Doom, but plots instead to cause the pair to become enemies, and snatch back the prized Ring.

It is hard to sum up, in just a few sentences, exactly why the three *Lord of the Rings* books have had such broad and long-lasting appeal since they were first published in the mid-1950s, but they certainly offer several universal and lasting themes: the dilemmas about right and wrong, the unshakeable belief that good will ultimately defeat evil, that humanity will display courage in the face of opposition, and that there is a willingness for people to sacrifice themselves for the greater good.

The Lord of the Rings may have been read by millions of loyal readers worldwide, but Andy Serkis was not one of them. He had leafed through *The Hobbit* when he was about eight years old as a way of making the bus journeys to and from school seem slightly more interesting, but it was his wife, Lorraine Ashbourne – who *had* become engrossed in its trilogy sequel when young – who urged him to proceed with the audition.

Even so, was he wasting his time? *The Lord of the Rings* seemed to be a long way from the sort of screen work in which he had flourished over the previous few years, what he later described as 'socially relevant drama, with powerful characters, facing titanic struggles in living day to day'.

Uncertain that this sort of project represented a suitable career move for him, he tried to reassure himself that it was nothing more than a gimmicky role. 'It'll probably be a load of old crap, anyway,' he told himself. With the casting audition fast approaching, there was insufficient time for him to familiarise himself with Tolkien's full text. In any case, he confessed to being no speed reader, and he had not long become a parent, so even thinking about opening a long book seemed foolhardy. Instead, he decided to concentrate on the character he was reading for – Gollum – and his very individual backstory.

It was Tolkien's description of Gollum's gurgling, anguished rasp of a voice that first fascinated Serkis, and he spent some time considering the options on which voice to use – in terms of timbre, tone, pitch, accent. Attempts at simply voicing random creatures seemed rootless and unsatisfying. He was no mimic. He knew he needed a psychological basis for this voice, so next he thought about the character's isolated state, his self-pity, and the way he would mumble to himself. Perhaps Gollum's pain could be lodged in his throat! Having killed his cousin Déagol, he could have been eaten away by the resulting guilt to the verge of feeling choked.

While Serkis was thinking about all this, one of his three cats, Diz, began to cough up and spit out furballs – the result of a cat swallowing loose fur after licking itself clean, then finding the fur collecting in its throat. But it was only later that night in bed, as he lay unable to sleep and remembered Diz's involuntary coughings and convulsions, that he had a brainwave – the key to Gollum's constricted voice. 'Maybe he sounds like a cat being sick!'

So the inspiration for the voice of Gollum's whiney gurgle came from Serkis's pet cats. The frustration and constriction and guilt within Gollum could physically lie in the throat. The guilt associated with killing his cousin Déagol could almost choke him. He thought of his feline pets at home.

When Serkis met casting director John Hubbard at the audition, he began to realise that this project was going to be more than just a whirl of special-effects pyrotechnics and underwritten characterisation. Plus, he was intrigued that the man adapting *The Lord of the Rings* was Peter Jackson. Serkis regarded Jackson's *Heavenly Creatures* as a 'sublime, dark and wonderful film'. Serkis's enthusiasm was boosted some more when he was shown some illustrations for Gollum's character, drawn by Alan Lee.

Jackson was still on the other side of the world in New Zealand preparing the film's screenplay. So Serkis had to record his audition on tape in London. His audition scene was an early draft of the scene in Emyn Muil, where Gollum swears on the 'precious'. But this was to be an unusual performance, which went far beyond simply delivering the 'cat-being-sick' voice that he had been working on. He climbed onto a chair, and hunched his shoulders so that he was perched in a low stooping position. It was this bent, gnarled and twisted posture, acting out the pained, wretched and manipulative nature of the hobbit's persona, that was in keeping with the voice he had created. As he delivered the creature's speech, he contorted his face into some bizarre expressions.

John Hubbard looked startled, even shocked, leading Serkis to assume he had made a terrible blunder. Quite the opposite, as it turned out. 'Andy, how do you do that?'

Hubbard wondered aloud in astonishment. 'I absolutely fell off my chair,' He told *USA Today* in 2003. 'He had done so much research. It was one of the finest auditions I've ever been in.'

Serkis's audition tape was duly dispatched to New Zealand. The next thing he knew, Peter Jackson and his co-writer, co-producer and wife Fran Walsh were planning to visit London, keen to meet their Gollum. It turned out that Serkis's relatively low profile in the international film world would be to his advantage: Jackson preferred not to cast 'a star' in such a role. And, in any case, would 'a star' be ready and willing to spend three years having his face and body disguised and distorted by special effects? Andy Serkis had no particular interest in stardom, anyway. 'It was not going to make me a new Brad Pitt,' he deadpanned to the *Sunday Times* in 2005.

In April 1999, Serkis met Jackson and Walsh at the American Church on Tottenham Court Road in London's West End, by which time Serkis had been cast as Bill Sikes in *Oliver Twist*. Filming for that was just about to start near Prague in the Czech Republic. But he clicked immediately with Jackson and Walsh. And now he started to discover just how far they wanted to go in making Gollum as believable as possible. While this small, emaciated ball of malevolence would be far less obvious in the first of the three films, *The Fellowship of the Ring*, he would be a key component of the second one, *The Two Towers*, and would be absolutely central to the final instalment, *The Return of the King*.

Out of 65 speaking parts required for the three movies, Gollum was the only one that would be realised entirely through computer-generated imagery (CGI). 'There are all sorts of creatures and monsters that will be created on the computer,' said Jackson, 'but Gollum's different because he says dialogue and has to have an emotional connection in the story. He's very much a real character.'

'I wanted to do it as an on-screen character,' Serkis told *Time Out* in 2002. 'I didn't think I needed the CGI. But Peter Jackson had a very specific idea of Gollum.' Very specific, in fact: emaciated, centuries-old, and a mere three foot six in height – some two feet shorter than Serkis.

Jackson and Walsh felt that, even with prosthetic make-up, it would be unrealistic to cast an actor in such an unusual role, and retain any sense of authenticity. However, they were also determined that whoever they cast would need considerable acting abilities, someone who needed to inject into the scenes an emotional and psychological level of credibility. 'Peter had the idea to do something unprecedented,' Serkis told *Variety* in 2002. 'Even though Gollum would be computer-generated, Peter wanted all the emotion and the physicality to come from a single performance.'

As Peter Jackson outlined plans to marry acting and CGI like no one before him, Serkis now knew that he wanted to accept the challenge and participate. What he couldn't quite grasp, at this early stage, was this technique of mocap that Jackson and Walsh were trying to explain – something to do with dots being stuck all over his body and face in a special studio. It wasn't as if he knew a great deal about special effects in the first place. Not that Jackson was that much more of an expert when it came to computer technology, as he would later laughingly confess. 'I'm absolutely hopeless on computers. I understand what they do, I understand how they do it, but I can't actually type in the instructions myself.'

Born at Hallowe'en 1961, Peter Jackson developed a fascination with escapism, fantasy and filmmaking in his childhood in Wellington. He loved Adam West as *Batman* on TV, and, even when very young, was busying himself constructing monsters out of rubber and wire, and persuading his parents to appear in various homemade short films. He became a fan of fantasy TV shows like the British puppet series *Thunderbirds* and *Stingray*, as well as the groundbreaking comedy work of *Monty Python*.

On leaving school, he had become a photo-engraver for the *Wellington Evening Post*. This steady job, which he held over several years in his late teens and early twenties, enabled him to scrape together some money to shoot a debut feature film with some of the actors drawn from his co-workers. This was the low-budget gory horror comedy *Bad Taste* (1987), and it led to the zombie flick *Meet* the *Feebles* (1989) and 1992's *Brain Dead* (retitled *Dead Alive* when it was eventually released – to no little acclaim – in the United States).

Jackson's international breakthrough, though, came in 1994 with an emotive drama based on a real-life murder case that had shocked New Zealand in the mid-1950s. *Heavenly Creatures* told the story of how two teenage girls – Pauline Parker and Juliet Hulme – plotted cold-bloodedly to kill Pauline's mother. Jackson was intrigued by how the girls' brutal actions were born of uncontrollable fantasising about what it might be like to kill someone – a fantasy that many people may have but very few translate into reality. The film consciously used sweetness the way other dramas about murder might have chosen to use malevolence, and the effect was every bit as chilling. Jackson could identify with the testimonies of both Parker and Hulme, who confessed to an almost feverish fantasy life. 'If you're an only child you spend a lot of time by yourself and you develop a strong ability to entertain yourself, to conjure up fantasy.'

Parker and Hulme had fertile and even outlandish imaginations, devising ideas for what they called their 'fourth world' – a fairytale kingdom called Borovnia, in which their violent and bloodthirsty fantasies could be explored. In Jackson's telling of their story, these fantasy sequences combined Plasticine figures (representing the kingdom's population) and digital technology. He had originally planned to use actors in medieval garb, before learning that Juliet Hulme had actually constructed Plasticine figures herself at the time. It was an inspired idea for Jackson, and truly in the spirit of the interest he had in special effects.

With powerful showings from Melanie Lynskey (as Parker) and the young British actress Kate Winslet (then just 19), *Heavenly Creatures* was an international success, even landing an Academy Award nomination, but Jackson was insistent that he would not bow purely to what he regarded as the homogenised values of Hollywood. He continued to make films in New Zealand, including the ghostly thriller *The Frighteners* (starring Michael J. Fox, which the director summed up as '*Casper* meets *Silence of the Lambs*'), arguing that, while his productions would inevitably be small-scale compared with the blockbusters of Steven Spielberg and

James Cameron, he could exercise complete control on his creations, from conception, through development and filming, to its completion and release.

All the while, still dazzled by the tales of Middle-earth's hobbits (or halflings, as they are sometimes called), trolls and orcs, he dreamt of making a film version of *The Lord of the Rings*. Apart from an animated version in 1978, no one had attempted one, and for many years it seemed that the only way of taking Tolkien's world away from the printed page might lie in a sound adaptation. To this end, BBC Radio 4's epic 26-part dramatisation in 1981 was well received, but Jackson still longed to make a screen incarnation.

In 1998, a golden opportunity arose. New Line Cinema, a division of Time Warner in the USA, agreed to bankroll an adaptation: three films, to be made concurrently over a period of more than three years. But how would they please both those who were new to Tolkien and those who virtually knew the books inside out? For Jackson, who believed there had never yet been a classic film in the fantasy genre, it was a formidable challenge. His main aim in the early stages was to avoid what he called 'that American heavy-metal look. It's a style that I don't think is appropriate but it's been used on a lot of Tolkien artwork and I think Tolkien would have been appalled.' Jackson sidestepped the issue by approaching the film as if it were a historical drama rather than a fantasy epic. And New Zealand seemed to be an ideal location in which the entire tale could unfold.

There were other good reasons to confine the making of the film to New Zealand that went beyond Jackson's wish to retain complete control. He was realistic about how fellow filmmakers would continue to live and work in New Zealand only if the government pumped more money into the islands' film industry. 'The average American has never heard of the All Blacks [rugby team] and doesn't know anything about our sporting success,' he said. 'Yet they all know New Zealand from movies like *The Piano*, *Once Were Warriors* and *Heavenly Creatures*, which were made here with a tiny amount of support from the government.'

Financial backing for *The Frighteners* had come from Universal Pictures in the USA, which had also promised to help fund a new lavish remake of *King Kong*, but plans for the latter were scuppered at the start of 1997, when it was discovered that Hollywood was set to release a *Godzilla* remake, and another revival about a gorilla – Disney's *Mighty Joe Young*. For now, *Kong* was a dormant project, subsequently to be revived in a saga we'll come to in Chapter 9. But at least Jackson and Walsh's company, Wingnut Films, had been given the green light to start work on the *Lord of the Rings* trilogy. Almost every Hollywood studio had passed on funding it. Only two (Polygram and New Line) remained in the frame when Jackson and Walsh flew to Los Angeles in August 1998 with some props and a special 40-minute teaser tape of test footage of locations, creature models and special effects.

Rather than a two-picture epic, which Miramax Studios had previously agreed to, New Line would permit a trilogy to be made: three films to be made simultaneously, which would premiere over three consecutive Christmases between 2001 and 2003. The total budget would finally reach $280 million. Going ahead with this plan was a risk, but making each one separately (quite apart from being more expensive in the long run) could have had a nervous studio pulling the plug if the first film had underperformed. 'Shooting three separate movies back to back has never been done before,' Jackson accepted. 'But I think it's unfair to say to an audience, "Come to *The Fellowship of the Ring*, and, if it's successful, we make Part Two.'

As Jackson continued to beaver away on the screenplays in Christchurch with co-writers Walsh, Philippa Boyens and Stephen Sinclair, the start date for *The Lord of the Rings*' shooting schedule was moved from the summer of 1999 to the autumn. Work would finally begin on 11 October on a project its director felt honoured and privileged to be in charge of. Technological breakthroughs and increasingly sophisticated computer equipment now suggested that the most extraordinarily vivid footage could be created to rival almost any vision that could be held in one's imagination. Jackson would work at the centre of the gargantuan operation, directing sections of the story, and overseeing footage beamed in by satellite.

Not that much information about *The Lord of the Rings* would seep out for some time: beyond the announcement that the project was happening at all, almost everything was shrouded in the utmost secrecy, owing to the terms of the contract that had been signed. With such immense sums of money involved, the element of surprise for press and public would be a crucial part of the film's power and charm.

When a casting call requested candidates who were either under 4 feet 2 inches (1.28m) or over 6 feet 8 inches (2.07m) in height, it fuelled rumours that Jackson was scouting for people to play halflings or elves. In fact, the point of the search was to find people of the right physical dimensions in order to develop special effects, rather than to cast actual actors. It had been expected by some that Jackson might cast authentic people with restricted height. Instead, they cast actors they wanted, then used prosthetics and computer trickery to reduce them in size. 'I certainly don't want to use puppets or CGI characters,' said Jackson, 'because this is a story about real people.'

As for who might be cast, there was a flurry of chatter on the Internet about who would star in the trilogy. Sean Connery's name was supposedly a possibility for the part of Gandalf, but Jackson dismissed this. 'Whoever will be in all three of these movies will basically be spending most of 18 months in New Zealand. So it's much better to work with unknown actors, who are happy just to do the work.' Ian McKellen, who landed the role of Gandalf, was apprehensive about spending so long away from his homeland, but was delighted to have committed, later described it as 'being the most fulfilling and enjoyable job that I've had in 40 years of professional acting'. And it wasn't as if the likes of McKellen, or Ian Holm (Bilbo Baggins), Christopher Lee (Saruman), Cate Blanchett (Galadriel), Elijah Wood (Frodo) or Sean Astin (Sam) were *unknowns*. But the main thing was that Jackson had been allowed by the studio, New Line Cinema, to cast the best people for the job rather than the most famous or obviously bankable.

Andy Serkis was now confirmed in the role of Gollum. Returning from the Czech Republic, where he had been filming *Oliver Twist* as Bill Sikes, he arrived home in London to find a mysterious package. Carefully tearing open the package, he found three film scripts entitled

'Jamboree': 'An affectionate, coming-of-age drama, set in the New Zealand boy scout movement during the years of turmoil, 1958–63.' Taking a slightly closer look at the scripts, he realised the cover sheets were fakes. There was no such film as *Jamboree*. It was to stop the scripts getting into the wrong hands, typical of the level of secrecy being practised at Wingnut Films. And, when Serkis finally reached the *Lord of the Rings* set in New Zealand, he would find lots of location signs that suggested that the fake film *Jamboree* was being shot there.

The actor was near note-perfect when it came to reproducing Gollum's voice, and he had used his audition to convey his crouching physical awkwardness. But there was still plenty of work to be done in researching Gollum's psychological motivations, and Serkis would spend weeks and months deep in research and contemplation, trying to get to grips with how to make him as credible as possible.

Gollum was in the grand tradition of such biblical figures as the fallen angel Lucifer, or Cain, who after killing his brother Abel is cursed with the words 'You will be a restless wanderer on earth.' Then, there were such literary antiheroes as Caliban in Shakespeare's *The Tempest*, Uriah Heep in Dickens's *David Copperfield*, the Hunchback of Notre Dame, Frankenstein's creature and Dracula. Additional inspiration for Serkis, though, came from his interest in art. Twentieth-century painters such as Otto Dix (1891–1969), the Austrian Expressionist painter Egon Schiele (1890–1918), Francis Bacon (1909–1992), Lucien Freud (b. 1922) and the American fantasy artist Gerald Brom (b. 1965) had all succeeded in capturing on canvas the faces of tormented human beings. But there was one much older painting that had haunted Serkis since childhood – a fifteenth-century work by Leonardo da Vinci depicting St Jerome: 'The memory of the anguish on his face and his semi-naked, ageing body jumped back at me and became part of the physical vocabulary.'

Another package to arrive from New Zealand contained some shots of sculptures of Gollum's face. He looked like an alien, 'bald with huge eyes' in the words of Serkis. There was also one pencil sketch of Gollum by artist John Howe, which was to inspire how Serkis as Gollum would move in the film. To Serkis the sketch depicted Gollum as 'a cross between a homeless junkie and a survivor of a concentration camp'. The notion of Gollum as an addict would be a major influence on how Serkis would play him, and Peter Jackson and his co-writers agreed that the concept of addiction was a very useful way of showing 'the obsessive, craven lustful nature of Gollum's behaviour'.

'It seemed logical to take this idea of lust to a very dangerous, psychotic level,' Serkis later wrote. 'Gollum is, in my opinion, dealing with a level of obsession and addiction that most people thankfully don't ever have to face.' Nevertheless, in order to make Gollum someone that an audience could identify with, it seemed necessary to Serkis to bring in a more human level of addiction. 'What if you were addicted to shoplifting, gambling, drugs? Or to violence, crime or murder? Imagine only feeling satisfied, calm and at rest by killing? So, instead of having to rush out and buy a packet of cigarettes because you were desperate, you had to assault and kill someone. How much would you "love and hate" yourself then?'

Gollum's addiction was towards the Ring, what he considered the ultimate and only prize. He was, in Serkis's words, 'a Ring junkie'. Everything about Gollum – mind, body and soul – was driven by the craving for his fix from his 'precious' Ring. 'Peter and I agreed early on that Gollum was an addict,' Serkis told the *Independent* in 2003. 'It was important for me to root him in reality, to treat him as human, because he looks so extreme. I thought it was a good idea to use the Ring as a metaphor for addiction. He's suffering cold turkey.'

And he told CNN in 2004, 'People like that cannot help themselves. You realise that the addiction is so strong, they're as helpless as a child.'

He told the *Japan Times* in 2004, 'The crucial thing was about how that addiction would affect him physically, and the whole pathology associated with addiction: the lying, the withdrawal, his passive-aggressive side. I wanted him to be physically torn apart by this thing. And the voice really came about by thinking of involuntary reactions. He's trapped in his throat, from this moment in time where he kills his cousin, so it's like Tourette's, an involuntary spasm.'

Gollum's addiction to the Ring was a weighty compulsion that would render him little more than a 'crawling wretch'. So desperate was he for his fix that he would crawl anywhere and everywhere. 'I strongly felt that Gollum should be on all-fours at all times,' said Serkis. 'It just seemed wrong that he could walk on two feet – his descent into madness was like the evolution of man in reverse.' There was the feeling of vengeance too: Gollum's pain, believed Serkis, 'is like that of a wounded, psychotically jealous husband whose wife has left him, and who imagines a million ways to get revenge.' Above all, though, Serkis had to keep in mind at all times that Gollum was complex and that, had he not become consumed by the need for the Ring, he might be very different. He was not so much an evil being as a flawed one, and, as long as the man playing him could hold on to that thought, Gollum could be redeemable.

Most of the others in *The Lord of the Rings* tended to be more easily categorised as good or evil than Gollum. Yet surely human beings are a collision of qualities and drawbacks. 'We're not heroes on the whole,' suggested Serkis. 'Most people don't have the ability to hold onto principle. They're challenged constantly and I think that's what people respond to in [Gollum].' Happily, Peter Jackson and Fran Walsh were in agreement with the idea of empathising with Gollum. They were not interested in portraying him as purely Machiavellian.

Serkis was originally supposed to jet off to Wellington in October 1999, but it soon became apparent that his services would not be required for several months. Aside from some test dialogue recordings he made for the film's animators (which began from December), for the time being he worked on two other film projects in his homeland: Julien Temple's *Pandaemonium* (in which he played the eighteenth-century Jacobean revolutionary John Thelwall) and *Shiner*, the boxing gangster thriller starring Michael Caine. Finally, on 5 April 2000, it was time for him to bid farewell to his wife Lorraine and his young daughter Ruby, to board the flight to New Zealand.

'Saying goodbye was awful,' Serkis later recalled. His journey to Wellington would take more than 24 hours, but it would not be one of sleep or relaxation. Throughout the flight, Serkis feverishly filled time by rereading the scripts and preparing himself for the months ahead. His industrious mindset meant that, by the time the plane touched down in Auckland, he was 'absolutely trashed'. But on the final leg of the journey – from Auckland to Wellington – a jet-lagged but excited Serkis met Elijah Wood (Frodo) and Sean Astin (Sam), the two actors he would be working with constantly. Both had already been on the film set for six months.

In Wellington, Serkis was greeted by the film's producer Barrie Osborne, the visual-effects team and animation crew (led by animation director Randy Cook), and then, the team at the Weta Workshop (named after a large ancient insect native to New Zealand that was thought to be indestructible). And then, finally, Andy Serkis was face to face with various versions of his new alter ego: Gollum models made of clay, including a full-sized naked sculpture that had been designed as a template for the character to be computer-generated. The detail of the model was considerable: bones dug against its flesh and there were lacerations and scars on its skin to illustrate the torture it had experienced.

Meeting these models brought home to Serkis how different this would all be from his previous acting experiences. 'I had the first dawning realisation that, unlike any character I'd ever played before, one of the major challenges would be the fact that I didn't totally "own" the role.' This created a little bit of a conflict of interests for Serkis. While the act of acting is necessarily a selfish one, where the performer has to know their role better than anyone else, in this case he would have to share the creation and development of Gollum: 'You're the voice and emotions, and eventually the movements, but the body will be taken care of by many very talented people, with their own equally valid opinions. Your body will vanish into thin air and be replaced by digital ones and zeros . . .'

Andy Serkis's first full day on the *Rings* set was spent familiarising himself with 'Gollum's physical vocabulary', considering some of the rich imagery that Tolkien had used in describing him: comparing his movements to those of spiders, or grasshoppers or frogs. But there was still more meeting and greeting to do too. Next, he would meet Orlando Bloom (who was playing the elf Legolas). Serkis found that Bloom was 'brimming with an almost insane energy that you'd imagine vampires to have before a night on the town'.

Bonding with the other actors in order to draw the best out of each other was just as vital on this shoot as any other. Sharing a car journey of several hours with Elijah Wood, whom Serkis had enjoyed seeing in films such as *The Ice Storm*, was important, given that their very first scenes together would be among their most intense and dramatic. 'He just *was* Frodo,' Serkis remembered. 'I was to find out on set that his energy, focus and consummate professionalism really gave power to all around him.'

And then there was the meeting with the epic project's director. Serkis has described Peter Jackson as 'a man clearly on a mission of Herculean proportions', who required remarkable powers of leadership to oversee a total of seven film units across New Zealand's North and South Islands.

Jackson may have been in charge, but there were so many people working on *The Lord of the Rings* that a sense of community spirit was vital. There was very much an ethos that everyone involved in the operation of making the film – actors, writers, production staff and technicians – was part of a colossal extended family. One regular daily feature during the shoot was watching the rushes of the previous day's material back at the hotel. Some directors would never share such material with actors at this early stage of filming, but Jackson was different. 'This was just one example', said Serkis, 'of the feeling instilled by Peter that we were all filmmakers trying to create this story together. It was almost like watching your own family in home movies.' It would eventually lead to the making of a Sean Astin short film, *The Long and the Short of It*, which would star some of the crew and would be made by the actors. Serkis was appointed location manager on the shoot.

Indeed, despite the armies of cast and crew present, Serkis felt that Jackson's project had its own sense of intimacy. 'There was never a sense of being in this huge unwieldy thing,' he told the *Japan Times* in 2004. 'There was a lot of on-the-hoof stuff. Pete says it was a bit like shooting the biggest home movie in the world.' Meanwhile, Jackson would be beavering away on the main plot, the key storyline scenes that he would be directing himself. Serkis had no doubt about how much Jackson trusted his actors to explore and show their own initiative: 'He really let you run with the ball. That's his greatest skill: to trust his actors.'

Serkis had done plenty of theoretical research into Gollum, but now he had to put this into practice on the set. To play Gollum properly did not just require perfecting the voice and understanding the psychological motivation, but locating a physical empathy too – 'being inside his head, his skin, his bones'. His commitment to getting this right was total: wearing specially constructed Hobbit feet to get used to how he moved, or shaving his head to 'feel the wind against my skull, like Gollum, to feel more vulnerable, brutal and dehumanised'. Even the night before the shooting of his first scene, when he found sleep impossible, he jogged down to Tawhai Falls to 'get into character' for a couple of hours. He made his return trip back to the hotel as Gollum, crouched on all-fours. As it turned out, the following day's shooting was postponed, to Serkis's great frustration, but all was not lost. Animation director Randy Cook wanted some reference footage of Gollum, whereupon Serkis was able to let off steam and put all of his preparation (including that of the previous night) to good use.

At long last, Serkis's first scene on the film was shot for real on 13 April 2000. It was the sequence from *The Two Towers* in which Gollum would lead Frodo and Sam out of Emyn Muil. Beginning the location shoot, though, was in some ways an embarrassing experience for Serkis. Wearing 'what amounted to a homemade, tie-dyed fetish outfit' before a sniggering film crew totalling around 100 people, while clinging to the side of a volcano, ranked as one of the most mortifying moments of his life to date. 'In the future, this "costume" was to be dubbed a "unitard", which I have to tell you describes exactly how I felt wearing it.' Peter Jackson's arrival at the scene was no help to the hapless actor: he simply joined in the giggling. But everyone fell silent when first assistant director Caro Cunningham ordered the laughter to stop.

Jackson's plan was that any location scene involving Serkis as Gollum would be shot in three stages. To begin with, filming took place with Andy Serkis appearing 'on camera' with the other actors, usually Elijah Wood and Sean Astin. This version, known as a 'reference pass', was captured for the benefit of the visual-effects department to work on later. A motion-controlled camera was used so that the shot could be replicated a second time. Next, the same scene was shot again, for real. This time, Serkis was off-camera, but delivering the same lines of dialogue at the same points. Wood and Astin still acted as if Serkis were still in the frame reacting to them, which required immense levels of concentration, especially if it was a fight scene, for which Serkis would have to call out descriptions of his physical moves – moves he had wordlessly made in the first take. (His fellow actors would have two stages to perfect their performances. Serkis had the added pressure of having just one.) Finally, a third version of the scene was shot, with no actors present. Now, the camera replicated the move to give a clean background 'plate' for the benefit of the animators.

Serkis began to wonder what he must have looked like from the perspective of his fellow actors. It was relatively straightforward to watch Wood and Astin and play off each other. 'But when they look at me,' he thought, 'all they must see is a man in a gimp suit, with a face that makes Jim Carrey's look relaxed and a voice that sounds like a cat being sick.' This way of working became a little easier with time, but, to begin with, reviewing the daily rushes back at the hotel was an excruciating and bizarre experience for Serkis. 'There were Frodo and Sam walking through the blasted rocky landscape of Mordor, everything working perfectly to create a magical reality, then suddenly the bald lunatic in pale green spandex comes lolloping into view.'

But, if nothing else, work for Andy Serkis had begun. 'At last, I was no longer a Gollum virgin.'

The shoots would be tough for him. Ahead lay a day when a surprise snowfall hit a location shoot of a scene that was meant to look like summertime. The crew spent a whole morning armed with blowtorches, hoses and heaters to rid the location of snow – before a shivering, wet-suited Serkis had to catch a fish as Gollum by hurling himself at the rocks in the still-icy stream. Peter Jackson was pleased with his efforts – but only after four perishing takes.

Jackson knew he had found the right man to play Gollum. He knew that Serkis's performance extended far beyond a voice artist's contribution. There was a physical and a psychological dimension – 'an emotional backbone' – to the Gollum he had cast.

CHAPTER 7

LORD OF THE RINGS II:
SERKIS IN MOTION

Only a fortnight after Andy Serkis's arrival at its nerve centre, the whole of the *Lord of the Rings* operation stopped for an Easter break. Most of the cast and crew headed back to Wellington, but he opted to stay in the grand New Zealand wilderness during the holiday interlude. Many times before, he had ventured into mountainous environments, on climbing expeditions both solo and in groups. 'To be dwarfed by nature always gives me a sense of connection and a feeling of being truly "in the moment". New Zealand wilderness really offers that possibility on a grand scale.'

It was starting to become clear to him that his role of Gollum, an outsider figure in *The Lord of the Rings*, was reflected in his isolation as an actor on the film. Without his fellow actors, and many thousands of miles away from daughter Ruby and wife Lorraine (who was now heavily pregnant with their second child), he was feeling a genuine sense of loneliness, which was both an advantage and a drawback. Although Gollum was indeed supposed to be an isolated creature, Serkis too couldn't help but feel rather cut off from the film's communal spirit, a status not helped by the fact that he had come relatively late to the shoot. 'The other cast members had all bonded through their roles – they were the Fellowship or the Hobbits and I was this weird unknown quantity which people didn't really know how to deal with.' In fact, during the whole of the shoot, Serkis would work directly with only four actors: Elijah Wood, Sean Astin, Thomas Robbins (who played Déagol), and – for a mere two scenes – David Wenham, who took the part of Faramir.

Recording the dialogue would also be a novel and slightly unsettling experience for Serkis. Ordinarily, an actor would stand at a podium and, via earphones, would be fed the audio track from filming. Then they would try to lip-synch the dialogue from the footage being shown in front of them on a screen. For Andy Serkis, capturing Gollum's dialogue would be a much more physically arduous task. First, he would be crouched on all-fours so that he could deliver the guttural rasp of Gollum in the best way. He had no pictures to react to, as they weren't ready yet. And, to add to the difficulties, he found it hard to hear his own voice through the earphones because of the highly individual noise he was producing. 'The way I produce the sound, by constricting my vocal chords, somehow resonates in my ears. If my ears are covered it makes me feel as if I'm semi-deaf!' There was also the worry of tiring out his voice, but what seemed to help was frequently treating himself to a concoction that came to be known as 'Gollum juice', a mix of lemon, honey, ginger and hot water.

Serkis was starting to feel uncomfortable, however, about the dialogue-recording process. He felt isolated, and unable to relate sufficiently well to the material that had been shot. There had still been very little discussion with Peter Jackson, the director, about how his efforts were faring, so he decided to write a letter to the producers expressing his doubts and concerns. Fortunately, their response would indicate that the whole point of the sessions was to experiment. Now, Jackson had plenty of versions of Gollum to choose among, and he could decide which one would work best in the context of the films.

The actor had mixed feelings about what had been achieved so far. In some ways, he delighted in the unconventional nature of the shoot, and enjoyed it as a challenge and adventure. Similarly, he understood that this was a long, complicated project and it would take up to three years to see how the sum of its many parts would fit together. This was never, he felt, going to be a film where he could say with conviction, 'Well, I certainly nailed that scene!' mere seconds after a take.

The biggest doubt of all, though, was this. Millions had been invested in *The Lord of the Rings*. But there was no guarantee whatsoever that the film would be a hit. Not only could it be a box-office flop, it could fail with the critics. And what about Tolkien's loyal band of readers who wanted something that could withstand comparison with the books? All that Andy Serkis could clutch onto right now was the trust he had for Peter Jackson's vision. 'I thought, if anyone can pull this off, he can,' he told *Adweek* years later. 'But I also thought, if this goes wrong, I'm going to have to go live on an island somewhere or just dig a hole and hide away.' Like Gollum in the Misty Mountains, perhaps? *The Lord of the Rings* looked like either making or breaking Andy Serkis's international career, and, at this early stage, 18 months before the first film would open, he could not imagine how it would fare.

* * *

Gollum was a fallen Hobbit. Before he was corrupted through possession of the Ring for hundreds of years, he was the innocent Sméagol. It was felt appropriate that Serkis should also play the part of Sméagol for a sequence that showed how he had transformed into the damaged and twisted Gollum. Consequently, Serkis's own face would appear in *The Two Towers* after all, in illustrating the split personality of Sméagol/Gollum. This schizophrenic-like relationship between the two sides of Gollum would rise to the surface most memorably in the final moments of *The Two Towers*, in a duologue where Gollum persuades both his psyches (both portrayed by Serkis) to lead Frodo and Sam to their deaths.

In May 2000, Peter Jackson, Fran Walsh and Philippa Boyens agreed that Serkis should play Sméagol as well as Gollum. So now he could play both parts – in a transformation scene from one to the other – and also in a flashback scene later. It was decided that Sméagol's voice would be distinguished as a more nasal tone, clipped and curt, as opposed to Gollum's lower, slower, growled delivery.

The split personality of Gollum and Sméagol seemed

extreme, but Serkis always felt that the entity's psychological state was only a heightened version of the conversations anyone has in their own mind every day. He told the *Japan Times* in 2004, 'Whenever we shot those scenes, where Gollum and Sméagol would be having this back and forth, I'd do the whole thing, and it's really the connecting breaths between the two that make him one person with two personalities.' Serkis did not believe, however, that Gollum was actually a schizophrenic. 'I think he's like me, able to turn on a sixpence. I talk to myself, want to throw my computer out the window, or get road rage...I think we all exist within a hair's breadth of doing very violent, dangerous things.'

In June 2000, Andy and Lorraine became parents for the second time when their son Sonny was born. Just as his furball-coughing cat had been the inspiration for Gollum's voice, the behaviour of both young children – switching between temporary bursts of aggression and vulnerability – would be a major influence on how Serkis developed this crawling, emaciated creature. If an infant throws a tantrum for not being allowed sweets, the outburst is not simply about being forbidden. It is also a lack of awareness and understanding about a bigger picture, a wider world. With no context, needing sweets for that briefest of moments became the child's only goal, only ambition, only purpose in life. The same was true of Gollum's addiction to the Ring, except that he had had the obsession for centuries.

As children gain a little self-awareness, they can also become manipulative. One day in the autumn of 2000, Andy's daughter Ruby, who was still not quite two years old but gaining greater self-awareness and independence every day, bit the finger of her baby sibling, Sonny, who was still only a few months old. Later that same day, she repeated the attack. 'I looked at my daughter with fresh eyes,' Serkis later wrote. 'It was as if she had lost some of her innocence. She had discovered a new power and was learning how to wield it.' But what truly startled her father was that she had consciously bitten Sonny's finger a second time, an expression that relished the power over someone smaller and more vulnerable. Maybe, thought Serkis, it was a gut survival response to feeling usurped.

Gollum was never far from Andy Serkis's mind, even when he wasn't at work with Peter Jackson and co. in New Zealand. As he later uncomfortably recalled, the first sighting of his newborn son Sonny had made him think of Sméagol, 'a squashed-up, old-man face on top of a pristine white baby body', or 'wretched Ring junkie'. But it did help to clarify in his mind how the characters of Sméagol and Gollum represent, respectively, the innocence of childhood and the loss of that innocence.

In addition, it made Serkis recall and explore again his own bad behaviour as a child. He thought about summer holidays in the Middle East in the 1970s, when he had found himself 'knocking the tails off tiny lizards with swipe from a bamboo stick'. Is anyone – Ruby? Andy? Sméagol? – born with a malicious streak, or do they acquire a fascination with power? The irrationality of childhood naughtiness does not necessarily fade for ever in adulthood. It bubbles under the surface of decency and courtesy, and occasionally rears its ugly head, usually when the person is under stress or being threatened.

Serkis had spent more and more time analysing Gollum's 'addicted' persona, by exploring his sense of isolation and alienation. Perhaps he could be a collector, an individual obsessed with the roots and beginnings of things. 'Objects became more important than people,' Serkis later wrote. 'At least they couldn't hurt him.' The most important object to Gollum – the only important object, of course – was the Ring. It added another dimension to Gollum; he may have been dysfunctional but it would have been reductive and misleading to have played him as unadulterated evil. Serkis had thought of him as an antihero in the vein of Travis Bickle, played by Robert de Niro in *Taxi Driver*, his soul corroded by a 'morbid self-attention'.

One of the centrepieces of the trilogy would be the transformative scene of *The Two Towers*, in which we witness the shunned young Sméagol fall, degenerate and emerge as the aged and damaged Gollum, destroyed by guilt as a result of killing Déagol. In preparation for the scene, extensive make-up was applied to Serkis's entire head and body, including a latex mask that covered his head and shoulders. Serkis was a little concerned, when Lorraine brought his children to visit that the sight of him might disturb them. Would they be freaked out? Ruby merely let out a sigh and said, 'Silly Daddy.'

But perhaps Serkis's greatest acting achievement of the trilogy occurs at the end of the second film: a three-minute *tour de force* of a scene in which he delivers a duologue between the split personality of Gollum/ Sméagol, where the former tries to persuade the latter to lure Frodo and Sam to their deaths in the lair of Shelob the spider. Serkis, who performed it as if he were delivering monologues on stage, regards it as his proudest *Lord of the Rings* moment.

Andy Serkis played the dual personality of Gollum/Sméagol with such aplomb that, in retrospect, it seems incredible that the original plan was to cast a different actor to play Sméagol. 'I said I really wanted to play that role,' he said. 'It makes no sense to not play Gollum all the way through. After I'd been working some time on it they decided that it was a good idea and would make total sense.' So impressive had Serkis been during the original shoot and motion-capture sessions of 2000 that Jackson, Walsh and Boyens caved in. But giving Serkis both roles now meant that the team at Weta had more work to do for the mocap scenes. The existing CG model of Gollum's face required a complete overhaul. It just didn't look enough like Andy Serkis. Gollum would have to be redesigned in Serkis's own image, which explains why the brief glimpses of the character in *The Fellowship of the Ring* are markedly different from how he looks in subsequent films.

The first press conference for *The Lord of the Rings* took place in a tent on set during the closing weeks of 2000. Invitations were restricted to local journalists, to underline just how important Wellington was in the making and development of the films. 'This is going to be bigger than *Star Wars*,' declared cast member John Rhys-Davies (Gimli the dwarf), which made Andy Serkis a little nervous, 'even though many of us actually believed he could be right.' Given that the first of the *Star Wars* prequels, *The Phantom Menace*, had been disappointingly received by some of the public and many critics in 1999, there was the possibility that *The Lord of the Rings* could make a bigger splash. All the same, it might be unwise to make such comparisons when the opening of the first instalment, *The Fellowship of the Ring*, was still over a year away.

The trilogy's mammoth 14-month stretch of principal photography ended on 22 December 2000. To commemorate the occasion, a wrap party was held on the waterfront. Three thousand people attended, all of whom had some input into making the film. As well as a feast, there was music from Kiwi bands, a cast performing a *haka* (a traditional Maori dance) and a compilation of outtakes and bloopers from the shot footage.

The Christmas and New Year break that followed found Serkis, plus family and friends, in a camper bus on a whistlestop tour of the sights of South Island. Serkis had to admit his obsessive nature did tend to make him get carried away when it came to organising holidays. The preparation required for going away on climbing expeditions, plus the anticipation of exploring somewhere new, made him – by his own admission – 'a complete control freak'. Plans for a further holiday in Fiji had to be abandoned, as Serkis received a call from his agent about a film role that, on the face of it, could hardly have been more different from Gollum. In January 2001, he had to go back to Manchester to portray the eccentric record producer Martin Hannett in *24 Hour Party People*.

That same month also saw the official *Lord of the Rings* website go live, which housed the first teaser trailer for *The Fellowship of the Ring* – a film whose premiere was still almost a year away. But would this mark the end of Serkis's duties as Gollum? Far from it. Unlike most of the other actors in the film, he would have to return to Weta's nerve centre many more times over the next couple of years, mainly for mocap work. As late as summer 2003, new scenes for *The Return of the King* – the third and final part of the trilogy – would still be being filmed.

* * *

August 2001: The past eight months had seen Andy Serkis playing an eccentric record producer (*24 Hour Party People*), a psychopathic killer (with Jonny Lee Miller in the thriller *The Escapist*) and a tormented wife beater called Jake in the Sam Shepard play *A Lie of the Mind* at the Donmar Warehouse theatre in London – described by one critic as 'wonderfully wired and desperate'. Now, however, he was at Pinewood Studios, Buckinghamshire, where he needed to cleanly rerecord Gollum's dialogue from the previous year's shoots – in a process called ADR, or automated dialogue replacement. Compared with the shoots in which Serkis would tumble down the sides of volcanoes or leap into icy streams, ADR sessions were relatively undemanding. The only snag was that Jake's voice in *A Lie of the Mind* required a different vocal range. Now, Serkis had to readjust his voice to meet the timbre, tone and pitch that Gollum's rasp required. 'It was obviously crucial to get the throat working in the same way,' wrote Serkis, 'as the voice would be the audience's main introduction to the character, more so than the images.'

Indeed, Gollum would make only a relatively brief contribution to *The Fellowship of the Ring*, mostly through sound only, and so when the film opened across the world in

December 2001, while he was not directly involved in the press tour, he could watch it objectively. 'I was so overwhelmed by the emotional power and magnitude…[that I was] completely drained by the experience. There aren't many films in one's life that have this kind of impact. I started to realise how much work needed to be done on Gollum over the course of the next year.'

What can't have harmed the fortunes of the trio of films was the unprecedented success of J. K. Rowling's *Harry Potter* series of books, which began transferring to the big screen in 2001 with *Harry Potter and the Sorcerer's Stone* (*Harry Potter and the Philosopher's Stone* in the UK, as is the title of the book). One reporter summed up the openings of both *Fellowship* and *Sorcerer's Stone* as 'the winter of the wizard'. Both stories addressed epic struggles between good and evil for millions of near-obsessive fans.

Having already grossed millions at the box office, in February 2002, *Fellowship* won the BAFTA Awards' Best Film of the Year award in the public vote. The critics were, if anything, even more smitten. When the nominations for the Academy Awards were announced, *Fellowship* received a staggering 13 nominations, including those for Best Motion Picture of the Year, Best Performance by an Actor in a Supporting Role (for Ian McKellen as Gandalf), Best Adapted Screenplay and Best Director (Peter Jackson), plus those for achievements in everything from cinematography and sound to makeup, costume design and visual effects. Even the original song, Enya's 'May It Be' was nominated for an Oscar.

Most of the actors had long departed *The Lord of the Rings*, but for Andy Serkis, along with Peter Jackson and the postproduction team, there was still a long way to go on both the second and third films. For Serkis, the laborious process of mocap would take up a fair bit of 2002 and the first half of 2003 as well.

As already outlined, during principal photography, Serkis had worn a skin-tight suit and crawled around as Gollum while two versions of each scene were shot: first, one on camera with Wood and Astin, then a second version where he would step off camera, whereupon 'Sean and Elijah would act to the void where I once was, and I'd do the voice off-camera, giving as much vocal energy.' Serkis would also describe his physical moves so that they could react at the right moments.

From these shot scenes, Peter Jackson would have two ways of enhancing them. They could rotoscope Serkis's movements – painting over them frame-by-frame. An alternative would be to work on the second take (the void where Serkis had been) in the mocap studio. 'It's acting as a virtual puppeteer,' he told IGN Filmforce of the second option in 2003. Wearing a suit covered in sensory dots, crouched on a podium and with arms outstretched, he would perform each scene again, as cameras from all angles captured his body movements via the dots. Covering his eyes were goggles, through which he could see a computer-generated image of Gollum. 'If I moved my right arm, then Gollum in real time would move his right arm.'

It was essential for Serkis to be as emotionally truthful in mocap as he had been on the shoot, as the technology would pick up the tiniest fluffs or physical stumbles in his delivery, which an animator would not think to insert. It meant that there was an honesty and spontaneity to a mocap shoot. In addition, sensory dots covered Serkis's face, and his facial expressions and reactions (many of them based on those of his tiny son, Sonny) were – separately – also digitally converted into the CG Gollum, which had been redesigned to look more like the actor playing him.

Thanks to mocap developments, it would now be possible to be more flexible in postproduction. Whereas Serkis had had to rerecord dialogue several months after shooting, he could now do so the following day, when the dialogue was fresh in everyone's mind. It also meant that new mocap scenes could be filmed, so that Wood and Astin could be called back to reshoot scenes later. 'It felt like the technology was finally bowing to the creative possibility,' wrote Serkis later, 'and that was a joyous departure.' It was undoubtedly hard work, but Serkis was thrilled and fired up by the progress of mocap. Throughout the process, he told the *Mirror* at the end of 2002, he felt like 'the emotional guardian of the character'.

It turned out that 15 years of regular stage work had unwittingly prepared Serkis for the challenge of playing such a physical part as Gollum. 'That kind of work was the best preparation,' he told the *Glasgow Herald* in 2004, by which time he had spent innumerable hours on all-fours. 'On TV you can end up acting only from the neck upwards. I've been destined for that part, I think, because the character brought together so many elements of how I like to perform – embodying a character physically and mentally in an extreme way.' The pressure of theatre work had taught Serkis to focus on being Gollum. 'Working on the motion-capture stage is very much like working on the theatre stage. I think had I not been a theatre actor, I would have done it all differently. You can stay in character for longer periods of time without being thrown by motion-capture dots and 25 cameras. You can just kind of settle into it and be the character.'

Jackson refused to feel intimidated by special effects and technology, which unnerved some other directors. 'They can't imagine what they can't see. It doesn't scare me. I don't know how to use computers but I know what they can do.' And he was fully aware that special effects onscreen were a very long way from reaching their full capacity: 'When watching the metal man in *Terminator 2*, I didn't think that just 18 months later we'd see those amazing dinosaurs in *Jurassic Park*. They made the *Terminator* effects look crude.'

Actors working on films like those made by Jackson would find it a challenge to work with computer effects. 'It is a new skill that actors are going to have to learn. Many find it difficult to work with nothing, knowing that it is going to be three months before a ghost is put in alongside them when they have long left the set.'

Serkis's colleagues on the trilogy paid tribute to his efforts, isolated for months in mocap work. 'That guy had such a lonely journey,' said Elijah Wood. 'So my heart goes out to him and my hat's off to him because of the work he had to do!'

'He was incredibly committed to Gollum' was Fran Walsh's feeling on Serkis, 'and would go to places where you wouldn't necessarily expect an actor to go. Andy is thoroughly part of the final CG character in that he's not just a voice: he's a powerful physicality.'

For the crew, it was a privilege to watch Serkis and Peter

Jackson working together on mocap. They were frequently moved by what the actor achieved, later writing that because of what they called his 'exceptional work ethic, we were able to evolve the process to the point where it would be disturbing to most actors – most actors wouldn't be able to endure the rigours of working within a virtual reality.' They were also touched by how unfailingly friendly and charming the actor had been during the process.

While it had been exhilarating for Serkis, it had also been exhausting. Such was the addictive pull of Gollum's personality that Serkis found himself abandoning his vegetarian diet, and had started eating fish again. Partly this came as a result of feeling perpetually drained, as well as reading about processed soya being carcinogenic, and the temptations of having fresh seafood up for grabs on the set. What did it mean? Was the effect of playing Gollum such a negative one that Serkis would soon wind up as, in his own words, 'a voracious red-blooded, war-mongering species supremacist'? 'Gollum, I blame you,' Serkis said to himself.

CHAPTER 8

LORD OF THE RINGS III: THE PRIZE

In December 2002, as *The Two Towers*, the second *Lord of the Rings* film, was about to wow cinema audiences around the world, Andy Serkis felt tense. Having helped to recreate the character of Gollum with such dedication, hard work and creativity, he was nervous about the audience reaction. He felt it was a little bit like one of his children going to school for the first time, the feeling that something of his does not belong to him any more. It has its own independence, and how the public will react is not something one can control.

Serkis attended premieres in Paris, London and Los Angeles, but began with a trip to the New York opening night, which he attended with Lorraine and several long-time friends. Unaccustomed to receiving star treatment, he presumed he would not be recognised on the red carpet. Instead, the moment he climbed out of the limousine, he was faced with a barrage of photographers and their flashguns. How ready was he for the massive press interest in *The Two Towers* and his somewhat mysterious involvement in it? He had just signed with the Gersh management agency in the US, and there was optimism that his role as Gollum might land him some more regular work in Hollywood pictures.

A publicist offered him guidance on the best way to approach the many media interviews that were lined up for him – up to 70 every day – in which he was likely to be asked the same questions over and over again. While many journalists would express genuine, sincere interest in how Serkis had become Gollum, others either could not or would not grasp how involved he had been in his genesis and development. It would become galling to Serkis how many reporters and news organisations would assume that his contribution to *The Lord of the Rings* amounted to no more than contributing a voice in a dubbing suite. Even when he tried to explain patiently the ways in which he had developed the character movements on set, it was assumed by some that he was a mere stand-in actor. Movie fans on Internet websites could be even more presumptuous. 'He's the guy who mimes Gollum,' insisted one. 'He doesn't mime him, he does the movements,' disagreed another.

For a time, even the most respected of film critics underrated Serkis's achievements, comments they would later retract. Writing in the *Observer* in December 2005, BBC Radio's Mark Kermode blushed to recall, 'I made a fool of myself on Radio 5 a few years ago by crediting Serkis only with providing "the voice of Gollum" – before an army of indignant fans explained the physical rigours of this new-fangled "performance capture" technology to me.'

Serkis would come to find such reductive misunder-standings dispiriting. It was one of the triggers for his writing *Gollum: How We Made Movie Magic*, which was published at Christmas 2003 to coincide with the release of *The Return of the King*. A behind-the-scenes guide to the process of making the trilogy from a Serkis perspective, it would succeed in helping to explain his unusual role in proceedings. For now, though, the explanation did not suit the soundbite culture favoured by reporters who wanted a snappy summary in 10 seconds or less.

In having to face so many press interviewers, Serkis had to prepare some kind of digestible summary of how Gollum was created. A sensible tactic, he felt, was to stress that playing Gollum was no different from playing anyone else. The only variation came in being unrecognisable onscreen. It caused much discussion, with critics asking where an actor's performance ended and where enhancement began. The development of CGI and its relationship with acting meant that some new rules might have to be drawn up.

In a flurry of positive critical notices for *The Two Towers*, there was special mention for Andy Serkis's contribution. The *New York Times* film critic Elvis Mitchell described Gollum as 'the most fully realized' character of the whole film, summing him up as 'an emotional and physical shambles' and 'a hissing, bitter child-man whose paranoia keeps him breathing, and plotting'.

It was vindication that the marriage of technology and creativity had been a successful one. For previous films that used digital characters, they rarely displayed the psychological sophistication that audiences could relate to. Instead, the intention was simply to dazzle the viewer. 'We sit and go, "Look, how clever!" ' said Richard Taylor, the special effects supervisor at the Weta Workshop. 'With Gollum, because of his reality, his subtleties and Andy's acting acumen, we divorce ourselves from that need and accept him as another performer.'

In any case, there had been a long tradition of actors whose performances were used in creating animation. Animators at Walt Disney had often traced over actors to make their drawn versions seem more believable. Hans Conried (who played Captain Hook in *Peter Pan*) and Adriana Caselotti (Snow White in *Snow White and* the *Seven Dwarfs*) both gave complete performances in costume. In the late 1980s, making *Who Framed Roger Rabbit*, Bob Hoskins acted opposite an actor on set who was wearing a rabbit costume. More recently, in the three newer *Star Wars* films, Ahmed Best (as Jar Jar Binks) performed next to Ewan McGregor and Liam Neeson. But in many ways the development of Gollum was the most satisfying achievement yet of taking an extraordinary character from literature, then having imaginative screenwriters to bring that character to life, and combining that with emotionally charged acting, before mixing that with motion capture and animation. All in all, Gollum was a long way from merely bombarding an audience with dazzling special effects.

At the BAFTA Awards 2003, the visual effects team of *The Two Towers* were rewarded with a gong for Best Special Visual Effects. They also received an Academy Award in March, as did the film's sound-editing crew. The 2003 Oscars was a tense time – just days earlier, US and British forces began bombing Iraq. Serkis, who had been strikingly aware of the situation in Iraq for decades, and who was not yet quite established in the USA, showed up brandishing a protest: a poster that read 'No war for oil'. 'I nearly got lynched,' he later told the magazine *Little White Lies*. 'My agent said to me, "Andy, you could have waited until you got your green card."'

Both Peter Jackson and New Line tried the best they could to emphasise Serkis's unique contribution to the computer-generated Gollum, but, when it came to recognition at the Oscars, the actor's eligibility for a Best Supporting Actor gong was in doubt. The Academy Awards panel for the 2003 ceremony argued that, as Gollum was computer-generated and Serkis did not physically appear on screen, he could not be part of the nominations list. '*The Elephant Man* had John Hurt buried under rubber,' argued Jackson to *USA Today*. 'Whether it is foam latex for John Hurt or a skin of pixels for Andy Serkis, the actor still drives the performance.' A few pundits questioned Serkis's suitability for a supporting-actor nomination not because his work as Gollum lacked excellence, but because they saw it as a team effort: an actor working with a visual-effects crew and group of animators. However, disqualify an actor from inclusion because of technical collaboration and no actor would be eligible for, say, an Academy Award, because they would be working with a director, a cinematographer and a film editor who would have brought their own considerable skills to a picture.

The Academy Awards omission for Serkis rankled, as well it might. The slight implied that Serkis had put in less work than his fellow actors on *The Two Towers*. Far from it: it was estimated he worked three times as hard as anyone else.

At least the discussion was out in the open, though. 'I'm not so interested in receiving an award,' he insisted, 'but the reward for me is that people truly understand what I've done.' Just as with anyone else he had played, a large proportion of Gollum was uniquely Serkisian. In fact, he felt that there was even more of himself in the makeup of Gollum than in any of his previous roles: 'Instead of hiding behind a characterisation I had to do it without costumes or makeup. It required pulling it out from inside in order to get the character on screen,' he said.

'The debate's been opened up, it's been cracked open,' he informed one reporter. 'I think the debate will be ongoing until a point comes where there will be some formal way of acknowledging the work.' With other actors limbering up to play roles in a similar vein, he felt that the awards debate 'will continue until the point where [this technique] becomes mainstream, which it will be. It's just that this is the first time it's happened to this degree.' The hybrid of CG and animation had opened a door to a new thrilling kind of screen performance. 'Now it's been proved that using CG and live action can work. That you can play a human being, that you can play an animal, that you can play whatever, as long as you can scan an image.'

Some members of the Screen Actors Guild had expressed concern that future feature films might not require the services of live actors. Could their antics be replicated by computers alone? 'That's rubbish,' Serkis told *Time Out*. 'Why go to the time and expense of trying to exactly replicate something as cheap as an actor?' In any case, he estimated that he had worked longer hours developing and performing Gollum than any other actor working on the trilogy, even before adding up all the hours in post-production involved in voiceovers, mocap and so on.

Serkis did at least receive *some* awards for his efforts as Gollum. His first plaudit had come in January 2003, when he was voted Best Digital Actor by the Broadcast Film Critics Association. In May, the Academy of Science Fiction, Fantasy and Horror presented him with a Saturn Award. Then, on 5 June, he scooped an MTV Award for Best Virtual Performance, for which he sent a specially shot acceptance speech for the accolade from New Zealand. As he graciously thanked MTV viewers, the *Lord of the Rings* fanbase and everyone who worked on the film, the award he was clutching was snatched away by a disgruntled, profanity-spitting Gollum. Given that Gollum in turn proceeded to argue with the Sméagol half of his personality, Serkis's speech had become a three-way quarrel. 'I won it! It was me!' hissed Gollum to Serkis. 'We only won because of me! We're not gonna thank anyone, no, no! Not you, not MTV and not those pixel-pushing pindicks at Weta Digital!' 'Not listening, not listening!' groaned Sméagol.

The speech, a send-up that was hilarious, audacious and ingeniously made, became an Internet sensation. It was entirely fitting to make Gollum as hungry for the award as he had been for the Ring. It also underlined the concern that Serkis, Jackson and others had expressed when Serkis was deemed ineligible for the Academy Award Best Supporting Actor gong. Not winning wasn't a problem. Not being considered eligible was.

Then again, no other actor on *The Two Towers* (or the other two films, for that matter) was even shortlisted for the Oscars, which seemed logical for a film with an ensemble cast. 'The fact that no single actor was nominated for an award was indicative of what a team success it was,' offered Serkis. 'There isn't an Ensemble Award at the Academy, but we'd surely have got it.' You could read such an argument as self-effacing generosity that actors traditionally put forward to sidestep any accusations of egotism. But in Andy Serkis's case it was entirely in keeping with a career that throughout has been about collaboration – from his early days in university theatre, then rep stage work, then television and cinema, he was part of a team of actors, rarely hogging the limelight, but sharing it. Even in the years to come, when starring roles became more frequent, he would never lose sight of his belief that the business of acting should be a collaborative one. 'We've encouraged more and more the cult of applauding the individual, but *Lord of the Rings* has certainly taught me to think in terms of team work, and it was a privilege to be in that environment.'

There was still one more instalment of the *Rings* trilogy that fans were awaiting with bated breath. And it still wasn't finished. Yet another 28-hour flight took Serkis back to New Zealand in April 2003, where he learnt from Jackson, Walsh and Boyens a shocking twist to the Gollum character in *The Return of the King*. Previously, Gollum had been full of revenge and bitterness and hatred, while Sméagol had been the vulnerable, victimised underdog. Now, it was to be revealed that the tables would be turned: Sméagol would represent the more unpleasant side of Gollum's split personality – calculating, manipulative and scheming. Andy Serkis could scarcely believe what was being asked of him, and, even after accepting the challenge, found himself wondering how to portray irredeemable evil.

The Return of the King could have simply given the audience more of the same of Gollum. Instead, Jackson and Walsh opted to take him in a different direction. 'That was a more exciting way to go,' said Serkis, who likened the development of Gollum through the trilogy to the journey of a psychological thriller. 'You're not quite sure where you stand with him. Nor are you sure how to judge him.' Everyone involved in *The Return of the King* knew that it was the emotional payoff of the series. Even though material from all three films was shot simultaneously, the actors appreciated in particular the more emotional scenes integral to the final one. Its emotional punch resonated offscreen too. Two thousand and three was a year of farewells for everyone still working on the trilogy. Not only that: while the earlier films required considerable screen time to introduce everyone and set up plenty of plot exposition, *The Return of the King* was a 'race to the climax', in its director's words. 'The way I always thought about this one was that it's the reason why you make the other two. You just want to get to that last chapter.'

The opening moments of *The Return of the King* introduced the undisguised face of Andy Serkis to the trilogy – in a scene originally planned for Part Two. As Sméagol is fully introduced for the first time, he is shown in flashback fighting over the Ring with his cousin Déagol (Thomas Robbins) during a fishing trip. It begins as a juvenile squabble. It ends with Sméagol strangling Déagol. Then we see the fight's victor physically wither, and see his sanity dissolve, before he withdraws to the Misty Mountains, to mutate into Gollum. 'It's great for the character because you finally get to find out the roots of this guy. It's crucial that you see him as a human being and that this could have happened to anybody, this Ring could have landed in anyone's lap.'

The fishing-trip scene depicts the moment when the Ring 'finds' Sméagol, but, as Déagol is pulled into the water and panics, Serkis played the scene as if Sméagol was delighted, only then to have a nervous reaction himself. 'I imagined [Sméagol] rather prone to outbursts of *schadenfreude*,' wrote Serkis, confessing, 'I suffer from it myself. I can usually control it, but in the most dire scenarios which demand sympathy or sadness, I'm still capable of nervously reacting with a giggle.'

Andy Serkis finished his contribution to the trilogy in the summer of 2003. He was presented with various mementos: his motion-capture suit, the slate of his last shot, a gelatine fish, and – a birthday present – the ultimate in preciousss gifts: the Ring. It would last be seen at the end of *The Return of the King* when Gollum manages to regain possession of it, but loses his footing and tumbles to his death in the fires of the Crack of Doom, in so doing destroying the Ring and all its inbuilt powerful evil.

As production wrapped, he took stock of what he had achieved in the four years since he accepted the invitation to audition for Peter Jackson's casting director, John Hubbard. Back in early 1999, he felt comfortable (if unchallenged) with the idea that he could hide behind the characterisation of Gollum. But the ambitions of Jackson, Walsh and Boyens, coupled with his own extraordinary level of commitment and stamina in immersing himself in a role (as well as dealing with freezing waters, hanging from the sides of cliffs and crouching and crawling a great deal on all-fours), meant that he had surpassed his own career expectations. In his own memoir about the journey through the making of *The Lord of the Rings – Gollum: How We Made Movie Magic* – he wrote, 'As the process developed, I think, bizarrely, that there is more of myself in this role than any other role I've played, even considering that for the majority of the time, I'm transmuted into pixels.'

There were advantages to Serkis's unorthodox part in the films. While his co-stars were in makeup being plastered in latex, he could sleep in for a couple of hours and be pixelated instead. It was a challenge for any actor's ego, though – to know beyond any doubt that your efforts are up on the screen, but no one can see your face. Serkis was philosophical about being excised in favour of the pixels. 'In a way it's a bummer, but I honestly feel strongly that the essence of what I've done is up there,' he had told *Variety* in 2002. 'Much the way that John Rhys-Davies hardly looks like the dwarf Gimli after being shrunk and wearing heavy prosthetic makeup, I feel like I'm wearing CG prosthetics. There is a satisfaction in playing one of the great literary character creations, being able to play Gollum without being pinned down by him for the rest of my life. Some anonymity is the actor's greatest weapon,' he added.

'I still have the wonderful anonymity that will allow me to play other roles,' he told reporter Paula Nechak in 2004, before jokingly adding, 'But I probably will be the only one of the actors in the films who'll end up looking like my character when I'm 70.'

As he would tell a BAFTA panel, Peter Jackson had *felt* like a 70-year-old during certain days of making the trilogy.

The gruelling pressure of multitasking had caught up with him, and there were times when he felt compelled to step back and focus on just one thing at a time. His confession of weariness gained him yet more respect from the actors, but it was the postproduction schedule that was the worst – a punishing timetable that had denied him a single day off for six months. What devoured the time was perfecting the special effects: *The Return of the King* had nearly 1,500 computer-generated shots, as many as the first two films combined. Editing and shaping the film was another considerable challenge, and even after some scenes were kept back for a future extended DVD, *The Return of the King* clocked in at 3 hours and 20 minutes, twice as long as most movies released in cinemas.

Within six weeks of its opening – at Christmas 2003 – *The Return of the King* had grossed nearly $600 million worldwide at the box office, while the three films had collectively taken in more than $2.3 billion in little over two years. DVD sales would be immense, too, especially as each film was presented in extended form on the format, adding as much as 40 minutes to an already generous three-hour running time. Peter Jackson believed that home viewing was a much more forgiving environment for the extended editions, featuring scenes that could have affected the pace of the theatrically released versions.

By the time *The Return of the King* had been released, Andy Serkis was gradually becoming used to the exhausting round of promotional tours. It was a rare interviewer, it seemed, who did not say to him, 'Do Gollum' or 'Say "My preciousss".' One journalist in Toronto, Canada, was even present when an argument raged between the two sides of

Gollum's split personality. One side would hiss that 'Toronto is the worst place I've ever been to in my life.' The other would counter 'No, no, it's not, precious, it's the best, it's a *beautiful* country.' 'How do you know?' came the retort. 'You've just seen the inside of a hotel room!'

In terms of being recognised on the street, however, Serkis found he could live life to the full in relative obscurity. He was rarely harassed. If he ventured outside his front door, he learnt to carry with him some glossy photographs of himself as Gollum so that any autograph hunters – especially his youngest fans – would not be disappointed. 'I know it's cheesy to carry those pictures,' he apologised to film reporter and critic Ryan Gilbey, during an interview with the *Independent* in December 2003. Gilbey did not agree with the word 'cheesy'. 'It's sweet, perhaps because the unassuming Serkis is the last person you would expect to see signing photos for spooked and star-struck nippers.'

The one aspect of Gollum that would always garner Andy Serkis attention from the public was his creepy, lisping voice. Requests for him to say lines like 'My preciousss' had become common. 'People come up all the time and ask me to do the voice, but it's flattery to an extent, and I try to oblige whenever possible. But you have to choose your moments. Sometimes it's not possible if you're on a bus.'

And he told an interviewer from the *Mail on Sunday*, 'I often get people saying to me, "Doesn't it irritate you that you hardly get recognised?" As though I sit there enjoying a nice meal in a restaurant thinking to myself, "The only thing that would make this lovely meal complete is if I were to be interrupted by a long queue of autograph hunters!" '

The effect of *The Lord of the Rings* and *King Kong* meant

that Serkis became a semi-regular at fan conventions. At one, the Elf Fantasy Convention in Amsterdam, he was faced with 10,000 people dressed as elves. 'I get recognised a lot,' he accepted, but maintained that a project like *The Lord of the Rings* was 'not about all the special effects – it's about great stories and characters. And often that means a very subtle mix of digital work and the physical reality of makeup and so forth, and using those tools to tell the story.'

The international market was only just becoming properly aware of Serkis, so it was more disconcerting to be approached outside his home country. 'I suppose people have now watched the behind-the-scenes specials and making-of featurettes on the DVDs,' he acknowledged, 'and I've done a lot of publicity, so they know who I am. In the UK, people have known me for other works. But it is bizarre to be walking around in America, where I have not done a lot of work, and have people recognise me on the streets.'

Serkis was slowly edging into work in Hollywood. He had already lent his voice talents to an episode of *The Simpsons* in 2003, but now had a substantial role in a teen comedy called *13 Going On 30*. Released in the spring of 2004, it tells of Jenna Rink, a girl who feels so humiliated at her own 13th-birthday party that she cowers in the closet. When she plucks up the courage to venture out, she discovers she is just five days away from turning 30 years old (and has been reborn as Jennifer Garner, star of the TV series *Alias*), has a boyfriend who's a professional ice-hockey ace and lives in a plush apartment on New York's Fifth Avenue. Furthermore, she's working as an editor for a magazine called *Poise*. But she can't truly act her age, and all the while her 13-year-old self is bubbling under the surface.

Andy Serkis, who played Richard – Jenna's control freak of a boss at *Poise* – believed firmly that Garner had excelled herself as an amusing, engaging and credible actress. 'It's a really big acting challenge to carry off, [being] a 13-year-old in a 30-year-old's body and to make that believable.' It was a new experience for Serkis, too, who was more used to playing the villainous and the psychotic than being slap-bang in the middle of a romantic comedy. It was yet another project that interrupted his work as Gollum down in New Zealand. 'It was strange to step out of Gollum and put on a pair of trousers again.' But even here there were unusual elements to this romcom as Serkis suggested. 'Gary Winick, the director, had done a lot of independent digital films, he's come from an art house background, so he gave it a different sensibility.' Even in *13 Going On 30*, Serkis's physicality was exploited for its comedy. In one of its set pieces, a re-creation of the enduring video of Michael Jackson's 'Thriller', he performed an impressive moonwalk. It was a far cry from the creepy identities Serkis was known for playing.

Could Serkis have found himself typecast as Gollum, given that playing that admittedly unusual role had made him an international star? It seemed unlikely, he told *Adweek* in 2004, a year in which he played a rock star (for TV's *Spooks*) and a priest in the occult horror film *Blessed* with Heather Graham. 'I've played a great array of parts and had a fantastic range of roles over the years, but Gollum is pretty special. I suppose if you're going to get lumbered with a part that people are going to remember you for, it's a great character to be remembered by.'

When asked by *Time Out* if it was galling to break

through in Hollywood 'as a cartoon', Serkis insisted quite the opposite. 'It's not galling. It's a great character, and playing characters is what I do. I tend to look different in everything I do and Gollum is one of the biggest players in this story.' He saw the experience of playing Gollum as broadening his horizons as an actor, a way of adding another string to his bow, and something that brought a new range of possibilities for his future screen work. He urged other actors not to dismiss work like this purely 'because it's cyber-acting'.

Why did Gollum capture the imagination of critics and public alike? The actor who defined his screen persona believed that director Peter Jackson allowed the performer to be creative and not be overwhelmed by technology. 'Pete had the wisdom to let the acting dictate everything. Pete never allowed the CG effects to dominate the true emotional power of a scene, and that's why it works. I mean, look at *The Hulk*.' Serkis felt disappointed that Ang Lee's big-screen version of *The Hulk* in 2003 did not capitalise on using the actor to play the Hulk in mocap. 'For me, the fact that Eric Bana never got to play the Hulk killed that movie for me,' he told *Adweek* the following year.

The Hulk and Jar Jar Binks were two CGI cautionary tales warning what could have happened if Gollum had not been rooted in human psychology and had prioritised technology over creativity. Serkis admitted to *Adweek* in 2004, 'It was nerve-racking when I took the job because there were no examples of it working.' Gollum could have been a disaster.

The *Lord of the Rings* trilogy had been a roller-coaster ride, a marathon experience on the other side of the world from Serkis's London home, and one that he had often spent removed from the experiences of the other actors. 'The hobbits were very bonded and the fellowship was bonded strongly and I was a bit of an oddity, and it stayed with me throughout.' His family had become the animators and mocap specialists. It wasn't just the long hours that had made the project prey on his mind constantly, either. 'I've just about stopped dreaming about it now. Leading up to the opening of *The Return of the King*, I went through the sense of reliving all the scenes, wondering how they were going to play because it's not just like a normal scene in a film.'

The Academy Awards ceremony of March 2004 was the point at which all those involved in *The Lord of the Rings* trilogy bade farewell to all things Tolkien – for now, anyway. 'That night was great closure, rather than relief it was all over or anything,' said Serkis only a few weeks later. 'But *Lord of the Rings* has had its life cycle and everyone is really looking forward to their next projects.' In fact, within six months of uttering those words, Serkis would be back in New Zealand, and back with Peter Jackson on yet another epic project: *King Kong*.

CHAPTER 9

CAPTURED ONCE MORE: *KING KONG*

In March 2003, on the morning after *The Lord of the Rings: The Two Towers* had won 11 Academy Awards, Andy Serkis nipped into the Four Seasons Hotel in Los Angeles to bid Peter Jackson a quick farewell. He found the director and his core creative team seated around a table, on which were placed the 11 statuettes. But this was no celebratory breakfast: it was a preproduction meeting for *King Kong*.

There were whispers, now Jackson was busy preparing to film a revamp of *King Kong*, that Serkis would be providing the human input to the ape himself. For the moment, he was denying that he was confirmed in the role, but accepted that, if asked, he would not refuse the offer. Jackson was equally tight-lipped at this stage, although he was interested in having a human representation for the ape. 'I think it's just better to have an actor be there on his behalf, as it were.'

ANDY SERKIS: THE MAN BEHIND THE MASK

Andy Serkis's direct involvement can be traced back to 20 April 2003, his 39th birthday, during the final pickups for *The Return of the King*. Jackson started showing him pictures of an albino gorilla at Barcelona Zoo named Snowflake. 'It dawned on me why he was showing me these pictures,' recalled Serkis, 'and by the end of the conversation he said, "We'd like you to come and work on *King Kong*."'

Even though their association on the Tolkien trilogy had been a creative triumph, Serkis was apprehensive. 'In one breath I was terrified, but also thrilled and flattered that he would ask me. But I thought, How do you create an arc, a journey for this character over the course of a whole movie?'

Jackson hesitated about teaming up with Serkis again for slightly different reasons. As he later told the *Sunday Times*, he was almost dissuaded from hiring Serkis for the part, ironically because of the colossal success of *The Lord of the Rings*: 'I thought, "The man I really want is Andy, but I can't use him because he is so high-profile after Gollum."' Then it occurred to the director that there was no reason why Serkis couldn't play Kong: he would be disguised (as he was as Gollum) via the techniques of motion capture and computer graphics. So, despite not being on screen as himself in the role of Kong, Serkis – represented by a creature weighing in at 800 pounds and aged between 100 and 120 – nevertheless would have a fearsome screen presence in one of the guaranteed box-office hits of Christmas 2005.

King Kong was the brainchild of Edgar Wallace, a remarkably prolific and popular British writer of crime novels, plays and journalism. At the end of 1931, he was paid £500 for delivering six scripts of *Kong* to producer Merian C. Cooper at RKO Studios; but, before the creation could reach the screen, Wallace's health deteriorated, and he died in February 1932, at the age of 56. If aspects of the film now seem primitive in terms of effects, the impact of the film at the time was sensational. It was considered such strong meat that it was banned in several countries, including Finland and Australia, and in Berlin, but was a popular draw in the cinemas of London when it opened in April 1933, and critics marvelled at the way it combined live action, models, superimposed pictures and animations. A sequel, *Son of Kong*, followed with a whimper the following year.

The 2005 *King Kong* was the story's third screen incarnation. Peter Jackson first saw Ernest B. Schoedsack's original 1930s version of *King Kong* on television when he was a schoolboy growing up in Wellington in the early 1970s. Its effect on the youngster was magical. It became his favourite film, and regularly kept him awake with excitement until, aged 12, he constructed a model of the ape – 12 inches in height – along with a cardboard version of New York's Empire State Building, and daubed a bed sheet with an estimation of the city's skyline.

By the mid-1990s, now firmly established as an internationally renowned film director, and flushed by the successes of *Heavenly Creatures* and *The Frighteners*, Jackson started to consider remaking it. He believed that there was room for a version that would not just satisfy new audiences who might be impatient at the relatively primitive 'jerky animation and scratchy print' of the original, but also please those who, like himself, had fond feelings for the original. He had no particular ambition to remake it, but two things pushed him to do so. First, he didn't want anyone else to do it. Second, he felt excited by the prospect of creating a 'computer-generated 25-foot silver-backed gorilla'.

But there was little point in remaking the original simply by replicating it. It needed a modern-day sensibility. 'I love the film for lots of reasons,' said Jackson, 'and some of them are to do with the 1933 vintage quaintness, its innocence and naïveté. But many of those things are not relevant for today, and I'm not trying to replicate that feeling because it just wouldn't work.' He also knew that just trying to remake it would unleash a critical drubbing. 'There's no critic in the world who's going to open their review of it with "This far surpasses the 1933 version . . ." Even in my wildest dreams, I know this isn't going to happen. I'm set up to lose!'

The plot of *King Kong* goes thus: Ann Darrow has just lost her job as an actress in vaudeville. Short of cash, she agrees to accompany a budding film director and a fighter pilot on a boat trip to Skull Island in the South Pacific Ocean, with the intention of shooting a film. However, Skull Island is a dangerous location, where women are ritually sacrificed by its natives, while Kong endures an existence of miserable isolation. Kong is captured and relocated to human civilisation, with tragic consequences.

In short, the best way to remake *King Kong* would be to aim for the utmost in realism, making the audience believe that the monster ape was real, rather than born of a computer. 'I want people to see the hairs on his arms ruffle in the breeze,' said the director. And, in order to convince an audience that Kong was believable, the whole film had to be imbued with an emotional depth. If *King Kong* 2005 had special effects but no beating heart, it would be a folly. One way would be to perceive the relationship between Kong and Ann as a take on an evergreen fairytale. Jackson regarded it as a relationship between 'a huge creature and a human being. It's basically the tale of Beauty and the Beast. On an intellectual and emotional level, he's like a child.'

There had been a previous reworking of the *King Kong* story in 1976, a tongue-in-cheek pastiche overseen by director Dino de Laurentiis, in which the heroine (Jessica Lange, no less) developed a soft spot for the ape. It was utterly panned by the critics, and, nearly 30 years on, few remembered it with much fondness. Colin Hanks (son of Tom), who was appearing in Jackson's new film, was shocked by its predecessor's limitations. 'It's painfully obvious that it's a guy in a monkey suit. I mean, he's literally walking around, looking in windows and going, "Where's Jessica Lange?"' Another touch of the de Laurentiis remake that would be reversed by Peter Jackson was his decision to use the World Trade Center as a clinging post for Kong rather than the Empire State Building. Not only did Jackson wish to stick to the original film's plot as closely as possible, to use the World Trade Center after 9/11 seemed in dubious taste.

Jackson's *King Kong* would not be played for laughs. It would reflect the same sort of 'dramatic sensibility' that had been such a hallmark of the *Rings* trilogy: believable characters in a fantastical world. A dramatic truth to any scene was essential for that scene to work, and the task for the director was to ensure that the art department did not run away with the story so that the audience could not relate to the film anymore.

Peter Jackson and Fran Walsh had hatched an original script in the mid-1990s, which was akin to a Hollywood-style action-adventure, not unlike *The Mummy* or an Indiana Jones story. The script leaked onto the Internet around the year 2000, but, when the duo returned to the first script three years after that, they binned it without hesitation and began work on a complete rewrite.

The new screenplay was a joint effort by Jackson, Walsh and Philippa Boyens, based on the 1930s original screenplay. For Jackson, the *Kong* story offered 'everything that any storyteller could hope for: an archetypal narrative, thrilling action, resonating emotion and memorable characters. It has endured for precisely these reasons and I am honoured to be a part of its continuing legacy.'

But this new version would not be set in the present day, as many movie-business executives might have preferred. To make *King Kong* believable in the twenty-first century meant placing the story's elements of fantasy within the social and physical context of 1930s New York during the Depression. It was a more innocent age, a time of discovery when a ship could conceivably have run aground on an unexplored island, or even that a giant ape could cling to the Empire State Building as biplanes buzzed around him. 'It couldn't work today with modern aeroplanes,' insisted Jackson, 'because Kong wouldn't stand a chance.'

Despite being based in the New York of the 1930s, *King Kong* would be almost entirely shot on a back lot in Wellington, as it would have been near-impossible to reconstruct that time in the very different New York of the twenty-first century. It was easier to start from scratch. The attention to detail in evoking the 1930s could hardly have been more careful: mocking up shopfronts, collecting vintage cars from all over New Zealand, then swapping the steering wheels from right side to left, creating stylised re-creations of front pages for the *New York Times* and the *Wall Street Journal*. Jackson stopped short of replicating the Empire State Building (that was confined to being computer-generated), but did mock up Times Square and Herald Square. There were even pipes and boilers installed under the streets so that real steam could be pumped up through sewer drains and manholes. The re-creation of New York in Wellington caused little offence in the eastern United States: they seemed to understand that there wasn't enough of the old-style city left to film. Plus, the finished film also triggered a warm wave of nostalgia for its past.

In preparing to play Kong, Andy Serkis was also striving for authenticity. He began by studying hours and hours of video footage of gorillas, and spent several weeks visiting the four gorillas at London Zoo in Regent's Park and San Diego Zoo in California. At Regent's Park, he was to find an unlikely admirer – a female gorilla called Zaire. 'She chose me,' he quipped, 'much to the chagrin of the alpha male of the group.' That male, a silverback named Bob, demonstrated his disapproval by throwing a pile of stones at his 'rival'. Fortunately, the only damage done was a scratched camera lens. Not that Zaire was averse to jealous tantrums. When wife Lorraine accompanied Serkis on one visit there, the female threw a water bottle at her. (Just as the film was opening around the world, Serkis made a return visit to the zoo, and found he had not quite been forgotten. 'She knew me but I think she's moved on.')

Being Andy Serkis, though, he felt unsatisfied by his research thus far into gorilla behaviour. What he really needed was to witness them in their natural habitat. A trip to the highlands of Africa, then, seemed the only way to find out what they were really like. Jackson, concerned for the actor's safety and welfare, refused to grant permission. 'Then one day we got a phone call from Andy in Rwanda,' he told a reporter from *Newsweek*. 'I thought, "Oh, the bastard's gone there without permission!" '

Serkis felt his journey to Rwanda was essential. To nail what made Kong tick, he felt he just had to watch the gorillas there at the closest quarters he dared. He wanted to observe the difference between gorillas in captivity and those in their natural environment. He found that, while those in zoos tended to reflect human behaviour because they were born and bred in a human environment, their more liberated counterparts in Africa were 'more enigmatic…They have an otherness about them.'

Serkis's journey to Africa was made possible after he contacted Rwanda's Tourist Authority and its ministry of national parks. They put him in touch with a research centre which had a team at the Volcano National Park in the Virunga Mountains. The American primatologist Dian Fossey – who was portrayed in the film *Gorillas in the Mist* by Sigourney Weaver in 1988 – had worked in the same area exploring gorilla behaviour.

Ordinarily, tourists were permitted to watch the gorillas for only an hour at a time, but Serkis was allowed to accompany the primatologists for three days. Although he was forbidden to actually touch the animals, his background in visual arts meant he could make effective sketches of them, and make notes on how they behaved. 'They were doing a survey on silver-backed gorillas, so I was very fortunate to be there at that time. I did nothing but eat, sleep and talk gorillas for the time that I was there.'

At times, he found himself in hazardous territory: some silverback gorillas lurched towards him. 'There were a couple of full-on charges by silverbacks and you do panic,' he told the Scottish newspaper the *Daily Record*. 'You are supposed to keep a seven-metre distance, but they don't know that. The instinct is to run and that is exactly what you shouldn't do. You should absolutely defer to them and not make eye contact. I have video footage of a couple of the charges, but on the whole they are incredibly peaceful creatures unless they are intruded upon. If they feel threatened they will attack with all their force.'

Studies by experts like Fossey and the American naturalist George Schaller had established that apes in the wild weren't simply bloodthirsty and aggressive. In the 1930s, when the first version of *Kong* was made, gorillas were a demonised species. 'They were a symbol of an uncultured, violent beast,' said Serkis. 'I saw a First World War American enlistment poster which was entitled "Destroy This Brute". It was a gorilla holding a woman and a club.' Genetically, of course, apes are more similar to human beings (an estimated 97 per cent) than some people might like to imagine. 'It doesn't take much, actually, to form a real connection with them.'

Serkis's trip to Rwanda resulted in his making some fascinating discoveries about gorillas, from how they communicate – 'They have a huge lexicon of about 17 recognised vocalisations' – to how they behave as a society.

A major entry point into understanding and empathising with Kong came when he realised that gorillas were essentially social animals that are happiest in bigger families. This finding was at odds with the withdrawn and isolated figure of Kong: the very last in his species, with no remaining kith or kin. At last, Serkis knew he understood the character. 'I'd really go down the road of making him as true to real gorilla behaviour as possible. Our choice was not to spoon-feed or anthropomorphise him.'

As *The Times*'s film critic Kevin Maher would acknowledge in his review of *King Kong*, its greatest achievement in its treatment of the gorilla came not 'in the realisation of Kong's loping walk or expressive features but in his simple scripted character. Like Darrow, he is an outsider in his own environment.' And, because Kong yearns for companionship rather than a sexual craving, the questionable sexual and racial subtext of previous *Kong* movies was no longer an issue.

Now convinced that gorillas possessed as much emotional intelligence as human beings, Serkis returned from Rwanda to Wellington with revealing tapes of their behaviour, evidence that the cast and crew would need to familiarise themselves with. He was extremely well informed about them, having also read many relevant books, so that, when the script called for Kong to chew into a dinosaur's ribs, he could query it as gorillas were vegetarians.

Even though Serkis stressed that gorillas had some emotional intelligence, this did not mean that the new *Kong* film would be 'softening Kong' in an attempt to humanise him. 'The power of the story lies in the fact that this is a savage beast from a hostile environment,' Jackson reassured concerned fans, 'and we don't intend to compromise that.' But nor would the creature be growling and cartoonish. He would be a battered, vulnerable survivor, the last of his race on Skull Island. Those watching were asked to empathise with a figure that had been unable throughout his lifespan to feel any empathy towards others.

Tempting as it was to drown the portrayal of Kong in waves of pathos, it was vital to remind the audience of Kong's terrifying presence and his natural instinct. Because he was an animal, he would react to the here-and-now, and would be unaware of his fate. So Kong had become, unapologetically and uncompromisingly, a wild animal. Jackson gave credit to Andy Serkis for remembering that Kong was, above all, a gorilla. 'He was very obsessively focused on making him as gorilla-like as he could possibly be.' He could frighten the cast, too. Jamie Bell, who played the part of Jimmy, the cabin boy on board SS *Venture*, remembered how intimidating Serkis was, once he was wearing the outfit suit, and living in the mind of Kong. 'There was no approaching him. We were just absolutely terrified of him most of the time,' he said.

New Yorker Adrien Brody (who had become the youngest winner of the Best Actor Oscar for his lead role in *The Pianist*) would head the *King Kong* cast as the pilot Jack Driscoll. Jack Black would also feature as ambitious filmmaker Carl Denham, who is determined to shoot a film on Skull Island. But for Serkis the most significant piece of casting concerned Ann Darrow, with whom Kong would form an emotional bond. Playing Darrow would be the Australian Naomi Watts, who had received much praise for her role in David Lynch's *Mulholland Drive*, as well as an

Academy Award nomination for *21 Grams* in 2003. Watts has pointed out that, although Darrow starts out as someone afraid, and Kong as a dominant creature, the balance between them shifts during the course of the film. 'Both of them have a major transformation. She builds this beautiful connection with a completely different species that is, in every possible way, threatening to her.' Watts also believed in Kong's power and masculinity, and, paradoxically, how this brought out the tenderness in their relationship. It gave the film a poignant weight.

Naomi Watts was quoted in one interview as feeling somewhat daunted about living up to the standards set by Fay Wray in the 1933 version, and Jessica Lange, too, from the much-maligned 1970s remake, both of whom had previously played the role of 'damsel in distress'. Describing both as 'a huge inspiration', Watts went on, 'It's a very iconic movie and iconic role, so there's a little bit of fear about that, but also intrigue.' Watts also felt fear and intrigue about performing to an empty space where the computer-generated Kong would later be placed, but was reassured by the director that Andy Serkis would be with her on the set as a reference for the computer-animation team, even though he would not be seen in that form on the screen. For Serkis, the beating heart of the film depended on how Kong and Ann related to each other. 'If it feels phoney, or if you don't connect, it'll still look great but the heart of the movie will be missing.' Watts felt relief when she was able to connect with Serkis. 'It's not just a pair of eyes but a soul,' she said. 'I was relieved that I wasn't going to be looking at a tennis ball on a stick moving around the stage.'

The only way in which Kong can empathise with any

other creature is when he views one in a different light. When he takes Ann Darrow to his lair in the jungle, she does not scream (as most would do). Instead, she confronts him. Serkis was adamant that the animal was not a psychotic killer who wants to destroy women out of sexual frustration: 'It's more to do with his inability to connect and the frustration he feels. Ann changes that.'

In order for the cross-species relationship to have any credibility at all, the idea of a sexual subtext between Darrow and Kong was out of the question. But she does charm him all the same, by performing for him a vaudeville dance routine. It inspires a curiosity and amusement in the gorilla. He pushes her further and further and eventually, when she tries to rebel, he is most resentful, but is soon embarrassed about his outburst, and then wants to protect Ann at all costs. 'It's an interesting dynamic in the story when she stops being a victim,' said Peter Jackson, 'and becomes a being that he empathises with. And of course the real tragedy of Kong is that those feelings are the beginning of the end. That's his downfall.'

'He has this kind of outburst,' said Watts, 'and then he's embarrassed. He goes through this huge gamut of emotions and has to run away and hide because he can't face her. And she sort of understands him in that moment, and sees him as this very isolated creature – and maybe just identifies with him.'

The shooting of *King Kong* would be a mixture of the exciting and the alarming for Watts. She would have to act many of her scenes long before the digitally created backdrops of New York would be completed. In one instalment of Peter Jackson's online production diary, she was shown hanging in midair clasped by two green 'fingers', interacting with Serkis, who was sporting black padding to give him the rough shape of a gorilla. 'What Andy brings to the party is like a whole other art form,' she said, and revealed that the secret of relating to Kong was looking into Serkis's eyes. 'It's not just a guy in a monkey suit. Other than the size, when I look into his eyes, I'm getting monkey,' she laughed. 'There's a lot of monkey.'

Sometimes it was difficult to escape the absurdity of the situation on set. Many scenes involving Serkis would find him wearing a black muscle suit described by Jackson as 'the worst Batman costume you ever saw', and perched on a crane some 25 feet above the ground. This was so that other actors reacting to him can be filmed looking at the exact spot where Kong's face would be. But regardless of how many props were around, or technical distractions, how they were positioned, or how Andy Serkis was dressed, he and Watts had no choice but to block out all distractions, and concentrate on the emotional connection of the scene. 'We obliterated everything out,' said Serkis, 'and played like two normal actors. The scenes were created on set with Naomi, and the real-actor connection was made so that she wasn't having to fake emotions. She wasn't having to make decisions about the character [of Kong] because I was there.' For Watts, Serkis had to be on that set in person. 'I'm reacting to Andy's truths, and that was my job. He made me go there, and he made me believe.'

The digital Kong would not be ready for a while. An early version of him was thought to be inadequate: Jackson felt it looked more like a bodybuilder on steroids. When improvements were made, it was to underline how Kong was bruised, elderly, past his prime. 'He's not the Hulk of gorillas. That's the charm of Kong,' said Peter Jackson. Decisions were still being made on how long and tangled the gorilla's fur should be, and how much grey colour should be applied around his eyes. The attention to detail in developing his physical characteristics extended to devising a snaggletooth for him, as if his jawbone was smashed in a fight a long time before, but had mended itself at a crooked angle. To help his physical performance as Kong on this front, Serkis had some extra teeth fitted, though these were not visible in the final film. Other evidence of a grizzled and scarred Kong included the added touches of some matted, filthy fur, bald patches and even a potbelly.

Then, of course, there was the roar of Kong, which was the roar of Serkis. In 1933, the Kong roar was achieved by combining the recorded roars of a lion and tiger, then playing the result backwards. Seventy years later, the various noises that the actor had learnt from gorillas could be amplified through an electronic contraption known as the 'Kongolizer'. Every sound that Serkis emitted (with his vocal pitch lowered by some three octaves) would be now be transformed into the sort of booming noise that could make the set shake. But there was a whole range of noises that he had employed. 'Gorillas have quite a vocabulary. They have a reprimanding grunt or song when they're happy and, yes, they do chuckle.'

Otherwise, Kong dialogue was not an option, a marked contrast from the restless hyperactivity of Gollum. 'He's mute,' said Jackson of Kong. 'His entire performance is in his eyes. Gorillas themselves don't move their faces very much.' So, with Kong it was very much a case of less-is-more. The main thing was that Serkis had placed 'a big thumping heart inside a digital body'.

Conveying Kong's back story to connect with those watching meant that the special effects, as well as the acting, had to be far beyond those used in 1933. Back then, Kong was a fur-covered model, just 18 inches in height, who could be brought to life only by being moved by hand, frame by frame. Then, the inspiration for the ape's movements came from those of wrestlers and boxers. And, when close-ups were required for the moment when the giant fist of Kong clutched Fay Wray's Ann Darrow, the only way it could be done was to have Wray held six feet off the ground by a model hand, measuring 8 feet across, and with rubber fingers. In contrast, 2004's Kong would come to life via the click of a mouse.

Once the scenes with Naomi Watts were complete, Andy Serkis began the motion-capture sessions, for which he donned a blue Lycra bodysuit, which was dotted with a total of 60 sensors. Then, all the while tightly holding a Barbie doll (representing Ann), he leapt around in front of a blue screen, tumbling and scraping his knuckles across the floor, while being filmed by more than 50 video cameras. With no actual dialogue for Serkis to deliver, the presence of more than 130 markers attached to his face meant that every facial nuance and movement – from internalising a thought to unleashing a full-blown rage – could be archived on Weta Workshop's software. A team of animators would then magnify and fine-tune the results. 'I can't pretend to understand the technicalities,' apologised Serkis to one reporter after the film eventually premiered. 'I just had to deliver a readable performance.'

It was relatively straightforward for Serkis to be mocapped as Kong: since human beings and gorillas are both primates, they have similar facial similarities. 'A lot of the similarities are in the face and the eyes,' said Christian Rivers, *King Kong*'s animation director. 'Gorillas have such a similar-looking set of eyes and brows, you can look at those expressions and transpose your own interpretation onto them.'

Kong's eyes became very important in conveying the character's emotions, explained Jackson. 'Even though his eyes are just a collection of pixels in a computer we wanted them to have depth, we wanted to see emotion in them. And so all of the muscles around the eye – the eyelids and the eyebrows – they are very, very complicated bits of computer modelling, and we can get a huge lot of expression.' To emphasise Kong as a battered, bruised figure, a sign of defeat and exhaustion was added. It was a drooping eye, which was caused by an encounter with a dinosaur in which Kong came a poor second. Everyone knew that this level of detail over Kong's face – which needed to be effective in close-ups – would be essential in order for the film to succeed. 'That was the scariest thing about making the entire movie, because if those shots didn't work the whole thing didn't work,' said Jackson.

Serkis had to be at his strongest and most agile when portraying the 25-foot Kong during the arduous mocap sessions. Weights were attached to both his arms and ankles, and he wore a heavy harness. 'It was to get the scale of [Kong's] movements, the inertia and momentum,' he explained. 'If he's swinging his arm, it's like a big wrecking ball on the end of a chain.' In order to express himself physically for the mocap process, he had to be in tiptop shape. 'I was pouring sweat every day. It was the most physically and mentally demanding role...much more demanding than Gollum, and that was pretty tough.'

His schedule meant that, even with Lorraine and their children flying over from London to join him (their third child, Louis, had been born in June 2004), he saw very little of them, although his wife gained a small part in the film as one of a group of theatrical actors. 'Lorraine was coping with three kids on her own and I was coming home drained. At weekends there wasn't much left of me.' From time to time, his children would watch him in action on the set. 'They would sit and watch me up on stage, and Kong taking form on the computer monitors. Seeing that Kong was behaving exactly like their dad was fascinating to them. We'd go home at nights and it would be hard to get them to bed because all they wanted to do was make monkey noises.'

Help for Serkis came from a physiotherapist, who had advised members of the All-Blacks rugby squad. Having moved around day after day for hours as if he were a gorilla was bound to make his frame feel strained. Mindful of his earlier back injury in *Othello* (see Chapter 3) he knew that such checkups were crucial, because, if he became injured, the very tight filming schedule might be delayed. 'My biggest fear was really injuring myself. They couldn't carry on without me.' It was a worrying, pressurised time, and, when each day's filming was over, he found it hard to unwind.

The demands of playing Kong weren't restricted to its physicality, either. If he wasn't nailing the emotional

A proud Andy Serkis at the Academy Awards after-party in March 2004. With 11 gongs, *Lord of the Rings: Return of the King* ties with *Titanic* and *Ben-Hur* as the most successful film in Oscars history.

Above: Andy and his wife – successful British actor Lorraine Ashbourne – at the BAFTA Awards in February 2004, after an evening of recognition for *Return of the King*.

Below left: Helping to launch east London's Dr Barnardo's Spark Centre in 2004, a rugged-looking Andy appears with his alter-ego, Gollum, on the screen. Andy is a staunch supporter and ambassador for Barnardo's.

Below right: Andy, Billy Boyd and Bernard Hill (a.k.a. Gollum, Pippin and King Théoden) at the *Empire* Magazine Film Awards, after yet more accomplishments for *Return of the King*.

Above: Andy shares the frame with Gollum at the launch of his book on making *Lord of the Rings*.

Below: Andy looking protective with a 'precious' Gollum figurine.

The cast of *King Kong* meets the press in New York, but they're unaware that a certain hairy giant wants in on the action...

Above: Andy and King Kong at the film's premiere in December 2005.

Below: Surrounded by fellow cast members, Serkis takes the mike at the *King Kong* premiere.

Right: A dapper Andy with *King Kong* co-star Naomi Watts, who is showing off a stunning deep blue dress by Christian Lacroix.

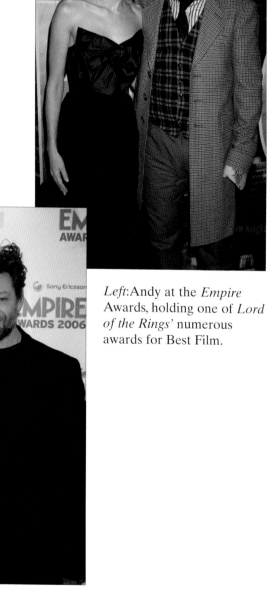

Left:Andy at the *Empire* Awards, holding one of *Lord of the Rings'* numerous awards for Best Film.

Left: Looking elegant in black, Andy and his stunning wife Lorraine in 2010 at the Orange British Academy Film Awards.

Right: With sons Louis and Sonny at the National Ballet's production of *The Nutcracker*. Andy apparently uses his Gollum voice if his children misbehave.

Above: The 2010 premiere of *Rise of the Planet of the Apes* in Los Angeles, in which Andy played the primate, Caesar.

Below: The whole Serkis family united at the premiere. From left: Ruby, Lorraine, Louis, Andy and Sonny.

essence of the character, it was hard to focus. 'There were no other actors to play off,' he told the *Daily Record*. 'So I would literally have to storm around until I felt the muse come back. That was pretty lonely. It was like Muhammad Ali in the ring, when the room starts spinning and you're going down.'

There were some physical consequences for Andy Serkis in the months after work on *Kong* wrapped. If kneeling down, for whatever reason, he could raise himself off the ground only by using his knuckles. He would have to lean forward on his arms, with elbows at right angles, and the palms of his hands facing back, before pushing down on his knuckles and lifting himself up. 'I keep looking at people on the floor after they've dropped something to see if they do it, too. It's something I can't stop.'

Serkis was cast in a second role – as Lumpy, the sweaty one-eyed cook aboard the SS *Venture* (the steamer heading for Skull Island). Lumpy would not be painted out in postproduction, and so his own face would be visible in the film. But even Lumpy's scenes were a challenge for Serkis. In order to create stormy waters around the ship, three tanks – each containing 250 gallons of water – were tilted so that the contents were sent down 20-foot ramps with angled kickers at the bottom. The resulting waves were powerful indeed – one that made contact with the ship sent Serkis overboard.

Lumpy comes to a sticky end when he is sucked face first into a colossal worm, although Serkis at one point revealed, with a chuckle, that Jackson had considered making the chef one of Kong's victims. 'Instead, he gave me a role who finally gets devoured by computer graphics – I don't know whether that is a comment or not.'

The released cut of *King Kong* is carefully paced. It is nearly an hour into the three-hour running time before Denham, Driscoll, Darrow and their fellow passengers on board the SS *Venture* reach Skull Island. As Kevin Maher, film critic for *The Times*, noted, the leisurely early scenes 'are simply a measured intake of air before one of the greatest dizzying sprints in cinema history'.

From the moment SS *Venture* reaches Skull Island, the pace is relentless and unstoppable: killer zombies, human sacrifices, executions, attacks from giant insects and slugs, a parade of dinosaurs (including a scene pitting Kong against three tyrannosaurs – and with Darrow stuck in the middle) – and that's even before the return to New York and the climactic tragic scenes atop the Empire State Building.

Kong himself does not appear for over an hour, which may have put off some impatient viewers (likely to have been the very same impatient viewers who would have grown annoyed at creaky black-and-white footage), but is necessary to establish the desperation faced by the struggling actress and the cash-strapped filmmaker.

The first of several premieres staged across the world's major cities took place in – where else? – New York City on 5 December 2005. 'There were tears,' admitted Serkis. 'It was deeply affecting. So much so that I felt numb.' This would be the first time that he had seen the final three-hour cut of the film, and it was an extremely emotional experience, not least the scene where Kong tumbles to his death from the Empire State Building – a scene Peter Jackson himself found too traumatic to watch over and over during editing. Players of the spin-off Xbox game, however (which featured the voices of all the main cast, including Serkis), would be given the chance to spare Kong. 'If you earn enough points,' said Jackson, 'you get to save Kong so he goes on to live a happy life.'

After the first screening, there was a party at a pier, where a replica of Skull Island had been constructed and 1930s-style entertainment was provided by a big band and dancers (both burlesque and ballroom). In the days that followed, the main players flew to openings in London, Berlin and Tokyo, and finally, on 14 December, to the home of the project, Wellington. The film went on worldwide general release that week, and its emotional punch resonated with many critics, even those who felt overwhelmed by other spectacular aspects of the film. '*King Kong* is never more captivating', wrote *Variety*, 'than when the giant ape and his blond captive are looking into each other's eyes.' 'Kleenex should be sold along with the popcorn,' advised one British paper, while the Australian title the *Age* suggested that 'Serkis has become to virtual acting what Marlon Brando was to method acting.'

Even though Andy Serkis had been relatively unsung when it came to receiving awards for Gollum, his Kong would be officially recognised by the Broadcast Film Critics Association (BFCA). On 9 January 2006, at the 11th Annual Critics' Choice Awards, he received the specially created honour known as the Distinguished Achievement in Performing Arts Award. The panel described the 2005 Kong as 'representing a revolutionary leap forward in synthesizing visual effects with an actor's performance.' The president of the BFCA, Joey Berlin, explained that many of its members 'were so impressed by the astonishing way in which [Kong] expresses love, lust, humour and rage in the tradition of the finest human actors'. In preparation for Serkis's accepting the award, Jackson and his team set about creating special new footage for the event, which was broadcast on television live and direct from the Civic Auditorium in Santa Monica, California, and hosted by US comedian Dennis Miller.

Within three months of its premiere, *King Kong* grossed over $215 million at the box office, and had been nominated for four Academy Awards, three of which it won. Although Serkis was not directly nominated, he was personally thanked for his contribution at the Oscars by visual effects supervisor Joe Letteri for 'really giving us the heart of Kong', while a victorious sound-mixing team thumped their chests in approval from the stage, as a homage to the great ape.

The DVD was issued in March 2006, selling a sensational 6.5 million units in seven days. A two-disc Special Edition set contained nearly three hours of behind-the-scenes footage, plus featurettes about the 'History of Skull Island' and the re-creation of 1930s New York. All underlined the sheer level of detail behind the making of the film. 'The film is kind of the tip of the iceberg,' reflected Serkis. 'There's so much extra that's gone on. If you could peel back the cinema screen and look behind it, there are another thousand creatures around the corner.'

Another bonus feature exclusive to the DVD was a documentary, made by Jackson in association with the International Gorilla Conservation Programme, to highlight the plight of gorillas in the wild. It was estimated that the species could be extinct within just 30 years. 'Gorillas are truly amazing animals,' said Jackson. 'Without them there wouldn't be entertainment like *King Kong*. It's really vital that we take this opportunity to realise how similar they are to us, and how endangered they are.' Serkis shared Jackson's concern, and had become a trustee of the Dian Fossey Gorilla Fund. 'The original *King Kong* film did a lot of damage to the reputation of gorillas and there was a big upsurge in gorilla hunting after that film. The tragedy of Kong is that the story is not too far from the truth, in that he is the last of his kind.' Several screenings of *King Kong* were organised in aid of the International Gorilla Conservation Programme, and over $100,000 (or around £55,000) was raised in total.

Although Peter Jackson had confessed that the cancellation of the *King Kong* project back in 1997 (see Chapter 6) had been 'the blackest day of my career', he was now grateful for the delay in getting the project off the ground. 'It worked out for the best. We wouldn't have done such a good job on *Kong* back then, and now we're able to apply everything we learned from *Lord of the Rings*.'

'In terms of achievement, it's immense,' said Serkis. 'It's very satisfying. It's like going to a great meal and you come out of it fully satisfied.'

In just a few short years, mocap technology had improved immeasurably. It had not been long since only one actor at a time could be captured, and even then that actor's face and body could not be captured together. By 2005, though, they could. As well as Peter Jackson's work, Robert Zemeckis's *The Polar Express* (2004) allowed Tom Hanks to play multiple roles, while Disney's *The Chronicles of Narnia: The Lion, the Witch and the Wardrobe*, which opened one week before *King Kong*, used mocap to create mythical creatures such as centaurs and fauns.

As far as Andy Serkis was concerned, though, it was still all acting. 'People say, "But we don't see your face." But my wife says she recognises almost every facial tick and mannerism whichever character it is. I do my thing for the cameras just like any other actor doing blue screen. It's just that I'm then digitalised down to four feet [Gollum] or up to 25 [Kong].' And as if to hammer home how he saw it no differently from any other sort of acting, when asked if he would have preferred to tackle a simpler role – 'something on a stage with a bare light bulb and a chair', he had a straight answer ready. 'That's all I was doing. I was on stage with a bare light bulb and on my knuckles for a year. That's the point.'

CHAPTER 10

NORMALISING THE EXTREME: ANDY SERKIS AND THE DARK SIDE

From his earliest stage appearances at Lancaster University in the early 1980s, via his television and film cameos, Andy Serkis has always relished portraying those with a dark side. He has argued throughout his career that there must also be another side to a villainous individual, and only by seeing glimpses of those other sides – vulnerability, tenderness, joy – can their actions begin to be understood. He has always been careful not to be judgemental of those with even the most negative traits. It would be all too easy to dismiss those who commit unpleasant acts as 'monsters' or to brand them as 'evil'. 'That is where the danger lies,' he wrote in 2003, 'in taking the moral high ground.'

There's no question that Serkis has played some deeply cruel, cold and violent individuals on stage and screen. 'My mum keeps asking me when I'm going to play someone nice,' he reported, having told her he was playing a wife beater in Sam Shepard's *A Lie of the Mind*. Is this a kind of typecasting? Then again, there are so many degrees and shades of evil behaviour that it is hard to define an all-purpose villain.

Serkis does not believe that the state of evil is a natural one. The acts of miscreants come about because of the circumstances of their individual lives. Those who commit shocking acts of violence have often either been surrounded by it at a very early age, or been neglected in other ways. Had Serkis portrayed Gollum as irredeemably evil and relentlessly aggressive, and not confronted his frailty or address the story behind his foibles, the power of the character would have been far less memorable and thought-provoking. 'It's a combination of keeping the audience on their toes, and finally handing back the moral responsibility to the audience to decide if he's good or bad.' He dedicated *Gollum: How We Made Movie Magic*, his own book born of triumph, achievement and success, to the unfortunate and isolated underdog of any society: 'To anyone who lives or has lived in a dark, lonely cave of their own, either driven by incurable obsession or powerless to change their course, "loving and hating themselves" like Gollum.'

Serkis has always been fascinated by those on the fringes of society, the outsiders, the supposed misfits. He feels his responsibility as an actor is to understand whoever he is portraying. Many do not have the best start in life, they may not have strong role models, and so may be subject to negative influences from an early age. His four years on *The Lord of the Rings* had made him think very hard about judging people; no matter how evil someone's actions seem at first glance, it is often the latest in a long successive chain of events. The experience had clarified and crystallised many of his ideas about the concepts of good and evil. 'I don't believe evil or good exists,' he told US reporter Paula Nechak in early 2004. 'I think there are very strong reasons why people are what they are.'

Of course, actors often say that playing a villain is far more interesting, even far more enjoyable, than portraying someone heroic. Without conflict, there is no drama, after all. But actors like Andy Serkis prefer to investigate the bad guys who also have other sides to their characters. Even in the context of fantasy films, his villains have recognisably human negative traits, whether it's the fascist dictator Capricorn (in the 2008 cinematic version of Cornelia Funke's novel *Inkheart*), or 'Dr Death', a.k.a. the shady psychologist Dr Adrian King, in *Death of a Superhero*.

When Serkis began to attract offers in films in the 1990s, they were often minor roles, playing people who would not appear on screen for long, and so, sometimes, there was not sufficient time for multifaceted figures to be represented. As he gained more prominent characters to play, so their complexities could be laid bare.

Sometimes, Serkis's villains operate as more extreme, morally bankrupt supporting characters to leading ones whom the audience can relate to more readily. In *The Escapist*, which was filmed in the Republic of Ireland in the spring of 2001, Serkis played a vicious sociopath with a nasty edge. Ricky Barnes gains entry to the house of commercial pilot Denis (Jonny Lee Miller) and kills his pregnant wife. Even though the baby survives, Denis is unable to recover from the trauma of his wife's murder and fails to bond with their child. For Denis, there is only one solution available to him. He fakes his own suicide and opts for a new life as a criminal, aiming to edge closer and closer to Barnes, the habitual violent criminal who has murdered his spouse, and who is now serving a 20-year sentence for the crime. But Denis is banged up not for murder but for mere vandalism. So he has to become more extreme to stand any chance of breaking into the maximum-security prison that holds Barnes. Denis, as the everyman with a family, is the 'hero' of *The Escapist*, the man we're asked to identify with.

For any actor, the eternal problem with portraying the violent and sadistic is the risk of overplaying the performance. Even in a career dominated by positive reviews and acclaim, Andy Serkis has just occasionally fallen foul of the charge of histrionic overacting. In the case of *Deathwatch*, a 2002 supernatural action drama set in the trenches of World War I, it was Jonathan Ross (then presenting the BBC's flagship TV film review show) who felt that Serkis's role as a barbarous soldier had strayed rather too much into the realms of caricature. 'I play this kind of desensitised, trophy-hunting nutter,' reflected Serkis. 'Jonathan Ross said that I overacted hugely. I might have gone one step too far on that character. I don't know.'

As Quinn, Serkis's psychotic persona was one of *Deathwatch*'s high points for some critics, although Ross was not alone in his views. The Scottish paper the *Daily Record* suggested that 'Serkis seems intent on transforming himself into Keith Allen rather than giving a decent performance.' But hysterical overacting or not, there was general revulsion at one of the film's set pieces where Quinn tied a German prisoner to a tree and beat him with a nail-studded club. 'A crucifixion scene worthy of Hieronymous Bosch,' gulped *The Times*.

Deathwatch gained acres of coverage in the British press long before it was completed, let alone screened, because one of its cast was Jamie Bell (then just 15), whose starring role in the smash hit *Billy Elliot* had made him a name to watch in British cinema. The film follows eight young soldiers who are – one by one – targeted by a sinister (and possibly nonhuman) killer. As well as Bell and Serkis, the cast included Laurence Fox, later the co-star of ITV's *Lewis*, and Kris Marshall, best known at that point for his appearances in the BBC sitcom *My Family*.

Described by its producer Mike Downey as 'a cross between *All Quiet on the Western Front* and *Evil Dead*', *Deathwatch* received a muted response from some on its premiere in December 2002, partly because the premise didn't seem too far removed from *The Bunker* – a movie that had opened in Britain only two months earlier. Veteran film critic Alexander Walker at the London *Evening Standard* accused the film of disrespectfully transforming the memory of British infantrymen into human ghouls. Ultimately, some of the most glittering notices were awarded to the gloomy, oppressive set design. 'You can almost smell the decay and hear the rats gnawing on the bones of the dead,' shivered the *Daily Record*.

The actors truly suffered for their art on that set, though, which in keeping with the setting was anything but welcoming or comforting. After some desolate land used for parachutists in the Czech army was hired by the production team, the set designers dug 400 metres of trenches and tunnels, littering the set with plastic corpses to represent soldiers, and replicas of rats. Then thousands of gallons of water, plus seemingly endless slabs of mud and silt from the nearby Vltava river, were poured into the trenches. Each day's shooting would begin with a drenching from a rain machine and fighting in the mud. Assigned to grab coffees for the actors playing his fellow soldiers in a moment of downtime, the cast's most junior member Jamie Bell found some reactions (in character, he hoped) to be somewhat unsettling but felt sure it raised his game for the next take: after Serkis spat out one sip of coffee and boomingly ordered Bell to get him another one, Bell told the *Daily Mail*, 'I wasn't quite sure how to play fear before that, but I [know] now.'

Bell must have hoped he was receiving a Quinn reaction, and not a Serkis one. Serkis himself has ruefully described another even more explosive incident on a London location shoot five years after *Deathwatch*. It was a moment when, by his own admission, he was so wrapped up in his violent persona that he could not control his aggression towards another actor when the cameras were not rolling. It happened during the filming of a low-budget urban drama called *Sugarhouse*, for which Serkis played Hoodwink, a former terrorist who was now a motormouth crime overlord on a rundown housing estate. In the firing line, as we'll see, was a young supporting player who misread the motivations of the characters around him; but, in order to explain how the incident unfolded, it is important first to explain the hectic context in which the film was made.

Location shooting is a tense business for anyone involved in it, especially for a film like *Sugarhouse*, which had only a few weeks in which to be shot, and a tiny total budget of only £250,000. The process of making the film – directed by former actor Gary Love (once a regular on TV's *Soldier Soldier*) – would be frantic for all concerned. The shoot, which began in August 2006, came less than six months after the production company Slingshot had first met the film's writer Dominic Leyton, who had adapted it from his own stage play, *Collision*. 'What matters', argued Slingshot's boss, Arvind Ethan David, in the trade paper *Screen International*, 'is the strength of your belief, the integrity of your approach and the quality of the material, not the size of your budget.'

Given that the budget for *Sugarhouse* was so modest, such conviction and self-belief was vital, and there was little time or space for anyone working on it to act the big star. The producer, Oliver Milburn, found he had plenty of unglamorous duties such as cleaning the toilet, a toilet that had been plumbed in by the film's 'water effects supervisor'. Above all, the crew needed to find a derelict warehouse in east London in which to film. What they secured consisted of two interconnected warehouses, one of which had a mezzanine level, an industrial fan and even some rooms that could be used as production offices. So, helpfully, the entire production could be based in one complex. Stunt artists and costumers had been lured into the project from the James Bond movie *Casino Royale*, but everyone was working for a pittance.

It all seemed a very long way from Peter Jackson's multimillion-dollar budgets, but Andy Serkis was more than happy with the varied nature of his career. '*Sugarhouse* is a great little film that deserves to do well,' he said. 'Obviously, it's not going to have mass appeal like *Lord of the Rings* but it's great to be able to switch from big blockbusters to small films like this.' But it wasn't just the low-budget nature of the film that would deny it mainstream success. Its sense of uncompromising brutality was always likely to alienate a large proportion of the British public, with its merciless gaze into desperate, drug-ridden and marginalised areas of society.

On such a shoestring budget and with time being so tight, preproduction on the film was equally pressurised. Serkis was on a much-needed family holiday in Italy when his agent forwarded him the script. Filming was just two weeks away. 'When you're in holiday mode, the intensity of this character seemed a million miles away. I knew there wasn't a lot of time to prepare for the part.' There was also the issue of perfecting a Northern Irish accent, for which he received a tape from a voice coach, and having his head shaved, but he was used to the latter by now. 'I've done that for parts before now. In fact, I got my kids to shave my head while we were on holiday. They each took turns with the clippers.'

The tattooing session, begun in earnest when Serkis finished his 16-hour drive back from Italy, took 20 hours to complete, and ultimately covered three-quarters of his body. The arduous task included the application of a giant Red Hand of Ulster, which extended up Serkis's back to his neck. 'They used a special jaguar fruit body ink that lasts for several weeks. They paint the dye on, and then you have to rip it off. It was applied all the way up the back of my legs, and up onto my backside – and I can assure you, it was agony. Once it dried, they pulled it off, which brought most of the hairs off my skin as well.' Even when filming was over, the tattoos remained – at least for a time. 'That ink doesn't come off. You have to wait for it to fade. So I had to walk around like that for a good six or seven weeks after we finished.'

But, for Serkis, never mind the semi-permanent tattoos, or the shaved head, or the accent he had to master. It was devising Hoodwink's high-octane temperament that was the most draining aspect of making *Sugarhouse*, even for an actor with the utmost dedication, strength and stamina. 'Once he's on his journey, there's no let-up for the man. And there wasn't any downtime to let the air out of it during the shooting day. We were all totally exhausted.' The most demanding scene of all found him going mad with a machete in a lift. Take one: 'I had been cranking myself up to do it all day, and we did it once…but I couldn't move a muscle after I did one take because I went at it so hard. And the camera just seemed to keep on going on and on, until I could not put one more stroke of that machete into that lift.' Serkis crawled out and collapsed next to director Gary Love. There would be no second take, and not just because the actor was spent. 'You know you've got only one go at it – because there is only one lift.'

Journalists reporting from the set of *Sugarhouse* couldn't help but comment on the marked, even disturbing gulf between the geniality of Serkis out of character, and the sheer foul-mouthed aggression when he 'became' the trained fighter, Hoodwink. 'He's the kingpin on this London estate, and everyone on the estate lives in fear of him,' he told one reporter. 'You wouldn't want to meet him in a dark alley.' But that explosive temperament could fizz at inopportune moments, a few of which weren't in the script. And it was at this point that Serkis would unleash Hoodwink's fury on one young supporting actor, Teddy Nygh.

It happened during the rehearsal of a scene in which Hoodwink had to confront three youths over the theft of a gun outside some garages. Nygh had decided that his character would 'front up' or show up Hoodwink, and started to deviate from the script, which Serkis didn't feel was appropriate for the characters. 'I was wired up to get this scene right,' he told the *Northern Echo*. 'I was pinning them all up against the garage door and everything. He sort of fronted me and I couldn't control myself, grabbed him, shoved him on the floor and started smacking him, saying, "Are you fronting up to the Hoody?" and this sort of stuff.'

Before Serkis knew it, an upset and shaken Nygh had beaten a hasty retreat. 'I said, "Teddy, look, mate, we're just acting and it gets a bit like that, it's a bit rough." I felt really bad and went a bit soft for a moment, trying to calm him down, and he was OK.' Serkis was determined to exercise Hoodwink's brand of authority to the younger actor, primarily to illustrate his tyrannical nature. Nevertheless, at the end of the shoot, as if to demonstrate that no single person there was more 'important' than any other, Serkis received a comeuppance of sorts. Having established how rewarding it had been to work with Serkis, Teddy Nygh had one final request. 'He said, "Do you mind if I just do this?" recalled Serkis. 'And he smacked me as hard as he could around the face. And I went, "I've really enjoyed working with you too, mate."'

Hoodwink begins *Sugarhouse* in a relatively secure position. He runs the estate, but is about to experience parenthood for the first time, with his wife Tania (Tracy

Whitwell). 'His wife is trying to bring out the "yin" in him,' said Serkis, 'taking him away from the alpha male that he is and trying to calm him down.' But Hoodwink was always a man with anger-management issues and a propensity for extreme violence. 'I've got a little bit of history playing monsters – but, once I was offered Hoodwink, I couldn't let him go. What really appealed to me is that he is very much a human being. He's so much more than a pantomime-ish villain.'

Just as with Gollum, or Kong, Hoodwink still had complexity, even vulnerability, as part of his makeup. And, while the man who had to play him described him as 'a beast of a man', he was at pains to explain his background, and why he had turned out the way he had. Hoodwink had been a member of the Ulster Defence Association, a paramilitary loyalist and vigilante group in Northern Ireland. 'He had a belief system. His violence was used in a political way. He was part of a brethren who believed they could achieve something through terrorism.' Once in London, though, the community of the terrorist organisation was gone, and he was isolated. 'He's lost his belief system and has become this *über* capitalist, a sort of survival-of-the-fittest Darwinian thug.'

Ashley Walters – a.k.a. Asher D of the group So Solid Crew – was playing a crack addict, and conducted research by hanging around at Stratford station in east London begging for food and spare change. As 'D' in *Sugarhouse*, he tries to sell a gun to a disillusioned middle-class city accountant called Tom (Steven Mackintosh), before Hoodwink – whose gun it is – enters the frame to create petrifying havoc.

Another novel factor in the film's development came with feedback in the form of an online test screening. In December 2006, three months after filming had been completed, 500 people were offered the chance to watch an early edit of the movie on the Internet. Those selected had a window of three days during which they could view it on a special site, and, influenced by their reactions to a questionnaire, the makers could then re-edit the film. Now filmmakers did not have to rely exclusively on test screenings at cinemas, but could garner responses by polling hundreds of people at once.

Serkis believed that director Gary Love had managed to establish an effortlessly natural authority on the production of *Sugarhouse*. 'He's driven in all the right ways and there's a real equality across the set.' This was a film where there were no stars. With no spare money sloshing around and only 24 days to make the feature, the cast could not retreat to personal trailers between takes. They had no choice but to stay on the mocked-up crack-den set. 'There was a real equality across *Sugarhouse*,' said Serkis. 'There was no chance of anyone throwing any kind of hissy fit. It was a fantastic environment to work in.'

Slingshot self-distributed the final cut. So many British films, as Andy Serkis knows only too well, never find a distributor, and never open in cinemas, but *Sugarhouse* would show on 50 screens around Britain. Reviews were variable. 'So unrelentingly violent, it's like being beaten with a housebrick for 90 minutes,' groaned the *Mirror*. The *Observer*'s critic saw it differently, admiring 'magnetic performances and a script that bristles with threat and misunderstanding. If not quite Reservoir, then certainly

Walthamstow Dogs.' And further acclaim would follow in August 2007, when it debuted at the Edinburgh Film Festival, and was nominated for the Michael Powell Award for Best British Film. Others in the running included Anton Corbijn's *Control* (the biopic of Joy Division lead singer Ian Curtis) and another film set in an intimidating world with a minimal budget, which also happened to feature Andy Serkis in an uncompromising role: Jim Threapleton's political thriller, *Extraordinary Rendition*.

Formerly married to Kate Winslet, filmmaker Threapleton impressed many with his first feature film, which follows the story of a man who is taken to an unknown country and held hostage without trial. A British Muslim teacher, Zaafir Ahmadi (Omar Berdouni), suspected of being involved in terrorist activities, is transferred from his workaday life in London to an undisclosed country, where he is tortured in an unflinching way. Eventually, Zaafir makes it back to the UK to try to repair his shattered life. Andy Serkis played one of his captors and interrogators, a prison warder called Maro, who accuses the prisoner of financing the struggle to build an Islamic nation. He played the part in menacing but understated fashion.

The subject matter of *Extraordinary Rendition* was timely, inspired by – though not closely based on – the real-life story of the Canadian computer specialist, Maher Arar, who in 2002 was arrested at JFK Airport near New York and dispatched to Syria, where he was imprisoned and tortured for a whole year. Threapleton was so keen to make the film as quickly as possible that the project went ahead with no time to write a full script. This meant that the motivation behind its making was driven by character, not by plot. Cast members were obliged to improvise on camera, meaning that the story took shape during shooting, resulting in a vivid and difficult viewing experience. In addition, the human rights organisation Amnesty International was consulted closely throughout the production to give strong credibility to the political dimension of the film. Comparison was made in one review to the warped, dreamlike quality of the torture scenes in Michael Radford's mid-1980s screen version of George Orwell's *Nineteen Eighty-Four*. Indeed, Threapleton denied his film was a polemical mix of documentary and drama, preferring to think of it as a thriller in the nightmarish vein of Orwell or Franz Kafka.

Although the film was set in Jordan, representing one of the CIA's so-called 'black sites', to which terror suspects could be transferred through Western airspace to Middle East nations, shooting actually took place in Dalston, east London. The budget was a minuscule £50,000, far lower than even *Sugarhouse*'s had been, which meant that the film looked abrasive and rough to watch, with lots of flashbacks and flashforwards and plenty of use of a handheld camera. The content, too, was queasy, with some brutal beatings and grim torture scenes, including one practice – waterboarding – that bordered on the unwatchable for many viewers. Waterboarding involves placing a cloth over the victim's face, then pouring water over it, to which the body reacts as if it were drowning.

To give the waterboarding scene shocking authenticity, the team carried out the practice on stuntman Jamie Edgell, who was also a skilful surfer. 'I surf a bit,' Threapleton told the *Evening Standard*. 'We both thought it couldn't be much worse than taking a fall off a board and being under for maybe a minute.' But, less than ten seconds after the water started pouring into him, the stuntman said to stop. 'He was really shocked by it. The whole thing was fairly horrifying. Whenever we filmed those physical-abuse scenes, the tension levels were really raised on set.'

'It is unpleasant,' Threapleton conceded to the *Observer* in August 2007. 'But we really thought we had to portray the reality of what is at the heart of the story...without being tub-thumping or preachy. It's sometimes perceived as being a dry, political subject, and we amassed a whole archive of evidence on it, but from that kernel we wanted to extract the real human drama.'

The film also has a lot to say about the information age: the incriminating material that traps Zaafir takes the form of a series of emails and personal detail that the authorities misinterpret. The idea of being held prisoner and being tortured was only one aspect of what made the film disturbing. Also at its heart was what the *Observer* described as 'a metaphysical question: What happens when someone else is let loose with the facts of your life and they make their own interpretation of what and who you are?' For director Threapleton, it was an examination of how our identity can be misused. 'Whether it's your credit card statements, or destinations you travelled to in your year off, or an email you may or may not have opened...Under scrutiny, that can be misinterpreted or appropriated to an agenda that can almost kind of mould you.'

Extraordinary Rendition never made it to cinemas, although it was shown at a film festival or two. It crept out on DVD in April 2008, and received its TV premiere within days. Threapleton was fully aware that what he had made was no commercial smash, and was cheerfully doubtful it even counted as entertainment. 'The bare facts for theatre audiences are quite simple: if you're out on a Saturday night and you're faced with *Knocked Up* versus *Extraordinary Rendition* you're probably going to go for *Knocked Up*.'

Whether it was exhausting himself as a machete-wielding gangland boss, or becoming involved in a political thriller's torture scenes, Andy Serkis could certainly make the viewer shudder with his visceral portrayals of the violent and damaged. But, from time to time, playing figures that were defined by both aggression and vulnerability could be a strain on his spirit and drain him.

In the late summer of 2002, while still working on Gollum's dialogue recordings for *The Lord of the Rings*, Serkis was opening (with wife Lorraine) in the stage production of *Othello* in Manchester. He was playing the very epitome of envy, the sergeant major Iago, who is so eaten away by jealousy when his friend Othello falls in love with Desdemona that he sets about plotting to sabotage their relationship. Even before injuring his back – and passing out in front of a matinée audience at the Royal Exchange – Serkis wondered if taking on Iago again for the first time since university days in 1984 was wise, given that his time as Gollum was not yet quite over. 'Playing Iago and Gollum at the same time is bad for your mental health. It means you are consistently full of hatred.'

Nevertheless, just as Serkis had spent a good deal of time and energy working out how to make Gollum empathetic and rounded, so he tried to see past the obvious evil veneer of

Iago. He argued to himself that Iago was once a good soldier, but had simply become addicted to the concept of power. 'He's you or me feeling jealous and not being able to control our feelings. Iago manages to thrill the audience so much with his scheming that they almost want him to succeed. They are then forced to question their own morality.'

There were times when Andy Serkis got to play a slightly more recognisable everyman, or at least someone the audience could identify with, 'like the straight man in the middle of all these weirdos'. In the gory British horror-comedy *The Cottage*, which opened in March 2008, he played the bungling, all-too-human David who – in a bickering double-act with weedy brother Peter (Reece Shearsmith) – plans to kidnap a young woman called Tracey (Jennifer Ellison). Once this is achieved, they intend to hold her for a £100,000 ransom in a deserted cottage, with the help of her treacherous stepbrother Andrew (Steven O'Donnell).

The whole point of the kidnap is to squeeze money out of Tracey's club-owning gangster of a father, but she turns out to be far feistier than her bumbling captors anticipate, delivering kicks, headbutts and profanities. Finally, she overpowers Andrew and, as she escapes from the cottage, takes him hostage. Soon, though, the most threatening character of all – a disfigured farmer – enters the picture, running amok with some very big knives, and the film becomes gorier and gorier: spilt blood and the dismemberment of body parts. At one point, a spinal cord is ripped out. At another, Tracey is decapitated. 'It was all prosthetics,' Jennifer Ellison reassured. 'There was a full body cast and I had to have a head cast.' Director Paul Andrew Williams, previously at the helm of the cult drama *London to Brighton*, preferred to use prosthetics than CGI effects.

However, Williams knew that gore had no meaning without a sense of context or strong characters the audience could relate to. 'Unless you've got good characters, people won't care about them or what happens to them. That's when it just becomes mindless gore.' He was careful for the film to avoid toppling over into crass parody. 'I wanted to make something that was very aware of how silly it is at times, but without sending itself up completely. Just don't go to the cinema expecting to see a thought-provoking, groundbreaking serious drama.' Some critics would be less sure of *The Cottage*'s tone, oscillating between broad comedy and garish horror, but Serkis was regarded as one of its saving graces. The film overall had its admirers, although, even there, it was perhaps more for the sheer audacity of its ambition. 'This film is fabulously deranged,' was *The Times*'s verdict.

The part of Tracey had been conceived for someone much older than an actress in her mid-twenties. 'It was written for a 40-year-old,' Williams told the *Daily Telegraph*, 'but to get the project financed I was told I had to cast someone young. I hadn't really seen Jennifer act but, after she came in for the audition, the producer and I literally hugged each other and said, That's her, that's Tracey.'

Ellison, still just 24, had come to prominence in her teens as the sparky Emily Shadwick in the Merseyside television soap, *Brookside*, and had since diversified into reality TV (she had triumphed on the celebrity cooking show, *Hell's*

Kitchen) and then stage work (*Chicago*). Her ubiquity in the popular press and men's magazines ensured that her presence at the premiere for the film in March 2008 overshadowed that of her co-stars.

In contrast, the six-week shoot a year earlier could scarcely have been any more uncomfortable. Filmed first on the Isle of Man, and then in Yorkshire in the grounds of the historic stately home Harewood House, it involved a large number of night shoots. In the cold conditions of early spring, the cast and crew felt the full blast of the elements. 'It was really hard work,' said Andy Serkis, 'because it was entirely a night shoot and we kind of lived in this weird netherworld for six weeks.

'It was all-night shooting,' said Ellison. 'So we started at five in the afternoon and went on until nine the next morning.'

Even during daylight hours, there was little time to rest, as this was when rehearsals took place. Shooting each scene could be very tiring, as Serkis detailed to Scottish paper, the *Daily Record*: 'A lot of the scenes are very dialogue-driven, and we were doing the big scenes in one take, so you had to be really on the ball trying to remember five or six pages of dialogue at four in the morning.'

But filming in the countryside gave the production an expansive feel, in the view of Paul Andrew Williams. 'I think the fact that we've found such great, real locations rather than shooting it in a warehouse, is a complete bonus.' That said, he vowed that never again would he make another film that relied so heavily on night shoots.

More recently, Serkis was regarded as flamboyant light relief when he made a brief but exuberant appearance – as the crime boss Mr Colleoni – in the 2010 cinematic adaptation of Graham Greene's novel *Brighton Rock*. Starring Sam Riley and Andrea Riseborough, this cinematic remake was noticeably darker for the most part than the famous 1947 version starring Richard Attenborough, and the action was transplanted from the 1930s to the mid-1960s. For Colleoni's costume, the film's designer Julian Day had referred to photographer David Bailey's unforgettable shots of the Krays and Michael Caine – to make Colleoni look both sensual and predatory. Serkis's Colleoni cameo was regarded by a few critics as light relief. 'I cherish him spouting "Restless youth: the ravaged and disrupted territory between the two eternities!" as he spins a spoon in boredom,' marvelled *Time Out*'s reviewer. The *Independent on Sunday* gorged on the film's overall campness, pausing to class Serkis's Colleoni as 'a cross between Oscar Wilde and Jabba the Hutt'.

There is a lighter side to playing villains, of course. Films popular with younger audiences need to portray the badly behaved in order for a story's hero to triumph at the end. Serkis would portray several such nemeses – or their associates – on celluloid. Even some of these figures, however, were by no means one-dimensional or reductive, and often had the sort of vulnerability common to Gollum *et al*.

The animated *Flushed Away*, which began production in 2004 and reached cinemas in late 2006, was a rare foray for Serkis into voice-only work. He provided the voice for Spike, a rat who acts as a hapless 'henchman' (or 'henchrat') to the villainous Toad (voiced by his *Lord of the Rings* co-star Ian McKellen). It tells how pampered British rat Roddy St James (voiced by Hugh Jackman) is accidentally flushed out of his penthouse flat into the sewers lying beneath the streets of London. He finds himself in the middle of a vast subterranean metropolis, where another rat, Rita, is on a mission of her own. But both are in danger from Toad and henchrats Spike and Whitey. 'He's a lowlife, rather neurotic gangster,' Serkis said of Spike. He based the rat's character on various self-important figures he'd encountered in his past. 'We've all known people who were too big for their boots, whose attempts to take control of a situation always backfires. Spike is the little guy trying to be scary, even though his mum washes his knickers.'

The animated film was a co-production between the mighty DreamWorks corporation in the US and Aardman Animations, based in Bristol, and best known for Nick Park's almost universally popular films featuring inventor Wallace and his faithful dog Gromit. Serkis was quite a fan of Aardman's previous output and jumped at the chance of being involved in one of its projects, because of the team's commitment to bringing out the reality in its extraordinary, outlandish characters. 'The world they've created is so rich,' he told one American newspaper. 'There isn't a frame where there isn't a hundred things going on.'

Aardman's previous output had relied on clay-model stop-motion animation. *Flushed Away* marked a move into computer-generated filmmaking, with intensive work spent on creating an underground sub-London city of rats. 'I think they enjoyed their first CG venture. It's part of the future,' commented Andy Serkis. In fact, the original plan was shoot the whole film as a stop-frame production. 'But then common sense kicked in,' said producer Peter Lord, all too aware of how long the stop-frame process had taken on previous Aardman productions, 'and we thought, It's just not going to happen.' What changed Lord's mind was accepting that very few materials in stop-frame animation production could mimic the appearance and movement of water.

Some of Serkis's fellow performers on *Flushed Away* could relate to some of the assumptions and received wisdom that had dogged him on CG productions over the previous five years. Bill Nighy – who provided the voice of a more philosophical lab rat named Whitey – realised just how like 'real acting' this voiceover work was. '[Andy] heard I'd been doing some of this stuff. I said [to him], "Well, now I understand what's been happening with you." So there's an immediate bond between us now.'

Although most voice actors on films work on their own, Serkis and Nighy did one voice session together, in order for them to work out how their characters' personalities and voices differed. 'It's always better when you have someone to play off,' Serkis commented. Even so, although animators on the production filmed the actors on reference cameras, this was not strictly a computer-generated project. 'It's a very different challenge, doing an animated movie,' said Serkis. 'You only come in to do the voice every so often.' Indeed, Serkis was juggling his commitments on *Flushed Away* during 2004–5 with his duties on *King Kong* in New Zealand, and so was frequently globetrotting between London, Los Angeles and Wellington.

Even though *Flushed Away* was animated via computer,

both Aardman and DreamWorks were keen to keep the spirit of Aardman's earlier techniques involving clay puppets and stop-motion animation. 'They've got the whole story aspect and the reality of the characters,' said Andy Serkis, 'and yet they've got the ability [with CGI] to take it where they want. So I think as a marriage of their old style and the new realm – I'm a little bit biased, of course – I think they've done a brilliant job.'

Serkis's Spike – a rat with delusions of evil – made it to the screen in *Flushed Away* in time for Christmas 2006, capping a period that had just seen him also open as assistant types in two other films. In *Alex Rider: Stormbreaker*, adapted from Anthony Horowitz's best-selling teenage-spy series of books, he was henchman Mr Grin, who reported to the megalomaniac Darrius Sayle (played by Mickey Rourke). *The Prestige* – a Disney-made period drama about two feuding magicians – saw him playing the assistant to the engineering pioneer Nikola Tesla, who was played by none other than David Bowie. 'I am playing Igor to his Frankenstein,' commented Serkis, thrilled to be working alongside one of the icons of his youth.

Spike in *Flushed Away* was one of Serkis's lighter versions of villainy, but, even there, he was more than a snarling, one-dimensional rat. As usual, Serkis preferred to take on a figure with complexity.

For Serkis, what was fascinating about playing a villain was to try to understand someone's origins, to try to track how they had made decisions and choices (whether those choices are right or wrong ones). It could be said of many of his stage and screen roles: Gollum, needless to say, Phil in

Hurlyburly, Bill Sikes in *Oliver Twist*, Hoodwink in *Sugarhouse*. 'You could play them all as pretty nasty guys, really, who've got no redeeming qualities. It's important to find redeeming qualities in these characters to make audiences ask questions, really, and do a lot of work for themselves, and not feel like they're being served something.' And understanding them was something he felt that was the responsibility of everyone, not just actors. '[They] are not just fictional evil villains: they are part of humanity. We can choose to disassociate ourselves from them, we can choose to pretend they're not there, but they are there. We are all together in this.'

One part Andy Serkis was unsuccessful in securing was that of Adolf Hitler, a role he auditioned for in 2002, which would have featured in a CBS drama in the United States. To Serkis's great fascination, the script was curiously sympathetic towards him. '[It] just treated him as a human being, and I guess that's what I try and do with acting. Just normalising the extreme, and finding as much range to what you would consider that you'd know about a character. Normalising someone like that is far more interesting, really.' The idea of Serkis's tackling Hitler is indeed an intriguing one, but he has been given plenty of other opportunities to play real people over the years, all of them with their own complex histories.

CHAPTER 11

SERKIS AND BIOPICS

With Andy Serkis's investigations bringing back rich insights into the denizens of fiction, even ones who had been played many times before, it is logical that he might have turned his attention to the portrayals of real people. It would be stretching a point to describe all of the Serkis figures that follow in this chapter as 'famous', but what they have in common (perhaps the only thing they share) is that they were all real people. Yet they also demand interpretation, research work that he revelled in undertaking.

The fact that some of them are not famous (and all but one of them are deceased) is irrelevant. What matters is that, like the fictional, they demand reinterpretation, re-evaluation and research, work that he would revel in undertaking.

After his experience of working on Mike Leigh's 1997 film

Career Girls, for which he had conducted several months of thorough research – living as a futures trader – Andy Serkis was invited to work with him again in 1998 on a project that became the vivacious film *Topsy-Turvy*.

Librettist W. S. Gilbert and composer Sir Arthur Sullivan were the most popular exponents of light comic opera in late-nineteenth-century England, with appeal for productions like *H.M.S. Pinafore* and *The Pirates of Penzance* also spreading to America. *Topsy-Turvy* documents how the duo and their many associates and colleagues created *The Mikado*, which opened at the Savoy Theatre in London in March 1885. It came at a time when the twosome's previous offering, *Princess Ida* (1884), had been damned with indifference, with one critic branding Gilbert (played in Leigh's film by Jim Broadbent), to his chagrin, as 'the king of topsy-turvydom'. Sullivan (Allan Corduner), meanwhile, was tiring of populist appeal and yearned to write something more serious.

Yet, despite this, the duo were able to write *The Mikado*, a fantastical tale about love and mistaken identity in Japan. Leigh constructed the story as if it were a symphony: one section concentrating on Sullivan, a second giving Gilbert the spotlight, and a third examining the whole of their opera company, the D'Oyly Carte – performers, producers, managers, costumers and other staff. A coda sequence acted as a reminder that behind all of these people lay spouses and families, some of whom also make sacrifices.

It was in this third section that Andy Serkis's contribution featured. He used the same process as before to reduce a list of possible 'touchstone characters' down to one persona, which he would base everything on. This time, though, he faced an additional responsibility: like those of the rest of the cast, his character would not be fictional, but someone who had actually lived. Serkis chose the choreographer John D'Auban, and so began some painstaking and fascinating background research. He discovered that D'Auban, a whirlwind of physical and creative energy, was not only a pantomimic dancer, but also taught classical ballet, and pioneered a then-popular kind of dancing called legmania.

By the end of nine months of rehearsal, Serkis's knowledge of D'Auban was encyclopaedic. 'I knew every piece of choreography for every single Gilbert and Sullivan opera that he programmed, through finding old copies of scripts with his notations on.' Much of this knowledge had seeped into the rehearsals: Serkis would physically choreograph some of the improvisations that grew out of research. He studied Irish dancing and ballet as part of his preparation. And, when he discovered that D'Auban also played the violin while choreographing to keep the tempo, the only option was to learn the instrument, at least at a rudimentary level. It was one of his most complete investigations into a character yet.

Even then, Leigh was not finished. Now that Serkis and his fellow cast members – including Alison Steadman, Timothy Spall and Lesley Manville – had found out as much as possible about their own characters, the next step was to conduct group research. Discussions took place on how people talked in the 1880s, what food they ate, what the political attitudes might have been like at the time. 'You had the accumulated knowledge that all these characters would have known about each other in the Savoy Company . . .' explained Serkis, 'which all had to be thoroughly researched.'

Eventually, the 70-strong cast would be able to improvise, which they did with gusto at the Savoy Theatre, while Leigh watched and shaped the structure and content of the final film. 'We had some of the most incredible improvisations, just being in character for hours and hours on end,' Serkis recalled fondly.

Topsy-Turvy set out to show how the most enjoyable and accessible entertainment requires enormous levels of dedicated work from those who make it. In making it, Serkis would find, as he often did, that the preparation and process were as rewarding as appreciating the final cut. 'You certainly wouldn't work with Mike Leigh if you didn't enjoy process.'

Not all of Serkis's research – the violin lessons for one thing – was deemed essential for the released cut of the film. And he hinted in 2003 that, while he would love to work with Leigh again, the commitment and dedication required for any of his projects could rival the attention needed for one's own family. 'It's secretive work, and it wouldn't be fair to shield my wife and children from that.' When he said those words, he had admittedly spent nigh on four years as Gollum, but perhaps even that wasn't quite the same as the 'emotional secrecy' that Leigh's work demanded.

Topsy-Turvy required all involved to conduct their own research, hopefully to bring as much authenticity as they could to the historical and cultural Britain of 1880s Britain. A more irreverent take on the nineteenth-century biopic would come in 2010 with the dark comedy, *Burke and Hare*, for which Serkis became a last-minute addition to the cast. It tells of how two Irish grave robbers discover that they can make a more-than-decent living out of handing over corpses to a medical school in Edinburgh.

Originally slated to play William Hare (opposite Simon Pegg's William Burke) had been David Tennant, who was due to start shooting in the Scottish capital in early 2010, just after his swansong as the Doctor in TV's *Doctor Who*. But on 21 January, ten days before shooting was due to begin, Pegg tweeted his many fans on the social networking website Twitter with the following message: 'No DT, but by sheer glorious serendipity, a legend of Middle Earth and Skull Island has come aboard. Welcome AS.' Tennant's abrupt departure came about because he had already committed to filming a pilot for NBC-TV in America, *Rex is Not Your Lawyer*, and the dates for both projects clashed. (The pilot was completed but did not result in a series.)

The director of *Burke and Hare* was to be none other than the American John Landis, whose track record had included the comedies *Trading Places* and *The Blues Brothers*, and the horror movie *An American Werewolf in London*, as well as the 15-minute promotional video for Michael Jackson's song, 'Thriller'. Landis had not directed a feature film in a decade, but leapt at the opportunity to 'make an historically accurate, very black, romantic comedy!' Having reportedly received several knock-backs from US studios, Landis was quoted at the 2010 Cannes Film Festival as saying that he had chosen to work in Britain instead 'because they still take risks and make interesting movies'.

Though Andy Serkis and Simon Pegg had not collaborated professionally prior to *Burke and Hare*, they had been near-neighbours in north London, as Serkis told *Time Out*. 'We used to live three streets away from each other in Crouch End, so the first time I met him was when I almost knocked him down with my people carrier.' Serkis, who dusted off for Hare the Northern Irish accent he previously brought to *Sugarhouse* three years before, joined the cast at the same time as Isla Fisher (playing Pegg's actress girlfriend), plus several people from Serkis's professional past: Tom Wilkinson (as Dr Robert Knox, the anatomy lecturer), actor and director David Hayman (from *Finney* and *The Near Room*), plus *Lord of the Rings*' Saruman himself, Christopher Lee, as Old Joseph.

Even the diminutive veteran comedy performer Ronnie Corbett showed up for a supporting role. 'Ronnie just cracks you up,' Serkis told the *Daily Record*. 'Every scene he is in he steals, but it is wonderful to work with him.' Serkis was similarly honoured to work with the film's maverick director: 'He's such a legend. He's a walking encyclopedia of old Hollywood and yet he's so connected to young filmmakers.' But how, *Time Out* wondered, did John Landis direct Ronnie Corbett? 'The way John directs is very forthright,' commented Serkis. 'He's not a subtle actor's director. It's all just, "Slower! Faster!" His words to Corbett were, "Don't act with your fucking eyebrows, Ronnie!"' For his part, Landis was a Corbett fan from long ago, having sampled *Two Ronnies* episodes in the mid-seventies while working in the UK as a writer on the Bond flick *The Spy Who Loved Me*.

Behind all the larks of *Burke and Hare*, though, lay a macabre, even grim, story. In the late 1820s, the body-snatching pair were busy digging up the dead from their graves and selling the cadavers at £10 a time (roughly equivalent to £600 each nowadays) to anatomy lecturer Dr

Robert Knox for dissection. But they soon discovered it was much easier to make money from killing anonymous vagrants. Seventeen murders later, Burke and Hare were cornered for their crimes. Hare, regarded as more sinister and cunning than his partner in crime, testified against Burke in return for immunity from prosecution. Burke was hanged in January 1829, after which his body was dissected in public, at the medical college where he had sold his victims. Hare was released from prison a month later, but he promptly disappeared, and ironically, given his line of work, his body has never been traced. Dr Knox managed to avoid prosecution. He was even one of the 55 witnesses at the trial, though, ultimately, he was not called to the stand. Burke and Hare's exploits have remained notorious in Edinburgh. The city's Dungeon, located on Market Street, has a whole section dedicated to the duo, while many of their haunts are explored in a special 'murder tour'.

Filming was a ball for the cast, it seemed. 'It is macabre, yet funny,' Serkis said of the twosome's grisly history. 'There are a lot of contradictions. These two guys, who were basically serial killers, helped contribute towards the enhancement of medicine. Hare is not malevolent or evil. Killing people is a job to him. He is totally amoral.' As William Burke, Pegg relished the 'moral playfulness' of the story, and how it challenged the audience. 'It's asking you to sympathise with two people who are effectively mass murderers.' For Andy Serkis, it was a satirical film in which the central figures are 'pawns in the medical industry'; the real villains of the piece were the doctors, played by Tim Curry and Tom Wilkinson, 'this self-serving, rather pompous pair who are the fat cats, really'.

Burke and Hare themselves were regarded by director Landis as 'kind of like an evil Laurel and Hardy', which reinforced the idea that this was, above all, comedy – albeit of the jet-black variety. But, then, John Landis had plenty of experience of mixing the hilarious with the shocking, most notoriously with *An American Werewolf in London*, where audiences would roar with laughter one moment, then shiver with discomfort the next. Laughing and screaming, he argued, were the same. 'They invoke an involuntary physical response: you gasp or scream or laugh, they're spasms. But they're both very difficult.'

How to make the audience like psychopaths, then, albeit of the comic variety? It was a tall order. Simon Pegg argued that their deplorable behaviour was almost an adventure in mischief that spiralled out of control. 'It is a gradual descent into homicide. They have a dead body that they sell, and then they try grave robbing, but that doesn't work because the bodies are so rotten. Then they start to kill people. The first people they kill are almost on their last legs anyway.'

'Really, we need the audience to like the main characters,' said Andy Serkis cautiously, 'and that's the challenge for us actors. I hope we get it right.' For some critics, he was sensible to voice a note of caution: they found the tone of the film too zany for the subject matter.

Burke and Hare died nearly two centuries ago, however. What to do about a killer who is still alive? Andy Serkis has rarely courted controversy, either consciously or accidentally, but there was some press concern early in 2006 when it was announced that he would be playing one of the most notorious murderers in twentieth-century Britain for a new television film drama, *Longford*. Between 1963 and

1965, Ian Brady, together with his then girlfriend Myra Hindley, abducted and killed five youngsters, aged between 10 and 17 in the Manchester area: Pauline Reade, John Kilbride, Keith Bennett, Lesley Ann Downey and Edward Evans. When they were tried and convicted of the crimes, at a highly publicised trial in the spring of 1966, it proved a most emotive subject for the British press and public.

For years after the pair's imprisonment, discussion of their ever being granted parole remained an incendiary topic of conversation in the media. The weight of newsprint, the accumulation of articles and documentaries, the resurgence of sadness and frustration and hatred every time their names are mentioned... For Andy Serkis, about to play Brady, *Longford* would be an intelligent take 'on a subject everyone thinks they know everything about'.

Myra Hindley maintained, right up until her death in 2002, that she had been 'misunderstood'. Lord Longford, who died a year before Hindley, agreed. Longford was a vigorous campaigner for the rights of prisoners, and regularly visited many prisoners, Hindley being one. He fervently believed that, no matter how severe the crime, no offender was entirely irredeemable. He also argued that Hindley had behaved well in prison and so was entitled to be freed, having served a far longer sentence than most who receive life. Brady, meanwhile, was declared criminally insane in the mid-1980s, and, at the time of writing, remains alive, despite stating on many occasions his wish to end his life.

The subject matter of *Longford*, necessarily tied up with the issue of Brady and Hindley (commonly referred to as 'the Moors Murderers'), was always going to mean the film would hit the headlines long before it was even screened. Even cast members had to think twice before agreeing to participate, like Samantha Morton, who played Hindley. 'Initially, I didn't even want to look at the script. I didn't want anything to do with it. But I believe it is my duty as a performer to raise issues we're afraid to look at.' Speaking at the London Film Critics Circle Awards at the city's Dorchester Hotel, Andy Serkis was even more adamant that the film should be made and he had no hesitation about taking part. 'The drama asks whether it's possible for people to be redeemed or whether people are truly evil. I haven't any problems playing the role as it's the job of actors to look at the darker side of society.' Kevin Lygo, head of Channel 4, who co-funded the drama (with HBO in the USA), insisted to the *Daily Telegraph* that *Longford* wasn't being made to linger on the crimes. 'The drama is about Longford and his Catholic-induced obsession with forgiveness. It follows his story and asks whether forgiveness is appropriate in this case.'

Traditionally, when violent crime takes place against children, the public are even slower to forgive women who have been convicted than men. And, even simply in taking the role of convicted killers, it's significant that Serkis (as Brady) was spared the full ire of the press directed towards Morton (as Hindley). It was a point that was not lost on Serkis, as he recognised why the pair remained representations of hate to so many people. 'It is how the media created them as iconic monsters and how much Myra Hindley, as a woman, would have been released earlier on parole had she been a man, as that is probably the case. She was demonised because she was a woman and women are not supposed to commit acts like that, whereas men can kind of get away with it.'

Serkis himself was relatively unflustered about how playing the role of Ian Brady might affect his standing as a public figure – even after photographs he had shot with Morton (in character) were released to the press. He wondered aloud to the *Mail on Sunday* about just why there was still considerable revulsion about their crimes five decades later. 'It touches a collective nerve, not only because it involves the murder of children but also because Brady and Hindley were from the era of black-and-white photography. It's no coincidence that the Krays became glamorised in their time by posing for photos with pop stars and movie actors, and that those pictures of Brady and Hindley are seared into people's memories.'

Such was Serkis's concern with confronting truth in the roles he played that not only did he research Ian Brady but also wanted to meet him, if only fleetingly, at Ashworth High Security Prison on Merseyside, though to his regret this was not possible. Quick to emphasise that he did not defend either the man or what he believed in, he nevertheless believed that Brady possessed fierce intelligence and a sense of moral relativism. 'He believes that the notion of good and evil is a construct of the upper classes to keep the working classes down. That's what I chose to play, someone who passionately believes in something as a way of making sense of his own life.' To Serkis, playing someone like Brady had the same appeal as getting to the heart of Gollum or Kong. In each case, it was about examining a character, then inviting the audience to draw their own conclusions.

Relatives of the deceased were understandably upset that

the film was being made, notably Winnie Johnson – by now 72 – whose 12-year-old son Keith Bennett's body has still never been traced, despite numerous appeals to his two killers. In the event, *Longford* was beaten to transmission by a second film about the crimes. *See No Evil* (made and shown by ITV), which starred Sean Harris and Maxine Peake, was made with the support of several of the victims' relatives, and was shown in May 2006 to coincide with the 40th anniversary of the trial and sentencing of Brady and Hindley. Advising the makers of *Longford*, meanwhile, was Longford's daughter, Lady Antonia Fraser.

Fears about *Longford* being a tawdry, exploitative production proved to be unfounded when it was broadcast on Channel 4 in October 2006. It was not going to reconstruct the actual crimes committed by Brady and Hindley. Instead, it examined just why Longford felt compelled to seek parole for Hindley, and why he believed so strongly in the concept of redemption. Even so, Serkis's sparing appearances in the film – he inhabits only three scenes – are restless and disturbing, highlighting the murderer's dark, persuasive power.

'Another outstanding performance from Andy Serkis,' wrote Nancy Banks-Smith, doyen of TV critics, in the *Guardian*. 'Before Brady, whose malevolence was like the breath of a furnace, even Longford's childlike shine was dimmed.' *The Scotsman*'s reviewer was floored by Serkis's 'eerily charismatic performance', though the *Independent* murmured concern that the Longford–Brady scenes 'relied on the sneaking pleasure of familiarity: this was Hannibal Lecter transposed to the real world.'

The mostly positive notices were mirrored by the

nominations released for the Television section of the BAFTAs in April 2007. As well as the production itself in contention for Best Single Drama, Samantha Morton's role as Myra Hindley landed her a Best Actress nomination. In the Best Actor category, two of *Longford*'s cast were featured: Jim Broadbent (as Longford himself) and Andy Serkis (as Brady). Battling it out against them were the other two nominees: Michael Sheen, whose eponymous portrayal in the TV film *Kenneth Williams: Fantabulosa!* was much-praised; and John Simm, star of one of 2006's big TV hits, the BBC time-travel fantasy drama series *Life on Mars*. When the envelope was opened on the stage of the London Palladium on 20 May 2007, Serkis, Sheen and Simm lost out to Jim Broadbent, although Serkis, Broadbent and Morton (as well as *Longford* itself) also found themselves nominated for Golden Globe gongs at the end of 2007. Serkis was shortlisted for Best Supporting Actor in Series or Miniseries, for which he was pitted against Ted Danson (for *Damages*), Kevin Dillon and Jeremy Piven (both for *Entourage*), William Shatner (*Boston Legal*) and Donald Sutherland (*Dirty Sexy Money*). Unluckily, once again Serkis did not win – the trophy went to Piven – especially unfortunate given that his two *Longford* co-stars (and the production) all won their respective categories.

It was inevitable that taking on the challenge of playing Ian Brady – and, of course, the acclaim it ultimately brought – would, for a time, almost guarantee him a question about Brady in a press interview. Ruminating on the task to the *Sunday Telegraph* in 2008, he was clear that it was no use simply approaching the part in a cold, calculating way. 'You can't just go into something like that just playing a normal villain. You have to find a comparison with yourself. For Brady, the moment when he was most complete, most joyful, was when he was on the moors with Myra. Mine was when I was with my wife and our children were being born. Bringing life into the world, taking life out: there's a connection.'

William Hare and Ian Brady were two men who used their wits to carry out murder, and whose acts inspired glaringly different screen biopics. For the most part, though, Andy Serkis's output in biopics has explored portraying real-life characters who have been pioneers, in music, in science, in art – and in literature. In 1999, while waiting to start filming *The Lord of the Rings*, he participated in Julien Temple's raucous, bizarre pantomime of eighteenth-century literary society, *Pandaemonium*. While the film speculated on the friendship and collaboration between Samuel Taylor Coleridge (Linus Roache) and William Wordsworth (John Hannah), Serkis took the more modest part of the revolutionary, writer and poet John Thelwall (1764–1834).

For an actor with a life-long love of painting, Serkis seemed a suitable choice for playing the popular epitome of 'the tortured genius': the ill-fated nineteenth-century Dutch painter Vincent van Gogh. A 2006 series for BBC2 called *The Power of Art* juxtaposed dramatic reconstructions with links on location supplied by the historian and presenter Simon Schama. It has often been said that Van Gogh's talent was overlooked during his lifetime, and recognised only after his untimely death, at just 37, in 1890. In fact, Schama revealed that Van Gogh's talent was starting to be noticed by the end of his life by both art critics and fellow painters. He took as his central point of study the painting *Wheat Field with Crows*, Van Gogh's last major work of art, and asked how the painter may have felt about his most revolutionary work. Another myth that was dismissed in the drama-documentary was the one that persisted about the painter chopping off his whole ear; it was, in fact, no more than a tiny chunk of the earlobe. Serkis's function in the drama-documentary was to read aloud, most movingly, as Van Gogh from some of the hundreds of letters the man wrote to his brother Theo. The painter was an insatiable bookworm who had abandoned a religious life for art, but this happened only when he was about 30 years old. He displayed the utmost faith in 'a life of the mind'.

German-born scientist Albert Einstein was, obviously, someone else who valued close research. *Einstein and Eddington*, made in 2007 for broadcast the next year, was a British TV single drama co-produced with HBO in the USA, and starred Serkis as Einstein. Taking the part of the British astrophysicist Sir Arthur Eddington was David Tennant. Eddington was the man who, in 1920, published an article that first told the English-speaking world about Einstein's theory of general relativity, introducing the notion of curvature in space-time. Prior to its publication in Germany, Einstein had taken several years to compile the theory, but the outbreak of World War One (which lasted from 1914 to 1918) meant that, as with other German scientific developments from the early twentieth century, it took time for the rest of the world to find out about it.

At the outset of *Einstein and Eddington*, the former is still an anonymous physicist in the midst of his research, while the latter is director of the Cambridge Observatory. The film goes on to demonstrate how their relationship flourishes and how Eddington comes to champion Einstein's work. 'It's about how science transcends national barriers, particularly at a time of war,' Serkis told one showbiz press correspondent, while also revealing a few more frivolous titbits about Albert. 'He was a bit of a one for the ladies, and he didn't wear socks. That kind of information helps an actor paint a psychological profile of a man.'

In addition, the experience of making *Einstein and Eddington* had an extraordinary personal impact on Serkis. Learning about the theory of relativity helped him face one of his own personal demons – a fear of death. Perhaps triggered by the remoteness of his own father, working away in Iraq during his formative years, he had had enduring, upsetting nightmares about losing his mother and father. 'When I was a kid I'd morbidly fantasise about my parents being killed,' he told the *Sunday Telegraph* in March 2008, several months before the film was first broadcast by the BBC. An atheist since his teenage years, he had held lingering worries about mortality ever since, to the extent that, now in his mid-forties, he had been concerned about what would happen to his three children if he or Lorraine was no longer alive.

As it turned out, with *Einstein and Eddington*, he was able to make sense of his neurosis. 'As we're sitting here, our planet is whizzing round at a huge, huge velocity. We're unaware of it, but, when you start looking at cosmology, that transference of energy is very exciting. The idea that your energy lives on after you, I find very relieving. People are either drains or radiators. And I just hate the idea that I'm not giving anything out.'

The rest of the cast included Rebecca Hall and Jim Broadbent, both of whom had worked with Serkis before. Hall's uncertainties were soon swept aside. 'When you get a script entitled *Einstein and Eddington*, you think, It'll just be a lot of people talking about science. But by page four I was riveted.' For David Tennant, it was like going back to school – in a good way. 'For this part, I had to learn real science rather than the fantasy stuff we talk on *Doctor Who*,' he told the *Stage* in 2007. 'Physics deals in things so beyond our ken and in astronomical distances which are impossible to get your head around, and yet some of the facts I learnt playing Eddington have actually stayed with me.'

'He was like a mad professor, a real pioneer, and just loved experimenting with everything.' Is this Andy Serkis quote about Albert Einstein? The rest of it suggests not. 'I loved the fact that he actually loved Abba. I think that's really funny.'

Abba fan Martin Hannett, whom Serkis played in 2002's *24 Hour Party People*, is not, perhaps, an instantly familiar name to people who do not scour the credits on album sleeves. But, in his own idiosyncratic, sometimes exasperating way, he was one of the great maverick record producers of the late 1970s and 1980s. Born in 1948, and a chemistry graduate from Manchester Polytechnic – 'a chemist and musical alchemist', Serkis would note – Hannett was a sometime bass guitarist and journalist before turning to record production in 1977. His many credits included tracks for punk icons Buzzcocks, performance poet John Cooper Clarke, the early days of U2, and Jilted John (a.k.a. Graham Fellows, a.k.a. John Shuttleworth). Yet it is his work for the fiercely independent Mancunian record company Factory and its three biggest bands – Joy Division, New Order and Happy Mondays – that has defined his reputation as one of British pop's visionaries.

24 Hour Party People, a dramatic reconstruction of the messy, chaotic and sometimes brilliant history of Factory under its founder, the journalist and TV presenter Tony Wilson (a supreme interpretation by Steve Coogan), was deliberately slippery with the truth, and irreverent with it. This was no hagiography, even with Wilson as 'special consultant' on the project. When Serkis landed the part of Hannett in 2001, he was taking a break from playing Gollum in Wellington. 'I went from this massive shoot, with such precision and complex technology, on *Lord of the Rings*, to this loose, everyone-kind-of-off-their-faces thing, wandering around in character, and the cameras, you didn't know when they were on or off! It was mad, but a great antidote.'

A day or night in the studio with the real-life Martin Hannett tended not to be smooth. Frankly, it could be downright difficult. He was prone to dispensing opaque advice to bands from behind recording-studio glass such as 'Do it again, but this time make it a bit more...cocktail party', or asking Joy Division and New Order drummer Steven Morris to play 'faster, but slower'. The time when Morris was obliged to record separately each component of his drum kit is semi-faithfully included in this entertainingly untrustworthy biopic.

In *24 Hour Party People*, Serkis as Hannett is sparingly but effectively deployed. We first see him pogoing at an under-attended Sex Pistols concert at Manchester's Free Trade Hall. Among his exploits later on, he is seen 'recording silence' by Tony Wilson, the same man whom he attempts to shoot later on. This was one of the many events in the film that had been mythologised, although he did once fire a gun at the telephone receiver during a conversation with New Order manager Rob Gretton. Wilson himself enjoyed the blurring of reality and invention: 'When you have to choose between truth and legend, print the legend.'

Hannett's life was blighted for several years in the 1980s by heroin addiction, and, even when he managed to beat that, he became ruinously reliant on alcohol and ecstasy. 'He was a huge consumer of all things chemical, and had that sort of potential for violence. He could scare the shit out of a lot of the bands,' commented Serkis. Bloated, blurred and aimless when not in the studio, by the time the producer died of a heart attack in April 1991 he had ballooned to 22 stone. He was just 42 years old, but so much of the output he produced continues to pack a punch to this day.

Perhaps the making of the film was most peculiar to Tony Wilson himself, a moving, confusing feeling that was highlighted when he went for a drink with Paddy Considine and Andy Serkis. '[They were] playing two of my best friends who are now dead, Rob Gretton and Martin Hannett, and that was shocking. They're so much like them. Very, very disturbing.' With a very sad irony, Tony Wilson would soon pass on too, dying of cancer at the age of just 57, in 2007.

Steve Coogan's portrayal of Tony Wilson, while undoubtedly very funny throughout much of 24 Hour Party People (there has always been a great deal of Wilson in Coogan's TV and radio presenter character Alan Partridge), has an ambiguity that has the mark of truth. It presents Wilson's faults unsparingly, but demonstrates how his shortcomings (wilful arrogance, outspokenness) are just as important to the story as his most brilliant qualities (originality, prepared to take a risk). Chutzpah can be a quality and a weakness, and, at different times in his eventful life, Wilson had felt its positive and negative consequences. The late Ian Dury had been a man of chutzpah too, and, when Andy Serkis came to play this inimitable British pop pioneer several years later, that life, with all its euphoria, misery and disaster, would also be well worth exploring.

CHAPTER 12

DURY

Though *The Lord of the Rings* and *King Kong* had brought Andy Serkis to the attention of international filmmakers and critics, it's debatable if either quite made him a star. Though much respected for how he had collaborated on such technically sophisticated projects and brought a beating heart to computer-generated characters, he was perhaps not in himself a *famous* name. The beginning of 2010, though, brought unprecedented press coverage for Serkis the leading man, as opposed to Serkis the cast member, when, in a homegrown biopic, he took on the role of a genuine one-off in British popular music.

Sex & Drugs & Rock & Roll was a colourful, boisterous and often moving drama based on the life of the inimitable vocalist and lyricist, Ian Dury. It was titled after one of his most enduring compositions, which had been released as a single in 1977. The seismic arrival of punk rock and new wave turned Dury from a cult figure on the live circuit, where he had fronted the group Kilburn and the High Roads, to a full-blown pop star. Major hit singles in the UK with his next group, the Blockheads, followed from 1978, including 'What a Waste', 'Reasons to Be Cheerful (Part 3)' and 'Hit Me With Your Rhythm Stick'. The last of these climbed all the way to the number-one spot in January 1979, selling nearly a million copies in the process. Meanwhile, his 1977 long-player *New Boots and Panties!!* was packed with earthy and witty offerings like 'Billericay Dickie' and 'Clevor Trever', as well as affectionate tributes such as 'Sweet Gene Vincent' and 'My Old Man'. It spawned no hits, but stayed in the album charts for nearly two years, and remains one of the great British pop LPs of the 1970s.

Ian Dury was born on 12 May 1942 in Upminster, Essex, the son of Bill, a coach driver, and Peggy, who was the daughter of an Irish country doctor and who had been a health visitor for Camden Council. When he was just seven years old, Ian contracted polio while paddling in the shallow end of a swimming pool in Southend-on-Sea, where his family had gone on a day trip. Not expected to survive, he underwent two years of physiotherapy, and was cruelly and permanently disabled, with a paralysed left arm and leg.

There were further traumas to come at a school for disabled children, Chailey Heritage Craft School. Pupils could be vicious and unsparing. The staff could be very strict and rather than Dury be on the receiving end of bullying, he became an aggressive force himself, which became glaringly clear at the High Wycombe grammar school he attended next. He was the only disabled boy in the school, but made an intimidating mark, even though he had to adopt a siege mentality to survive such an environment. His own survivalist streak meant he could be unforgiving. A stand-out scene in *Sex & Drugs* shows Andy Serkis as a grown-up Ian revisiting Chailey Heritage to meet the pupils. Here he learns that one particularly vindictive member of staff who had made his own schooldays so tormented has taken his own life. Dury's response is gleeful. 'That's made my day, that has.'

Dury would attend art college, later becoming a lecturer in art, and start playing in bands like Kilburn and the High Roads, but was already 35 years old when stardom beckoned with the release in 1977 of his breakthrough LP, *New Boots and Panties!!*. As with all supposed overnight successes, though, it had been a long night. And only a handful of performers – usually talented lyricists, interestingly – have become prominent pop or rock stars after the age of 30: Pulp's Jarvis Cocker, Pet Shop Boy Neil Tennant and Canadian poet, singer and songwriter Leonard Cohen. Ian Dury was another who defied the cliché that pop is a young person's game. His unique gift for wordplay, his working-class vernacular and his perceptive flair for characterisation were clear. But it took time for him to gain the self-belief to embrace stardom. The late broadcaster and author Charlie Gillett, who was Kilburn and the High Roads' manager for a while, told the *Observer* in 2009, 'He never seemed to have any real confidence in his abilities.'

Before punk rock invigorated the British musical and cultural landscape in 1976–7, Dury was already a mainstay on the live circuit in London, but his persona in the High Roads was too tough and threatening for any real chance of crossover success. The arrival of the Sex Pistols, the Clash and the Damned, all of whom were over a decade younger than Dury, meant he (like Elvis Costello) could also gain major recognition. Dury was, strictly speaking, not punk rock, though songs like the profanity-laden 'Plaistow Patricia' still have as much power and impact as anything the Pistols did. Punk rock was about being individual, not just controversial, but it was also about showmanship. Dury's act was shot through with music-hall comedy, and he once said that his idea of being in a band combined his love for Chuck Berry with that for Tommy Cooper. Also in the mix was his thirst for art, English suburbia and the East End of London. 'The way he put it all together on stage made it utterly unique and riveting. He was a one-off,' was the verdict of another of his managers, Peter Jenner.

Dury's time in the chart spotlight was relatively fleeting. By 1980, the hits were drying up, while his association with the Blockheads was deteriorating. His reliance on prescription drugs and alcohol, coupled with notoriety for being difficult, made him volcanic and unpredictable. He frequently unleashed his spite and bitterness onto those in his inner circle: musical collaborators, close friends, loved ones. Though he would never lose his edge and bite, a noticeable mellowing set in from the mid-1990s, and at least he did manage one more great LP, 1998's *Mr Love Pants*, before succumbing to liver cancer in March 2000, at the age of just 57. British pop had lost one of its true originals.

His death brought an outpouring of tributes from friends, musical associates and celebrities, and the warmest of obituaries from newspapers. His funeral at Golders Green crematorium in north London was attended by Labour cabinet minister Mo Mowlam, Robbie Williams and, as pallbearers, the members of the group Madness. In his last years, he had become regarded as a cornerstone of British pop culture, even though many of his songs had been too abrasive and confrontational for radio play, and his own persona had frequently been too much for some, including many of his friends and his family.

It's arguable that *Sex & Drugs & Rock & Roll* made Andy Serkis more of a star in Britain than his projects with Peter Jackson. In any biographical drama about a single figure, it would be unlucky indeed for the actor playing that role to avoid getting top billing. In the month before the film's British opening, in January 2010, Andy Serkis was everywhere, granting interviews to the press and TV shows. It appeared that, at long last, over 20 years since his television debut, and over 15 since his first appearance in a feature film, he was being recognised for his ability to completely inhabit a character in the most engaging way – which was summed up by how he reimagined Ian Dury. 'I think that a lot of things have come together with this role,' he told *The Times*. 'There's a lot that floats my boat in terms of Ian's style, Ian's persona and Ian's artistic endeavour.'

Serkis had first spoken about the role of Dury in detail at the start of 2009, three months before filming began. 'In a way, he was prior to the punk movement and part of that generation,' he said in an interview with National Public Radio in the USA. 'But he also had this love for his family, so this kind of schism between the passion for his music and the desire to shake everything up completely collides with his family and his children.'

Sex & Drugs & Rock & Roll would have a rough, grainy

quality about it, something it shared with Michael Winterbottom's *24 Hour Party People*. Mat Whitecross, the director of the Dury film, had been a production runner on the earlier picture (in which Serkis had featured, of course), and later worked as a director on the TV series *Spooks*, plus promo videos for Coldplay. In 2006, he had also co-directed (with Winterbottom) the drama-documentary *The Road to Guantánamo*, which was the story of three British Muslims from the West Midlands who were held hostage for two years in Guantánamo Bay.

Oxford-born Whitecross credited Serkis with bringing everyone on board for *Sex & Drugs & Rock & Roll*. 'There was no money, so his charm was key.' Whitecross estimated that, during its spring 2009 shoot, no other cinema films were being shot in Britain, 'which might have helped the great can-do spirit from cast and crew. It also helped with getting actors! You'd say, "I want a Ray Winstone type", or an Olivia Williams type – and be told the actors themselves were available.'

As with Serkis's collaborations with Peter Jackson and Weta Workshop in New Zealand, Whitecross owed a great deal to the development of digital technology during his apprenticeship. He told the *Observer*, 'A few years before, if you wanted to make a film, you had to blag a 16mm camera or a Super-8 and physically get your hands on some film. People I knew who had been doing that ran out of money or got tired of it because it was so painstaking. But I could blag a camera and film friends or make a spoof comedy and cut it on someone's laptop. You could practise and screw up by yourself, rather than making your mistakes in public.'

The actor-turned-writer Paul Viragh, meanwhile, was a

friend of Serkis's, and the two had acted together on Jim Threapleton's low-budget political thriller *Extraordinary Rendition* in 2007 (see Chapter 10). Viragh knew he wanted Serkis for the Ian Dury role, reluctant as he was to 'ask your mate to be in your stuff'. Finally, he contacted him to agree to the part before he'd written a word of the screenplay. Serkis became one of the film's executive producers.

Viragh had also approached Whitecross about turning his Dury screenplay idea into a film, but the director was a little doubtful at first. 'I didn't know much about Ian,' said Whitecross, 'and I initially knocked the project back because I felt you really needed to know the music and be a dyed-in-the-wool fan. I couldn't understand Ian. He was so mercurial, he had so many personalities.' What persuaded him to get involved was realising that a patchwork overview – '100 little films' – might be a better way of laying bare Dury's life than a straightforwardly chronological biopic.

It was the independent film producer Damian Jones who helped to facilitate the Dury project, aware that even a low-budget flick required a high concept. He'd already helped Alan Bennett's play *The History Boys* to the big screen, and while preparing *Sex & Drugs & Rock & Roll* was also preparing a film about Margaret Thatcher for Pathé and BBC Films. But it still took over two years for *Sex & Drugs & Rock & Roll* to reach the public. It was greenlit towards the end of 2007. Just as the shoot was being organised in 2009, a musical had opened in London, with the title of *Hit Me: The Life and Rhymes of Ian Dury*.

The eventual film drifted back and forth between two pivotal periods of Ian Dury's life – the aftermath of his being diagnosed with polio and his harrowing experiences at school, and the years between the mid-1970s and early 1980s, when he became one of the great finds of the British new wave music boom. 'We didn't want to bore people stupid with a conventional biopic, particularly people who had no knowledge of Ian and his music,' reasoned Serkis. 'So it was decided we would focus on the part of his life that would have universal appeal to the uninitiated, with the music being an added bonus.'

When real people are shown the results of fiction that draws on the lives of people they knew, they are often heard to say, 'That's not how it was.' It is usually assumed that this is because writers and actors exaggerate and distort, and make a person or situation far too grotesque to be credible. But it was quite the opposite when Andy Serkis and screenwriter Paul Viragh first showed an early draft of the script to Dury's children, Baxter and Jemima. It turned out they hadn't gone nearly far enough.

If the Dury family were to be involved in a biopic, then glossing over Ian's darker side was not an option. Before Serkis, Viragh and Whitecross contacted them, other filmmakers had tried to gain access to them for memories and approval. Baxter Dury: 'The last thing we wanted was some horrible rock biopic, because 90 per cent of them are a load of bollocks, just karaoke nonsense.' Knowing that the trio were not planning any kind of hagiography was utter relief for him. 'There's going to be some trepidation: are they going to get it right, are they going to be careful? But we worked closely with them.'

Serkis had experienced a little of Ian Dury's difficult, awkward side at first-hand. They had in fact met in the summer of 1993 in Leicester, where Dury was contributing songs to a Sue Townsend play (not featuring Serkis) called *The Queen and I*. It wasn't the most pleasant of encounters, as Serkis recalled 17 years later in 2010. 'He was very much out of order. He didn't suffer fools, put it that way, and he'd had a few to drink. But I was very glad, when I got to play the role, that I'd seen that side of him.'

But, then, all celebrities and public figures have off days. They all have the complexities and some of the neuroses and drawbacks that others do. Ian Dury was no exception, Andy Serkis learnt, while gathering memories and anecdotes from his surviving family. 'He could be very sweet and gentle and very loving and compassionate, and then he'd flip like a coin and be very visceral and nasty. But that came from being a very creative, driven man who got beaten around and loves to demonstrate and feel all those things. He's a million different things to different people.' Ultimately, Serkis did feel an affinity and a kinship with him. 'I've always felt very close to Ian's take on things and the way he thinks about the world, so I suppose I felt quite in tune with it.'

After Ian Dury tasted stardom in the late 1970s, his self-destructive antics grew wilder, with the sort of behaviour that continues to make his colleagues and surviving family wince. Baxter Dury, who himself is a singer-songwriter (and who as a small boy appears on the sleeve of *New Boots and Panties!!*), has acknowledged his father's wit and talent but could not forget how obnoxious he could sometimes be. 'It was all very complex,' he told the *Observer*. 'As he got older he could be extraordinarily difficult but he was saved from wankerdom by his humour and his honesty.'

Daughter Jemima dimly recalled Ian's late 1970s

environment as 'a scarily male world at times'. She continued, 'Some of the dubious criminal types turned out to be the most charming and thoughtful. The dicey ones were the rock'n'roll misfits that punk threw up who always seemed to find their way onto the bus and into the hotel room.'

The Dury clan would provide Andy Serkis with ample help and guidance in getting to know Ian – warts and all – during the making of the film. At every turn, they were able to inform him. Their candour in explaining his habits and behaviour, no matter how intimate, seemed to know no bounds – from how he got in and out of the car or the bath, and (thanks to his second wife Sophy Tilson) information about what he was like in bed. 'He was very physical!' was as much as Serkis was prepared to reveal.

Sometimes, though, when they could correct tiny errors was when the greatest self-doubt could creep into Serkis's performance. 'Once, when we were shooting [a] live concert bit at Vauxhall Palace, just as I was about to do the opening number, Sophy came up and adjusted my scarf. Ian used to tie his scarf in a very particular way.' It reminded him that those who knew Ian Dury best of all were present. 'That was particularly nerve-racking because it suddenly brought sharp relief that they were there watching.'

Other live footage for the film was shot early in June 2009 at the Palace Theatre in Watford, when Serkis led a team of actors playing the Blockheads in some jaunts through the Dury back catalogue. With tracks already laid down for the soundtrack with the real Blockheads, there was an abundance of audio and video footage lined up for the editing process. According to *Time Out*, Serkis also stayed in character on the Palace Theatre stage to exchange banter with the audience of extras, and didn't let up when – perhaps inevitably – one wag called out a reference to Gollum. 'Precious? I'm not precious…Fuck off!' barked Serkis as Dury. A ferocious live take of 'Hit Me With Your Rhythm Stick' ended with a surprise coda for the crowd of extras: the Blockheads' tight backing unravelled as a fight broke out, ending up in the sax player administering a headbutt to the keyboardist, and Serkis as Ian roaring 'You're all fired!'

In some ways, the scenes set on stage with the Blockheads' performances are the most magnetic and hypnotic of the whole film, conveying the thrilling, unpredictable nature of late-seventies British punk and new wave. For Serkis, it was the live energy of Blockheads gigs, with Ian Dury at his best, that was 'the real core of the film'.

One Serkis scene had to be unexpectedly shot when no other actors were available, something that (thanks to Peter Jackson epics) was becoming second nature for Andy. It is a Christmas Day scene at the dinner table where Dury mocks his former wife's new spouse, while Baxter and Jemima look on in embarrassment. Director Whitecross filmed the sequence with Serkis alone, with the remaining actors' performances dropped in later. Serkis reassured any observant viewers that their eyes had not been deceiving them: crew members – not his children – were passing him bowls of food. 'Notice the hands. Biggest hands you'll ever see on a 12-year-old.'

Playing Ian Dury's son Baxter in the new film was 14-year-old Bill Milner. Portraying Dury's ex-wife, the artist Betty Rathmell, was Olivia Williams, who agreed to sign up to the film when she discovered who was in the starring role. 'Andy

Serkis as Ian... That was the hook for me,' she told the *Independent*. 'I was actually in LA and he was on a radio show promoting another film. He wouldn't talk about the film he was supposed to be promoting and just said, "I'm so excited, I'm just about to play Ian Dury." I thought, "That sounds like something I'd love to be involved in."' In a curious coincidence, when Williams returned home, there was a message from her agent offering her a part in the same film.

One of the few drawbacks of the film is that it does sideline the female characters, which is especially unfortunate since it was Ian's mother and aunt who raised him in a comfortable middle-class background. Yet Ian's mother Peggy, ex-wife Betty (Williams) and his daughter Jemima are all given short shrift in the movie. Of all the key women in Ian's life, only Denise Roudette (*Pirates of the Caribbean*'s Naomie Harris), who became his girlfriend in 1973, receives generous screen time. Harris admitted to knowing little about Dury or his music on accepting the part, but learnt the bass guitar for her part as Denise.

Reality TV vehicles like *Britain's Got Talent* have purported to champion the unconventional in entertainment – witness the meteoric rise of the fortysomething singer Susan Boyle in 2009 – but it's hard to imagine they would know what on earth to do with someone with such an inimitable and untameable stage presence as Ian Dury. 'He is such a good antidote to the *X Factor* generation who only want the end result: the success, and the fame and to fit in,' Andy Serkis argued in the *Daily Telegraph*. 'What was unique about Ian was that he didn't really want any celebrity. For him, it was all about the craft, the graft, the art.'

A lesser actor than Serkis might have settled for an impersonation of Dury, like a variety turn, or a spot on the soundalike TV music show *Stars in Their Eyes*. It would have been much easier, but, quite apart from being in questionable taste (in conveying the man's physicality), it would have missed by a mile the need to draw on all the strands of the icon under scrutiny. Serkis's Dury was no caricature. There was too much depth for that. It was such a rich interpretation of him that, watching Serkis, you could easily forget you were watching an actor. For him, 'it's not about doing an impersonation, it's about finding the emotion and where you connect with that character.' At least Serkis, not a naturally technical singer, did not have to play Caruso or Pavarotti here. 'He would admit he was a dreadful singer. He thought of himself as an entertainer, so it's more about getting the lyrics across in an entertaining, challenging way.'

The big nerve-racking test for Serkis, though, with Dury's voice would come when he entered the recording studio with the Blockheads to rerecord versions of Ian's most famous songs for the film's soundtrack album. The group had played many live shows with guest vocalists, ranging from Robbie Williams to stand-up comic and TV regular Phill Jupitus, and even issued new recorded material, such as 2009's *Staring Down the Barrel*. But none of the guest vocalists had consciously claimed to be playing the Dury part, and so Serkis was worried. He need not have been. The Blockheads found his interpretation of Dury in song to be little short of miraculous. Their keyboard player and composer Chaz Jankel found it all spine-tingling, even 'quite scary. He can now mimic Ian with 100 per cent accuracy.'

Saxophonist Davey Payne was equally startled, being heard to remark at one point, 'Cor blimey! It's like being in a séance with Ian!'

Mastering the voice of Dury was one thing. Finding a truthful, authentic way of reflecting his physical disability would be one of Serkis's greatest challenges. It required a lot of background research, and, in striving to perfect his walk, stance and posture, Serkis was to experience severe discomfort. For starters, he lost two stone in weight, and had to have the entirety of his rather hirsute body waxed by a beautician, while he tried to concentrate on learning his lines. 'She started with my ankles. It was fine at first and I just read my script. Then she crept upwards. When she came to the inner thigh, it was excruciating. There were blood blisters all over my legs and she had to do the most tender parts three times. Never again.' It meant no sex – let alone drugs or rock and roll – for some months. 'My wife didn't like the way I looked,' he confessed. 'I think it freaked her out a bit.'

Six months of gym workouts – on the right side of his body only – gave him a weak left side, and taking the weight of a heavy calliper, which was attached to his leg, was exhausting. But it was a case of 'no pain, no gain' for Serkis and, besides, Dury had had to live the whole of his life in this way, not just for a couple of months. 'His widow Sophy said you have to imagine this is a man who has the energy of a *Tyrannosaurus rex* with a mangy arm and leg. He wouldn't let his disability get in the way of his life.'

Months after the film wrapped, he accepted that such efforts had been worthwhile, but he remained in pain nonetheless. 'I'm still recovering from it all,' he groaned to *The Times*. 'I've got a dodgy back at the best of times, but the weight of that calliper, throwing it about every day, it shoves your body off-centre. And it made this massive weird muscle develop in my groin.' Director Mat Whitecross paid tribute to Serkis's stoic but thorough approach. He told the *Observer*, 'Playing Ian is a difficult, intense role, and he did it with a method style while avoiding being in any way precious.'

The youngster who was portraying Ian in the film's childhood scenes – 13-year-old Wesley Nelson – also conducted his own research. Nelson, who hailed from South Wales, had cerebral palsy, and so already had to wear leg splints and walk with a stick. 'I read a lot about Chailey [school],' he said, 'but a certain degree has to come from you and your emotion. I drew on my cerebral palsy and partly used that to understand him, which you could say was handy.' Wesley also learnt more about Dury's musical past through his father's record collection. 'Wesley's an amazing young actor,' commented Serkis, who shared a couple of fantasy scenes with this teenage version of himself. 'His brief scenes are quite heartbreaking; the lad is a unique talent.'

Dury's career in music was colourful. The chaotic nature of the music – the sax break on 'Hit Me With Your Rhythm Stick' is the nearest thing to free jazz that has ever reached number one on the pop charts – was one reason for him not to get playlisted. The lyrical content was another reason. The song 'Sex & Drugs & Rock & Roll' had two words in its title alone to make radio programmers nervous in the late 1970s. The B-side of 'Hit Me…', entitled 'There Ain't Half

Been Some Clever Bastards', garnered some tabloid outrage. And we know about 'Plaistow Patricia'. But only in 1981 did a Dury single receive an official BBC ban.

'Spasticus Autisticus' is, in some ways, the most important Ian Dury single, an angry and playful reaction to 1981's International Year of Disabled Persons. Inspired by the 'I am Spartacus' scene in Stanley Kubrick's epic 1960 movie, it was a 'war cry' in Dury's own words. It is an unapologetic summing-up of what it means to be disabled, irreverent language and all. It was all too much for radio and television and the 45rpm, starved of promotion, sank without trace. But, then, Dury had always been direct about his condition, often labelling himself a 'raspberry' ('raspberry ripple' being rhyming slang for the word 'cripple'), and even considering titling *New Boots and Panties!!* with the commercially suicidal name of 'The Mad Spastic'. For Dury co-writer and keyboard player Chaz Jankel, 'Spasticus Autisticus' was his epitaph. 'People think of the humour of his songs, but, if you asked me which song defines Ian to me, I would say "Spasticus Autisticus".'

Watching the final cut of *Sex & Drugs & Rock & Roll* was a deeply affecting, emotional experience for the people who knew Ian Dury. His real-life son Baxter, by now himself in his late thirties, found that his fourth viewing of it was the first time it hadn't moved him to tears. 'When I first saw it, I didn't sleep for a week, he told the *Sunday Times*. 'I would dream about the film. I'd see dad as Andy Serkis.'

Ian and Baxter's relationship as father and son was closer than Ian's had been with his own father Bill – Bill had left the family home when Ian was still very young – but still turbulent enough, nonetheless. But was the film true to Ian's failings? It did, after all, contain a scene at Baxter's birthday party where Dury gets together with a fan called Denise, and sacks a drummer or two. A difficult balance between family life and rock'n'roll, then. So, was Serkis's Ian sufficiently flawed for Baxter and Jemima? Jemima seemed happy enough, according to Serkis. 'We got a lovely email from [her]. She said he would have laughed, and then slagged us off with great affection.'

'I don't think it glosses over a lot,' Baxter told the *Sunday Times*. 'It's an emotionally brave film. I can only judge it against my own experience. Dad was an arsehole sometimes, but he was a very rare form of arsehole. I think back on a lot of that chaos really fondly, and I miss it now it's gone.'

Ian Dury had written an affectionate but realistic paean to fatherhood in 1977's 'My Old Man'. His own father, Bill Dury (played in *Sex & Drugs* by Ray Winstone), was a boxer and bus driver from London's East End who became a chauffeur. By all accounts, Ian had seemed to inherit Bill's gift of the gab, and, while his dad had walked out of his life early on, his son continued to think a great deal of him. Some of *Sex & Drugs & Rock & Roll*'s most poignant scenes show a tough but supportive Bill, offering young Ian (played by Wesley Nelson) advice about how to stand up for himself and, most of all, how to *be* himself.

'My Old Man', one of the warmest songs on *New Boots and Panties!!*, remains a favourite of Andy Serkis's. It resonated with him partly because, like Baxter Dury, 'I had an old man I didn't see very often.' Serkis also loved 'Reasons to Be Cheerful (Part 3)'. 'I love the happy nature of it and the brilliant early rap.' A fan of jazz himself, he was also greatly pleased to hear the name checks for John Coltrane. But it was, inevitably, the number-one hit, 'Hit Me With Your Rhythm Stick', heard on that school trip over 30 years earlier, that had been his introduction to Dury's music.

Serkis felt a kinship with Dury over other issues, too. He felt that they shared a sense of being the outsider in their respective formative years: Dury for his disability, Serkis for his Iraqi background, which sometimes made him the target of racist bullies in the school playground. Above all, like Serkis, Dury was an art student before being diverted into his secondary career. Over 20 years before Serkis headed north from London to his visual-arts course at Lancaster University, Dury enrolled at art college in Walthamstow, later gaining an MA qualification, which helped him secure an illustrating job at the *Sunday Times*. By now a voracious reader and a fan of jazz and rock'n'roll – especially Gene Vincent, whom he would later immortalise in song – Dury had as a tutor one Peter Blake, who was about to design the sleeve of the Beatles' *Sgt. Pepper* album. He would later supply some of the material for the animated sequences in *Sex & Drugs & Rock & Roll*.

Although there were no period scenes in the film that directly referenced Dury's time in the art world, his artistic background did feed its shape and style. Not just crammed with wisecracks galore – 'Worst gig we've played since Sidcup crematorium' – the structure could also accommodate unlikely set pieces such as an underwater rendition of 'Hit Me With Your Rhythm Stick'. 'It's a collage,' suggested its writer Paul Viragh to *Time Out*. 'That pop art thing of collaging lives...It's an impressionistic version of Ian's life.' Serkis agreed with his screenwriter: a traditional biopic would not have captured the man or his existence. 'We wanted the film to have a raw, live feel and that would be the dramatic keyhole into his life. Our approach is very abstract and gives a more kaleidoscopic view of the man.' Too kaleidoscopic, possibly, for one real-life unnamed Blockhead, who might have preferred a more chronological portrait: 'I just wish it had begun at the beginning and finished at the end.'

Reviews for *Sex & Drugs & Rock & Roll* were mixed, but few were in any doubt that Andy Serkis had nailed the spirit and *joie de vivre* of its main subject. Writing in the *Daily Telegraph*, rock critic Mick Brown cheered: 'Serkis is simply stupendous in the title role, giving a performance which, in its kinetic energy and physical verisimilitude, seems to be less a matter of acting than channelling Dury from the other side.' And at least it was accepted that the film aimed higher than what *Time Out* called the 'sanitised, reverential' nature of recent biopics on Ian Curtis (*Control*) and John Lennon (*Nowhere Boy*), 'robbing them of power and mystery in an effort to "understand" them – a pointless and impossible task best left to the cultural scholars'.

The Dury bio was felt by some to share more of its qualities with *24 Hour Party People* or even Todd Haynes's *Velvet Goldmine*. In the London *Evening Standard*, novelist Andrew O'Hagan wrote, 'It's hard to think of another actor who could have done what Serkis does in the part, taking hold of a frenetic but guarded showman and showing us his internal life. If Serkis ever decides to do the same with Shane MacGowan, I'll be first in the queue to see it.' That's a possibility: in January 2010 when the *NME* suggested the

Pogues singer's name as a future role for the actor, he agreed, 'That's not a bad story.' What about other rock icons? 'I could do Bono,' he suggested. Although... 'Someone will have to write the screenplay.'

Sex & Drugs & Rock & Roll was first publicly screened in London on 6 January 2010. Those attending the screening included Coldplay's Chris Martin – a friend from Mat Whitecross's university days who directed several Coldplay videos – and the actor Emilia Fox. Also in attendance was James Jagger, who in the film had played Kilburn and the High Roads' John Turnbull. Asked who was the true embodiment of rock'n'roll – Dury or his own dad, Mick – he was cheerily disloyal. 'I'd definitely say Ian, as my dad's not here right now and I'm not going to get into any trouble. Ian went out with a bang.'

Andy Serkis was also at the first screening, as were members of Dury's own family. He had to admit, in the end, that it had been hard work playing Dury. 'He really touched a lot of people's lives, so that is quite a lot of pressure.' But he hoped that the film might interest a new generation of fans unaware of the depth and richness of the man's output. 'I'd love to think young people who've never heard of Ian Dury will become excited by him and become new fans. He was a force to be reckoned with, and there's been no one quite like him ever since.'

The controversies over eligibility at awards ceremonies, which had dogged the receptions of the *Lord of the Rings* film *The Two Towers*, would not be repeated in 2010. Nominations for Serkis's Dury poured in during the weeks following the film's premiere. In the London *Evening*

Standard Film Awards 2010 nominations list, unveiled in January, Serkis was, of the four Best Actor nominees, one of three who were playing real-life characters in their respective films, the others being Tom Hardy (prisoner Charles Bronson) and Christian McKay (Orson Welles). The other nominee, playing someone fictional, was *The Hide*'s Alex MacQueen. On 8 February 2010, Serkis would be victorious, sharing glory with other winners such as Andrea Arnold (whose *Fish Tank* won Best Film), Anne-Marie Duff (Best Actress for her role as John Lennon's mother Julia in *Nowhere Boy*), Sacha Baron Cohen (whose work on *Bruno* landed him the Peter Sellers Award for Comedy), and Armando Iannucci and his co-writers on the political comedy *In the Loop* (which took the Best Screenplay prize). The day after the prizes were handed out, Andrew O'Hagan wrote in the *Standard* of Serkis, 'He won it because he was able to embrace the character's steep contradictions. It is a performance with great, old-fashioned English music hall panache, a star turn from one of Britain's best actors.'

January had also brought the nominations list for BAFTA's British Academy Film Awards. Again, Serkis was favoured in the Best Actor category, competing against Jeremy Renner (*The Hurt Locker*), Colin Firth (*A Single Man*), Jeff Bridges (*Crazy Heart*) and George Clooney (*Up in the Air*). Serkis pronounced himself 'totally blown away' by the announcement. 'The whole experience of making this film with such amazingly talented, articulate, honest people has been a joy, and to get this nomination is not only a great thrill for all of us involved, but a fitting tribute at a time that we mark the 10-year anniversary [due on 27 March 2010] of the passing of the magnificent man himself, the unique Ian Dury.'

As Serkis prepared to appear at the BAFTAs, he warned that, if he had to take the stage to make a victory speech, he might still be limping slightly because of the pressures and strains he had placed on himself a year before in perfecting the role of Dury. 'The preparation took its toll physically,' he told the *Daily Telegraph*. 'I am only just fully straightening up now.'

And he told Hugo Rifkind in *The Times*, 'It's ultimately about putting your own life under a microscope and relating it to Ian Dury. And your life changes. You're altering yourself. And then you have to go through a decompression period afterwards.'

In the event, Serkis was not required to take the stage. He lost out to Colin Firth. His time as Ian Dury was not quite over, though. In March 2010, he joined Chaz Jankel onstage in Norwich as part of a benefit concert for the victims of the horrific earthquake in Haiti. Several months later, he was still occasionally reuniting with the Blockheads onstage in North London.

Dury's work did not tend to export particularly successfully from his home country, so *Sex & Drugs* faced a tough time in terms of international distribution. American critics were less enthusiastic about both the film and its star, with *Variety* even suggesting, somewhat absurdly, that Dury is an artist 'more admired than actually listened to today, even by aficionados of late-'70s rock'.

In fact, it was later revealed that director Mat Whitecross had struggled to find Stateside backers for the film. A screening was organised for the Sundance Film Festival in Utah in January 2010, where Whitecross learned that many of those in attendance were not *au fait* with who Ian Dury was. 'I didn't really understand the gist of the conversation. Their questions didn't make any sense. They kept asking me, "Who wrote the music?"' The penny dropped in Whitecross's mind. 'I realised, They don't know it's a real person.' Fortunately, enough movie bosses found the story of *Sex & Drugs & Rock & Roll* sufficiently engaging to pick it up for US release, and the film duly opened in America in May 2010.

As for Andy Serkis, even now – winning awards or landing nominations for the uncanny portrayal of Dury – there remained a reluctance to bask too much in his own glory. He gave thanks to Dury's family and the members of the Blockheads for their help while he was researching the part and developing his version of Ian, and of course was quick to speak warmly about the man himself. It was Dury's insistence on not fitting in – and perhaps his inability to do so – that made him a truly original force of energy and passion in British pop. 'He didn't want celebrity, didn't take to it particularly well, was 10 years too old to be a rock star, he had polio and he couldn't sing,' listed Andy Serkis, adding rhetorically, 'How well do you think he'd do on *The X Factor*?'

CHAPTER 13

A STORYTELLER FROM THE OUTSIDE: SERKIS THE DIRECTOR

Back in his days in Lancashire as a student actor and rep theatre player, Andy Serkis was made aware very early on about how performing is a collaborative and communal activity. Given how closely he has identified with crews as much as with fellow actors, it was perhaps only a matter of time before he would move into directing.

'Directing is something that's been brewing for many years,' he said in 2007 to the *Northern Echo*. 'I wouldn't want to give up acting. I have always wanted to be a storyteller from the outside as well. I'd like to do both.' To act or to direct? Whatever seemed appropriate to the job in hand. 'If it's a project I feel passionate about directing, that's what it has to be. And if it's something I want to act in, and my contribution will be better as an actor, I'll act in it.'

Tellingly, though, in 2004, he preferred to define himself

not as an 'actor' but the more all-encompassing description of 'filmmaker'.

Since the early 2000s, Serkis has been edging into directing. Having directed his wife Lorraine Ashbourne in the short film *Snake* (2001), he performed similar duties for a stage play two years later. *The Double Bass* was written by Patrick Süskind (author of the acclaimed novel *Perfume*) and was a psychological drama about an orchestral double-bass player who undergoes a breakdown. It ran for two weeks at the Southwark Playhouse from September 2003.

Hunt his own website or scour the Net, and you can find various film-directing projects for Andy Serkis, all of them presumably somewhere between conception and completion. Of particular interest is the biographical drama *Freezing Time*, documenting the life of Eadweard Muybridge. Muybridge had a colourful and controversial existence, clashing with the authorities, and put on trial for the murder of his wife's lover; but he is best remembered for being at the forefront of developing the art of photography (a nineteenth-century invention) into moving pictures – the beginnings of what came to be known as cinema.

The making of *Freezing Time* was first suggested as far back as 2005 (when it had the working title of *Muybridge*). It remains a work in progress, but in the meantime, Serkis's experiences working in motion capture and its successor, performance capture (PC), made him a good candidate for directing computer games. It was a curious connection that led to his working at the helm of *Heavenly Sword* (2007), a digital drama and martial-arts game for Playstation (PS) 3. Tameem Antoniades, the boss of British game developer

Ninja Theory, had a brother who just happened to be Serkis's mortgage adviser. Once Serkis was forwarded a trailer for the game, he couldn't wait to participate. Initially, he was pencilled in to contribute a voice (as an evil king), but soon he became a key part of the game's 'dramatic direction'.

As computer games had become technologically more sophisticated, so it was vital to make them seem as emotionally engaging as possible. With *Heavenly Sword*, Ninja Theory's intention was to bring the dazzling action and visual pyrotechnics of martial-arts films to the world of adventure video games. The production quality was so high that it was possible to approach people in the film industry, explained Antoniades, who announced that Serkis would be taking care of PC and casting and would even have a hand in the writing process. 'We've done facial tests with him to find out how to create believable performances in real time on the PS3.'

It was image-capture technology that was used to closely recreate the face of Serkis in the game's villain, King Botan. The team working on the game were able to ape the style of Hollywood blockbuster films as a result of the computer-processing capacity of Sony's new console. For Serkis, it all represented the perfect relationship between cinema and gaming. 'In the next few years there's going to be this huge transformation,' he predicted, 'where good story content, drama and narrative are going to come across in games more and more. This new generation of games is heading this way.'

Among the people whom Serkis approached for *Heavenly Sword* was musician Nitin Sawhney, who composed its score. 'The game is set in a culturally non-specific Asian world – about AD 700,' explained Serkis in the *Daily Telegraph*. 'It's great ground for him to work.' Sawhney at least was based in London, but otherwise Serkis faced a long plane journey to New Zealand, for six weeks of motion-capture directing duties at Peter Jackson's Weta facilities. 'I'm directing the performances,' Serkis promised, 'and we're using the same motion-capture techniques I used to play Gollum in *Lord of the Rings* and the ape in *King Kong*.' He also pointed out how the craft of 'cyber-acting' was becoming more common. 'Look at *Beowulf*, [with] actors of the calibre of Anthony Hopkins and John Malkovich, serious actors who've embraced the new technology.'

The 'Heavenly Sword' of the title refers to the religious relic that the hero Nanko must try to keep from being snatched by King Bohan. It was the first video game whose characters used subtle facial expressions in order to communicate. One previewer gasped, 'A flick of the eyes, an intake of breath, a slight downturn at the corner of the mouth...this is digital acting, in real time.' Serkis's role as Bohan received excellent notices. 'One of the best video game villains ever,' was the response of the *New York Times*'s gaming critic.

Again in the dual capacity of actor and director, Serkis reunited with Nitin Sawhney a couple of years later for another Ninja Theory mocap game, *Enslaved: Odyssey to the West* (2010). While Sawhney composed and orchestrated this post-apocalyptic adventure's lavish score, on co-writing duties was Alex Garland, whose CV included the novel *The Beach* and the screenplay of the zombie horror flick, *28 Days Later*.

Enslaved was loosely based on *Journey into the West*, an old Chinese tale in which a sage and his monkey embark on a quest to discover the wisdom of Buddhism. 'We looked at the original novel,' reported Serkis, 'and decided to make [him] less of a mischievous and chaotic figure and more of a gruff hobo, a loner not used to communicating with others, and quite selfish.' *Journey into the West* had in fact also inspired *Monkey* (also sometimes known as *Monkey Magic*), a Japanese TV series of the late 1970s which, in a dubbed English language version, had been a cult favourite in Britain, and the development team re-watched old episodes to help slot in some winks and nods to the series in the new game.

Enslaved is set in an almost unrecognisable and alarmingly quiet New York over 150 years in the future, with a human race that is fast dying off, and killer robots roaming the metropolis. Players are offered the chance to adopt the roles of a brute of a loner called Monkey (Serkis), and a female companion called Trip (*10 Things I Hate About You* star Lindsey Shaw). When they are captured by a slave ship, they have to try to escape, but Trip is aware that she can make it back home alive only if she enslaves Monkey to link them together. So the players have to ensure that Monkey and Trip cooperate so that they can work together against an uncaring and aggressive environment, as well as dodge the hazardous obstacles that await them in their journey home. But, because Monkey has been fitted with a headband that compels him to obey Trip's every order, if Trip loses her life at any point so will he.

'Along the route, they begin to affect each other,' Serkis told the *Independent* when the game became available in the autumn of 2010. 'They're worlds apart at the beginning [of the game] but they go on to form a strong relationship. The challenge of the piece in terms of an acting experience was how to make that plausible.' It was also essential, he suggested to another interviewer, not to make the characters too dominant in terms of directing the game player, so that the player could feel more involved. 'You don't want to lead the player too much in one way or another – after all, they are the character too. Your character can't lead the audience of players in one direction.'

The mocap shoot for Serkis and Shaw took six weeks, and could be emotionally draining, as Ninja Theory's Nina Kristensen explained to one Australian reporter. 'I stepped off the stage for a moment and, when I came back, Lindsey was crying. I rushed over to see what was wrong. It turns out she was just working herself up for an emotional scene.' Quite clearly, this was as intense and dramatic a scene as one that the two actors could have acted out on a theatrical stage. This was no mere voice-dubbing session, and gaming reviewers could see that. 'Wholly believable,' said one critic, referring to the interplay between Monkey and Trip. The same reviewer then paid tribute to the extraordinary facial-motion capture. The characters' facial expressions were remarkably vivid and detailed, epitomised by the moment when Trip asks Monkey to find his own way to the top of a building while she opts to climb via a shortcut. In response, there is the tiniest hint of disdain on Monkey's face, an expression that many film directors might not have bothered to focus on.

Associated Press reviewer Lou Kesten felt that *Enslaved*'s depiction of relationships was gratifyingly a world away from the clunkiness of much of the competition. 'When two video-game characters connect, it usually translates into a kind of grunting camaraderie.' But *Enslaved* had brought 'the most engaging game couple in years'. Serkis's inspiration for Monkey, incidentally, had come from an unlikely source, located not far from his north London home. 'I prepared for it by observing a man who walked his dog regularly on Hampstead Heath. He talked to his dog a lot but was really talking to himself.'

Just as in film, the spectacle of video games had to be balanced with a believability and authenticity of characterisation, to make the spectacle seem as if it were really happening. For Serkis, it was a journey of discovery for what was possible in gaming that was only in its infancy. 'We're really only at the beginning,' he told the *Independent*, 'but children and young games-players will receive stories and morals in gaming, and therefore games deserve a certain amount of investment artistically.'

Performance capture had become an integral part of storytelling culture for all those who love entertainment, whether they favour cinema, theatre or (increasingly) video games. It had come a long way from Serkis's experiences making *The Lord of the Rings* only a decade earlier. Then, PC was treated as separate from the rest of the filmmaking process, and its computer equipment was prone to faults and delays. Now, PC is no longer peripheral – a whole film can be made in a studio specifically designed to make a film including PC techniques. So, as Serkis told the *Guardian*, 'The methods of recording give greater fidelity to an actor's performance, and the technology can now capture multiple actors. It couldn't be more different.'

ANDY SERKIS: THE MAN BEHIND THE MASK

The fleshing out of characters and situations to make the fantastic seem more and more vivid and believable has given this new age of storytelling a biting relevance in the world of video gaming. Previously not a regular player, Andy Serkis now participates in gaming with his three children. 'Until recently, this huge gaming force has been neglected when it should have been treated with respect and invested with as much artistry as possible.'

The constant trips back and forth to and from New Zealand, however, to direct mocap for computer games as well as work on movies with Peter Jackson, had put an idea in Serkis's mind. He loved visiting the country, no doubt about that, whether it was to work at the Weta Workshop or just lose himself in the islands' awesome landscapes. But he had become puzzled that there were still no equivalent mocap facilities centre in the United Kingdom, even though so much of the original mocap technology had been developed in Cambridge and Oxford. Quite apart from that, it was becoming unrealistic and impractical to expect Lorraine and their children (all three now of school age) to relocate from London to New Zealand every time he had to work in performance-capture mode on a movie.

And so, in April 2010, he announced that he was planning on setting up the very first studio in Britain to specialise in performance capture: a kind of laboratory studio called the Imaginarium. There are those creative people who prefer not to share their secrets, but Serkis – always generous towards his collaborators and insistent that any acting project should be about teamwork – wanted to pass on some of the tricks of the trade he had learnt at Weta to aspiring young actors who were interested in working with PC.

The Imaginarium was to be an acting school and studio for the 3D era. Appointing himself as its head, Serkis intended not to restrict the studio simply to be used for films and video games. He also hoped to use the centre for live performances, where mocap could be used in ballets, rock gigs or clubs. There were plans for working with advertisers, too, but, above all, he desired that writers, technicians and artists could work in this environment to swap ideas and create some new kinds of entertainment. 'We need to encourage writers, directors and producers to think on a much larger scale,' he told the *Guardian*. 'People come out of film schools not equipped with the skills for doing anything other than shooting kitchen-sink dramas.'

Serkis felt it was time for the British film industry to confront, not shun, the technology of special effects and its growing importance. At the BAFTA ceremony in February 2010 (when he had triumphed in the Best Actor category for his Ian Dury), he couldn't help but detect a certain sniffiness towards any prize won by James Cameron's CGI fantasy epic *Avatar* – very much at odds with the cheers and whoops given to the accolades for *The Hurt Locker*, directed by Kathryn Bigelow. '*The Hurt Locker* is a great film,' he stressed to the *Observer* a few months after the ceremony, 'but it was very conventional in many ways and no director here could have got anywhere near to what Cameron has done with *Avatar*.'

He felt that the acting profession in general had often been particularly nervous about mocap developments. 'Actors, on the whole, are just really poorly educated about the whole process. There is still an idea that CGI characters are going to take over the world. It is not a question of an actor being smothered by visual effects. In fact, the exciting thing about it is that it means you can play anything.' Yet he understood some of the worries from thespians, which perhaps had more to do with career security than egotism. '[They think] if it's not the actor's face onscreen, they won't get the next job. There's a kind of vanity about that. Actors who care about the purity of acting and transformation are not worried about that.' He maintained that far from shrinking the number of potential roles, mocap could only expand the options. 'It enables you to play any manner of characters you might not normally be cast as.'

He also felt strongly that, as with stage acting, performance capture could not hide a weak performance. 'You can't rely on anything else but your own skill as an actor,' he said to the *Los Angeles Times* in 2011. 'You can't dial it up, lift the lip or the eyebrow. It has to be right at the core moment. If you don't have the performance, the rest is dressing.'

Crucially, though, Serkis believed that, far from being a strange new development in the world of performing and acting, technology was doing nothing more than catching up with the traditions of disguise and alter egos. 'It's part of the actor's journey. If you go back to Greek drama and *commedia dell'arte* – which used masks – I don't suppose audiences were questioning the technology or how the actor was cloaked. They were moved by the performance.' He felt that within a few years 'this strange superstition about performance capture will disappear when it's practised by more actors.'

Serkis would receive some criticism for his stance on

motion-capture. In late 2011, he was reported as saying that he had received negative correspondence from movie animators who accused him of taking too much credit for his characters in mocap movies. He told the *Hollywood Reporter*: 'I've been bombarded by hate mail from animators saying, "How dare you talk about 'your' character when all these people work on it after the fact? We're actors as well." He responded: 'They are actors in the sense that they create key frames and the computer will join up the dots, carefully choreograph a moment or an expression and accent it with an emotion. But that's not what an actor does. An actor finds things in the moment with a director and other actors that you don't have time to hand-draw or animate with a computer.'

In any case, Serkis has argued – to Scottish film critic Siobhan Synnot – that a form of performance capture has always existed on film for actors, 'in a million different ways, down to the choice of camera shot by the director, whether it's in slow motion or whether it's quick cut. Actors' performances do not stand alone in any film, and performance capture's no different.' In other words, no matter how an actor's performance is being technologically rejigged, its psychological energy remained. It went back to what he had learnt with director Jonathan Petherbridge in the Lancaster theatres of 1985: 'Any sort of role requires a certain amount of research and embodiment of the character and psychological investigation.'

CHAPTER 14

THE CGI CHAPLIN

At the time of writing, Andy Serkis has been a professional actor for over 25 years. Flexible and versatile, he has excelled in stage and screen work throughout that time. But such is his interest in collaboration, in the community spirit of theatre and filmmaking that stretches right back to the start of his career in Lancaster, that he continues to embrace new challenges at a time when he could settle for complacency.

For Andy Serkis, 2011 would be a year that juxtaposed grand and ambitious projects with small-scale ones. Whether working on low-budget films in London or lavish performance-capture work on the other side of the world, he delighted in a variety of commitments. The year began with his filming a cameo as a gangster kingpin for *Wild Bill*, the first film to be directed by Dexter Fletcher. It was an East End drama about a father who, following an eight-year spell in jail, is reunited with his sons, and it eventually opened in the UK in March 2012.

Two of 2011's most eagerly awaited movies would feature Serkis in starring roles. In 20th Century Fox's *Rise of the Planet of the Apes*, he would feature as the ape Caesar, who leads an uprising. Set in contemporary San Francisco, the film examines the battle between apes and human beings when one ape involved in laboratory experiments about genetic engineering rebels and leads an uprising. A group of scientists, led by Will Rodman (James Franco), are conducting experiments on apes into genetic engineering, in the hope that they can find a cure for Alzheimer's disease, which Rodman's father (John Lithgow) has now developed. In their efforts, they create an 'intelligent' super-ape with an unusually high level of sentience or awareness. Caesar (Serkis) leads an uprising of his fellow apes against humanity, and the primates run amok through San Francisco. It was described by Fox as 'a war for supremacy', with the human population placed at great risk.

Some wondered why Serkis had chosen to play another ape character so soon after Kong, but he was quite clear about his reasons for committing to the part. 'I hadn't intended to play another ape,' he told *The Sunday Times* in 2011. 'But I was sent the script and it was terrific – a really great, emotional origin story. The characters grabbed me.'

'With Kong, he was a huge technical challenge, because he was a 25-foot gorilla,' he said in July 2011. 'With Caesar, I actually believe it was even more of a formidable challenge. He realises that he is not the same as the human beings that he's been brought up by.'

Serkis had vivid memories of seeing the original *Planet of the Apes* film, made in 1968 and starring Charlton Heston and Roddy McDowall. It took him all the way back to his childhood. 'I watched it in the cinema in Ruislip where I grew up, and I'll never forget it,' he told the *Western Mail*. 'It was a really formative experience. Watching gorillas riding on horseback, ploughing through cornfields, rounding up humans in nets!' The film's shoot had taken place in Vancouver, Canada, then Los Angeles, over the summer of 2010 with Brit Rupert Wyatt directing. Cinematographer Andrew Lesnie had worked with Serkis on both *King Kong* and the *Lord of the Rings* trilogy. Other cast members included Brian Cox and Tom Felton, the latter previously Harry Potter's arch-enemy Draco Malfoy. But the prosthetic approach of Tim Burton's 2001 film of *Planet of the Apes* had been replaced in favour of creating and designing CGI apes, a process that developed at New Zealand's Weta Digital.

With Serkis now firmly established as a front-runner in performance capture, he was aware of how the special effects had grown more sophisticated within a decade. Now mocap action could be shot outdoors and on location, meaning that Serkis's contribution would not have to be enhanced later in post-production. No reshooting was necessary. 'It has become more of a transparent technology,' he explained to the *Western Mail*, 'which allows live action actors to play opposite performance capture roles played by actors on live action sets. That wasn't the case on the *Lord of the Rings*. Although I acted every single scene with the other actors on set, for any of Gollum's close-ups, I'd have to go back and do them separately on a small motion capture stage. It's a lot more fluid now and I can film on location. But it's changing every day.'

There had been early discussions in using real primates alongside Serkis's CGI Caesar ape. This plan was soon abandoned, for two reasons. Apes are not actors, and Rupert Wyatt felt there would have been 'moral problems' in using them in this way: 'There was no way we could put actors in simian suits... It would have been a bit of an irony to be telling the story of our most exploited and closest cousins, and use live apes to tell that story.'

Wyatt also argued that using real apes in the film would have had practical limitations. 'It would be virtually impossible to get them to do what we need them to do within our schedule,' he told *Total Film* magazine. 'The other Apes films dealt with talking apes, and apes that were humanoid in many ways. This film isn't about that. It's about apes as apes...' 'It's frighteningly realistic,' cast member John Lithgow said in awe of the 'zoological' authenticity of Caesar. 'This isn't corny ape makeup and leather jumpsuits. That's why it's so powerful.'

Serkis – described by Rupert Wyatt as 'our generation's Charlie Chaplin' for his commitment to CGI – regarded his experience as Caesar as one of the 'toughest challenges' of his career to date, because he played the creature in different stages of its life, from infancy to its adulthood as a revolutionary leader. Serkis explained: 'We very clearly charted his emotional intelligence, his physicality – moving from this young, innocent chimpanzee, seeing him grow in stature and become more physically upright and more human-like in his behaviour, without over-anthropomorphising him.' But the figure of Caesar was nevertheless cloaked in a recognisable form. 'The audience watching will be seeing a chimpanzee,' he emphasised, 'but it's a chimpanzee-plus.'

Some of Serkis's inspiration for the character of Caesar came from a real chimpanzee called Oliver. In the 1970s, the creature had been nicknamed the 'Humanzee'. 'You can see footage of him,' Serkis said. 'Basically he never went on all fours, which is totally unusual. He displayed a lot of human behaviour and was brought up by human beings. He was considered to be man and ape, they thought he was a hybrid. A lot of experiments were carried out on him and he became this sort of media freak and travelled all over the world. But when the experiments were finished, he was discarded, thrown into a cage and abandoned for about 30 years until he was rediscovered, completely psychologically broken down. He became the touchstone character for me on this film and with good reason.'

Critics were mostly very positive about Serkis's contribution. 'A bravura performance,' cheered the *Daily Mail*, for instance. But doubtful murmurs were aired about the notion of having Caesar speak. 'Suffice it to say that when the ape talks,' wrote David Thomson in the *Guardian*, 'his "liberty" is crushed by the simultaneous revelation of another all-too-familiar set of prison bars: he has wretched screenwriters.'

Rise of the Planet of the Apes opened in cinemas in August 2011, the same week as *Project Nim*, a documentary which chronicled an attempt in 1970s New York to raise a chimp as a child. In its first fortnight in US cinemas, it took nearly $105 million (around £65 million).

ANDY SERKIS: THE MAN BEHIND THE MASK

At a London screening of *Rise...*, a power cut two-thirds of the way through the film caused Serkis to wonder if it had anything to do with the riots which had broken out in various parts of the city that week. Several connections were made (some not terribly subtly) between the real-life events ('gangs of humans behaving like marauding chimpanzees' as one critic put it) and the film. Serkis had some sympathy for the way tensions had boiled over in London. 'There's been no leadership from the government,' he told one interviewer. 'And there's no cause on the streets. It's just a flailing around of pure anger.'

* * *

Autumn 2011 saw the opening of *The Adventures of Tintin: Secret of the Unicorn*, a film made in digital 3D and entirely in the mode of performance capture. Serkis would play Tintin's boozy and irascible sidekick Captain Archibald Haddock, with his immortal cry of 'Blistering barnacles!' Belgian-born Georges Remi (whose pen name, Hergé, came from reversing his initials) had written 23 books between 1929 and 1976 about the adventures of the young reporter Tintin, with Haddock introduced in the ninth book, 1941's *The Crab with the Golden Claws*. A 24th story – *Tintin and Alph-Art* – was unfinished at the time of Hergé's death in 1983.

The books have sold over 200 million units worldwide (their appeal never quite spread to the USA), but their author was never fond of French attempts in the 1960s to adapt them for film and television. He was, however, a fan of Steven Spielberg's *Raiders of the Lost Ark* (1981), whose hero, Indiana Jones, was very much in the mould of Tintin. Michael Farr, author of numerous books on the Tintin phenomenon, revealed that Hergé would have been thrilled at the prospect of Spielberg's remaking *Tintin*. 'He thought Spielberg was the only person who could ever do Tintin justice,' Farr told the *Sunday Times*.

It was in May 2007, almost exactly coinciding with the centenary of Hergé's birth, when the *Tintin* project was first announced to the press. It would be a trilogy, with Peter Jackson and Steven Spielberg directing at least one each of the three films. Jackson made an assurance that the trilogy would be respectful to the author's original designs, but that computer animation and mocap would be used in order to make the much-loved characters 'photorealistic'. The technology would enable the film to be directed as if it were live action as opposed to animation. 'We want Tintin's adventures to have the reality of a live-action film,' said Spielberg. 'Yet Peter and I felt that shooting them in a traditional live-action format would simply not honour the distinctive look of the characters and world that Hergé created.'

When Spielberg first had the brainwave of remaking Tintin, he thought of Jack Nicholson in the Captain Haddock role. In the end, the part went to a British actor: Andy Serkis. 'The whole thing was shot in one studio,' Serkis told *Time Out* in 2010. 'The idea is to create a three-dimensional rendering of Hergé's drawings. But the characters are truthful because they're acted, not just voiced over. It's the perfect tool to bring those stories to life.'

The performance-capture filming (based in Los Angeles) of *Secret of the Unicorn* would take just 32 days between

January and March 2009, but the postproduction work on the film would take another two years. The cast included Jamie Bell as Tintin himself (the third time he had worked on a movie with Serkis, following *Deathwatch* and *King Kong*), and Daniel Craig in the role of enemy Red Rackham. Simon Pegg and Nick Frost would feature as the Thomson and Thompson detective duo. The screenplay was originally to be co-written by three Brits: Steven Moffat (now showrunner on the BBC's *Doctor Who*), and the comic filmmakers Edgar Wright and Joe Cornish.

But little was revealed before its opening about the nature of the story or even what it would look like. Andy Serkis himself was mostly tight-lipped, bar describing it as 'extremely exciting' and promising that the characters would be 'animated 3D humanoids, essentially'. It was left to Simon Pegg to reveal one or two stories from the set and the performance-capture process. By now Serkis was so comfortable with the process of performance capture that it led Pegg to describe him as 'just the guv'nor. He's clearly at ease with the whole business, although I was reassured to see that even he doesn't look cool in spandex. Mind you, even Daniel Craig had problems rocking that look.' Pegg also told one American reporter in August 2010 that he was pinned to the floor by Spielberg during one rehearsal – although not for misbehaving. 'He demonstrated to Andy how Captain Haddock should beat me up,' he said. 'I was lying on the floor with him holding me by the lapel, shaking me, hitting me against the floor. I was just laughing because it was fucking Steven Spielberg!'

There were some disgruntled reactions when it was discovered that Serkis would be playing Haddock with a

Scottish accent. Aside from the character's love for Loch Lomond whisky, there was little suggestion in any of the books that he was anything other than English. Indeed, Hergé had been inspired to use the surname Haddock on seeing the word on a restaurant menu. Unaware of what 'haddock' was, he was enlightened by his wife, who told him it was 'a sad English fish'.

There were two very special surprise guests at a preview for the *Tintin* film in July 2011 at Comic-Con in San Diego, California. The 6,000-strong audience was thrilled to see what appeared to be a clip of Peter Jackson auditioning for the part of Haddock, but even more so when the director walked on to the stage for real. The next surprise came during a question-and-answer session when a disguised Andy Serkis asked the first question – shortly before his identity was revealed to the audience by Steven Spielberg.

Serkis had discovered that the global cult of Tintin was perhaps even more widespread than Tolkien. 'Recently I read that half the world or more has read *The Lord of the Rings*,' he told the *Daily Telegraph*, 'but then I found out that something like 75 per cent of the world knows the Tintin books. My children are starting to read Tintin now, so I am looking at them afresh. He has a forward-propelling curiosity, a simplicity and an innocence. He's a valuable role model.'

Of course, the problem with adapting something so popular for the screen is that while you're guaranteed a lot of attention and the likelihood of commercial success, affection for Tintin over the years meant that some critics would feel protective towards Hergé's creations. Some reacted strongly against the remake ('airless pastiche', 'painful'). A.L. Kennedy, author and Tintin fan, was more measured but noted: 'People get freaked out if people change anything they came into contact with as a kid. The filmmakers were almost already on a sticky wicket. The original was so beautifully drawn, I'm not sure how you would render that.'

When *Secret of the Unicorn* opened in cinemas in October 2011, some critics expressed astonishment at some of the action set-pieces, most notably a motorcycle chase through a market in Morocco. There were murmurs that the CGI effects had made the human characters unconvincing and lacking in personality. However, Serkis's Haddock was given mostly approving notices. 'Andy Serkis convincingly breathes life into his character's pixels,' said the *Daily Telegraph*, 'delivering a full-blooded and frequently hilarious turn.'

It was during some of the *Tintin* postproduction work at Weta in New Zealand that discussions were held about Serkis's part of Gollum in the project that millions of Tolkien fans had been awaiting since seeing *The Return of the King* at Christmas 2003. Ever since that *Lord of the Rings* final instalment, capping one of the biggest cinematic phenomena of the twenty-first century (which has now grossed close to $3 billion), some interviewers and fans had only one question. 'When are they going to make *The Hobbit?*'

Serkis had been fielding such questions for years. When asked in 2004 if he would ever play Gollum again, he was quietly committed, so long as Peter Jackson was. 'If Pete was to do *The Hobbit* – and I think he's keen on doing it,

I'm just not sure what the situation is like with the rights – I'd love to do it. I'd definitely play him again. He's still very much under my skin.'

It would have felt simply wrong to have cast anyone but Andy Serkis for the part of Gollum, but would his responsibilities extend beyond acting on *The Hobbit*? As late as 2010, Serkis remained cagey to *Time Out* magazine. 'We've discussed many things, but nothing's nailed down. Shooting *The Hobbit* will be completely different because it's an entirely fresh story, a new cast for the most part. I'm very excited about it.'

The Hobbit would not be just one film – for some time, it was intended to be two separate films. Initially, it looked as though Jackson would not be directing them, though he would have remained centrally involved in the projects. He told the *Daily Telegraph* in early 2010, 'I thought there might be something unsatisfying about directing two Tolkien movies after *Lord of the Rings*. I'd be trying to compete with myself and deliberately doing things differently.' So he appointed Mexican film director Guillermo del Toro, who opted to shoot *The Hobbit* as a conventional film. 'Which suits me,' said Jackson, 'because he wants to keep it in the same space as the original trilogy.'

However, in May 2010, del Toro left the project due to other commitments, and Jackson took his place as director after all. It was just one of a series of wobbles that delayed the start of the shoot to March 2011: there had been funding difficulties, major union disputes and a fire at the studio, which destroyed a number of the models. In addition, Jackson (only recently knighted in recognition of his services to cinema) had been admitted to hospital with a perforated stomach ulcer.

The first two *Hobbit* films – which are at the time of writing scheduled to premiere worldwide at Christmas 2012 and 2013 – were officially granted working titles in early 2011, namely *The Unexpected Journey* and *There and Back Again*. The first preview – a two-minute online trailer – appeared at the end of 2011, still around a year before *The Unexpected Journey*'s much-ballyhooed arrival. And at the end of July 2012, after shooting had wrapped, Peter Jackson announced an additional untitled third instalment for the summer of 2014, thus making *The Hobbit* a trilogy like *Lord of the Rings*.

The basic story of *The Hobbit* tells of how Bilbo Baggins is approached by the wizard Gandalf the Grey to set off on a quest to reclaim the Dwarf Kingdom of Erebor, conquered long ago by the dragon Smaug. With 13 dwarves in tow, he crosses dangerous territories, dodging orcs, giant spiders and sorcerers. The journey includes having to sneak through the goblin tunnels, and it is here that Bilbo meets Gollum, and gains possession of Gollum's 'preciousss', a Ring that holds the fate of Middle-earth.

Martin Freeman was cast as Bilbo Baggins. As well as Serkis returning as Gollum, *The Hobbit* would see Cate Blanchett (Galadriel) and Elijah Wood (Frodo) reprising their familiar alter egos from the *Lord of the Rings* trilogy. There were some other surprising castings, though, one being Bret McKenzie, half of the New Zealand comic duo Flight of the Conchords. They had already written a song called 'Frodo, Don't Wear the Ring', but McKenzie had also been an extra in *The Fellowship of the Ring* and *The*

Return of the King. In *The Hobbit* he was cast as an elf called Lindir.

Back in the guise of Gollum, Serkis found the first block of shooting on *The Hobbit* in spring 2011 a disconcerting experience to begin with. 'It was weird for the first couple of days,' he told *The Sunday Times*. 'As if I was doing a strange impression of a character I'd once played, which, over 10 years, had been owned by the public on a big level – so many impersonations, so many answerphone messages. It was a great place to start the shoot.'

While other performers were being hired for the marathon shoot – Stephen Fry (as the Master of Laketown), Barry Humphries (the Great Goblin), Benedict Cumberbatch (the voice of Smaug the dragon) – Peter Jackson was hunting for a suitable candidate to be the films' second unit director. He needed someone who would relate to the whole project, and who would sympathise with his vision. Andy Serkis seemed a logical choice, and even if he was startled to have been asked – 'There was this email out of the blue' – he half knew why he had been selected. 'I think I understand Peter's sensibility, and we have a common history of understanding Middle-earth. There really is a sense of Peter wanting people around him who totally understand the material and the work ethic.'

Nor would his directorial contribution be confined to directing performance capture. 'Yes, there is some performance capture,' he said, but I will be very much on the live-action sets and locations helping Peter to tell the story.' Because of the sheer scale of the project, his second unit contribution was almost as substantial as fully directing a feature. He was encouraged by Jackson to be bold, and to make strong decisions. 'You are shooting large sections of the movie, everything from big stunt sequences to drama to vista shots, everything you would do on a main unit. It's been amazing and Peter's put a lot of trust in me.'

Serkis acknowledged that the biggest challenge this time round would be getting to grips with 3D filmmaking and using it dramatically, to convey a point of view. But he would say very little about *The Hobbit*'s version of Gollum at this stage, other than offer the reassurance that he would appear in his 'truest form': 'He is very much a Gollum that people will recognise.'

At least, even on the other side of the world a dozen timezones away from Lorraine and his children, Serkis could still connect with them, thanks to other technological advances. 'I've had some interesting Skype moments where I'm cooking dinner in the evening, they're all having breakfast and everyone just wanders off. They're doing their own thing and I can hear them screaming down the hallway. I can just imagine myself being at home, but for now, I have to be there virtually – I'm a virtual dad.'

* * *

Despite so much acclaim for Andy Serkis's work in performance and motion capture, recognition at the Oscars continues to elude him. After working with him on *Rise of the Planet of the Apes*, fellow cast member James Franco had tried to drum up support to try and secure an Academy Award nomination for him, as a measure of how his motion capture work did not cancel out his 'real acting' ability. While Franco's efforts did not result in a nomination, Serkis appreciated the gesture nonetheless. 'I thought it was extraordinarily bold and honest,' he told *Movieline*, 'and quite frankly I was thrilled that James had written it. It just goes to show that an actor who is in pursuit of creating drama isn't prejudiced against live-action or performance capture, or any method of performing. [Franco] is one of the first actors who has been bold enough to really state, and in such a humble way, that the weight of the movie lies in Caesar's hands. I thought it was incredibly articulate.'

Serkis's skills and talents may have been ignored once again at the Academy Awards, but plaudits came from elsewhere. In February 2012, his role as Caesar landed him a Virtuosos Award at the Santa Barbara International Film Festival. That same month, he picked up a Visual Effects Society Award in the animated character category, also for Caesar. In March, he was nominated for the Best Actor category at the annual *Empire* magazine awards, though lost out to Gary Oldman (for *Tinker, Tailor, Soldier, Spy*).

Future plans for Andy Serkis seem both numerous and varied. He intends to continue developing the Imaginarium as the first British base for performance capture, and to direct a live-action feature for the first time. As if all this were not enough to satisfy his energies, other personal projects are pending: he announced in February 2010 that there was talk of his starring in a mocap film incarnation of Bertolt Brecht and Kurt Weill's *The Threepenny Opera*, for which Australian rock star Nick Cave would be contributing a music score. There is talk, too, of another teaming-up with composer Nitin Sawhney for the London stage work *Einstein/Tagore*, with Serkis in the role of Einstein for the second time in his career. And Caesar may also return to the big screen in another *Planet of the Apes* movie.

Serkis has even found time to co-found a film production company, Caveman Films, with the producer Jonathan Cavendish, to make comedy, horror films and thrillers. Caveman's first film, *All Good Children* – which brought Sam Taylor's novel *The Republic of Trees* to the screen – debuted at the Cannes Film Festival in May 2010.

Serkis still works incredibly hard, but is discerning with choosing projects. Occasionally, he commits to something he regrets and then retracts, as with a voiceover in 2009 for the Central Office of Information. 'It was about asylum seekers being tracked and it was really quite officious and nasty,' he told *Little White Lies* magazine the following year. 'Halfway through I was bleeding inside, so I said, "I'm really sorry, I know this has fucked up your day, but I can't. I just can't do it."' A man who, in his younger days, had routinely sold *Socialist Worker* on the streets, Serkis still has many of his principles firmly intact, although his feelings towards the Socialist Worker Party have cooled somewhat. 'I was involved in the party for some time,' he said in 2011. 'It just didn't work out with being an actor. That job demands that you empathise and see another person's point of view. I couldn't be that black and white. The characters I play are always in a grey area.'

Far away from some of the intense, furious personae of some of the work creations which lurk in that grey area, Andy Serkis continues to live quietly in north London with Lorraine and his three children, where he paints and practises yoga. Life at home is one of relaxation and stability. In Crouch End, he has occasionally appeared onstage at a local pub with members of the Blockheads, reviving some Ian Dury numbers for old times' sake. And for Christmas 2010 he led the crowd's countdown to have the festive lights switched on in Highgate.

He remains a disarmingly reluctant celebrity, politely tolerating the paparazzi at premieres, or being unfailingly charming when he's chatting about a film on *The One Show*, or handing an award to Dizzee Rascal at the BRIT Awards, or guesting on *Never Mind* the *Buzzcocks*. But one gets the sense that he appears at all not for his own self-gratification, but to gain recognition for the work – work that includes so many other people: actors, directors, writers, technicians.

For Serkis, there is little excuse for losing touch with what the business of acting involves and how it does not make one a big star. Without identifying the performer in question, he once told a newspaper about an actor on one of his many pictures, someone who was experiencing a career resurgence but could not relate to the job in hand. 'He had big tantrums, sat in his trailer for hours, leaving the crew sitting around doing nothing. His drug dealer was around, there were prostitutes on the set, all that kind of malarkey, just wasting people's time and being generally despicable.'

Philip Martin, who directed Serkis in 2008's TV film *Einstein and Eddington*, regards him as one of the great British actors of our time. 'He's incredibly intuitive. He can blend edgy and raw drama with the technical craft of acting, which is a rare thing. He can play charming, complicated, difficult, mercurial, dangerous and emotional characters. Or he can play all of them at the same time.'

Serkis remains keen to have a varied career. 'As an actor,

I'm very much like a billiard ball, bouncing around a table, never sure what kind of hole I'm going to drop into. I love the fact that my career has worked out that way.'

Serkis had received critical accolades for acting roles in human guises, but what perhaps set him apart from many of his contemporaries were his forays into acting from inside a hi-tech special effects suit. 'If a character moves and touches people, I feel very strongly that, within a few years, the audience will draw no distinction. We need to be a lot less Luddite in our approach to films. No one complained that those who helped John Hurt become *The Elephant Man* did so unfairly.'

In the long run, Serkis has been able to go about his daily business. For a brief period, he was besieged by *Lord of the Rings* fans to give autographs or to hiss like Gollum, something he was mostly happy to do. But his refusal to embrace celebrity outright means he can subsume himself into characters. 'That's what excites me about acting, being able to get inside another person's head and mind and body, and be that other person.'

He has claimed that 2003 – the year that *The Two Towers* swept the boards at the Academy Awards – was his first and probably his last experience of the Oscars. Could this be true? Does it matter, in fact? Versatile enough to excel at just about any well-written role – real-life, fictional or computer-generated – he is still only in his late forties, and so his varied career should roll on for years to come. 'You get that thing where people recognise you but can't quite place you,' he has said, but he welcomes the relative anonymity. 'I'm like a man in a mask,' he told the *Sunday Times*. 'And when the mask comes off, I can just be myself.'

ANDY SERKIS:
CREDITS

A ll entries refer to Serkis as actor or performer unless otherwise stated.

Some cast lists are selective and restricted to principal performers.

STAGE

1982–1985: *Productions at Department of Theatre Studies, Nuffield Studio Theatre, Lancaster University,* including:

Henry IV Part I by William Shakespeare (as Poins) (1983)

The Lucky Ones by Tony Marchant (as Tim) (1983)

Welcome Home by Tony Marchant (as Polo) (1983)

Gotcha by Barrie Keeffe (as The Kid) (1983)

Rosencrantz and Guildenstern are Dead by Tom Stoppard (role not known) (1983)

Othello by William Shakespeare (as Iago) (1984)

The Bundle by Edward Bond (as Tiger) (1984)

Paradise Sold, author unknown (as Stephen Craig) (1985)

Class Enemy by Nigel Williams (as Iron) (1985)

1985: *Jul–Aug:* ***Privates on Parade*** (role not known)
Dukes Playhouse, Lancaster
Directed by: Jonathan Petherbridge
Written by: Peter Nichols; music by: Denis King
Cast: Claude Close, Linda Dobell, John Fleming, Simon Gregor, James Quinn, Michael Roberts, Jon Strickland, Andy Whitfield

1985: *Sept:* ***Company*** (as Paul)
Dukes Playhouse, Lancaster
Directed by: Jonathan Petherbridge
Written by: Stephen Sondheim and George Furth
Cast: Andy Whitfield, Linda Dobell, Tricia Deighton, Jon Strickland, Diana Bishop, Hilary Cromie, Buffy Davis, Fenella Norman, Stephanie Sales, Claude Close, John Fleming

1985: *Oct:* ***The Winter's Tale*** (as Florizel)
Dukes Playhouse, Lancaster
Directed by: Jonathan Petherbridge
Written by: William Shakespeare
Cast: Tricia Deighton, Andy Whitfield, Robert French, John Fleming, Stefan Escreet, Claude Close, Gerard Bell, Hilary Cromie, Linda Dobell, Fenella Norman

1985: *Dec–Jan 1986:* ***Sleeping Beauty*** (role not known)
Dukes Playhouse, Lancaster
Directed by: Jonathan Petherbridge
Written by: David Cregan; Music by: Brian Protheroe

Cast: Ian Blower, Lizzie Queen, Dusty Hall, Linda Dobell, Tricia Deighton, Hilary Cromie, Jane Nash, Chris Larner, Andy Whitfield, Gerard Bell

1986: *Jan–Feb:* **The Dresser** (as Mr Oxenby)
Dukes Playhouse, Lancaster
Directed by: Jonathan Petherbridge
Written by: Ronald Harwood
Cast: Jon Strickland, Leader Hawkins, Angela Wyndham Lewis, Jane Nash, Ian Blower, Helena Paul

1986: *Mar:* **The Clerical Outfitters** (as Father)
Dukes Playhouse, Lancaster
Directed by: Jonathan Petherbridge
Written by: Elisabeth Bond
Cast: Denise Bryson, Anthony Deu, Rod Arthur, Ian Blower, Stefan Escreet, Jon Strickland, Andy Whitfield

1986: *Apr–May:***One Big Blow** (role not known)
Touring production from Dukes Playhouse, Lancaster
Directed by: Linda Dobell, Jonathan Petherbridge
Written by: John Burrows, music by Rick Lloyd
Cast: Rod Arthur, Roger Delves-Broughton, Stefan Escreet, Howard Ward, Andy Whitfield

1986: *May:* **Volpone** (as Corvino)
Dukes Playhouse, Lancaster

Directed by: Jonathan Petherbridge
Written by: Ben Jonson
Cast: Andy Whitfield, Roger Delves-Broughton,
Bev Willis, Linda Dobell, Liliana Baird

1986: *June–July:The Unexpected Guest* (as Jan Warwick)
Dukes Playhouse, Lancaster
Directed by: Jonathan Petherbridge
Written by: Agatha Christie
Cast includes: James Vaughan

1986: *Aug:* **Bouncers** (role not known)
*George Square Theatre, Edinburgh Fringe
Festival*
Presented by: Hull Truck Touring Company
Written and Directed by: John Godber
Cast: Dave Findlay, Tony Lound, John Collins
(*In 1987, Serkis would also tour the Republic of
Ireland in this play.*)

1986: *Dec–Jan 1987:* **Red Ridinghood** (as George)
Dukes Playhouse, Lancaster
Directed by: Jonathan Petherbridge
Adapted by: David Cregan
Music by: Brian Protheroe
Cast: John Fleming, Sandra Slinger, Andrew
Powrie, Angela Bain, Chris Larner, Bev Willis,
Jane Nash, Anna Skye, Pearce Quigley, James
Tavare, Melanie Sylvester

1987: *Feb:* **The Good Person of Sezchuan** (as Yang Sun)
Dukes Playhouse, Lancaster
Directed by: Jonathan Petherbridge
Written by: Bertolt Brecht
Cast includes: Chris Larner

1987: *Apr–May:* **Pravda** (as Doug Fantom and Hannon Spot)
Gateway Theatre, Chester
Directed by: Jonathan Petherbridge
Written by: Howard Brenton and David Hare
Cast: Nicholas Blane, Leader Hawkins, Claude
Close, Ian Blower, Michelle Butt, Roger Delves-
Broughton, John Fleming, Peter Forbes, Beccy
Wright

1987: *May–June:***Should Old Acquaintance** (as Jacko)
Gateway Theatre, Chester
Directed by: Peter Fieldson
Written by: Alan Bleasdale
Cast: John Ashton, Ian Blower, Michelle Butt,
John Fleming, Mark Brignal, Peter Forbes,
Beccy Wright, Roger Delves-Broughton

1987: *July:* **A Midsummer Night's Dream** (as Lysander)
Dukes Playhouse Company:
Play in the Park, Williamson Park, Lancaster
Directed by: Jonathan Petherbridge
Written by: William Shakespeare
Cast: Peter Forbes, Beccy Wright, Bev Willis,
Ian Blower, Claude Close, Jane Nash, Nicholas
Blane, Michelle Butt, John Fleming, Nick

> Murchie, Roger Delves-Broughton, Linda Dobell, Leader Hawkins

1987: *Nov:* **Berlin Days, Hollywood Nights** (as Maslow/ Mephistopheles)

> *The Place Theatre, London*
> Directed by: Pip Broughton
> Written by: Nigel Gearing
> Cast: Robin Soans, Fidelis Morgan, James Windsor, Josie Lawrence, John Atholl, Ted Richards.

1988: *Apr–Jul:* **Faust (Part I)** (as Tinker, Valentine, Frosch, A Minister)

> *Lyric Theatre, Hammersmith, London*
> Directed by: David Freeman
> Written by: Goethe/Christopher Marlowe, translation by Robert David Macdonald
> Cast: Simon Callow, Peter Lindford, Caroline Bliss, Paul Brightwell, Toby Davies, Jack Ellis, Linda Kerr-Scott, Robyn Moore, Alyson Spiro, Graham Walters, Ingrid Wells

1988: *Apr–Jul:* **Faust (Part II)** (as Emperor, Phorkyad, Nereus, Peter Profundis)

> *Lyric Theatre, Hammersmith, London*
> Directed by: David Freeman
> Written by: Goethe/Christopher Marlowe, translation by Robert David Macdonald
> Cast: Simon Callow, Peter Lindford, Caroline Bliss, Paul Brightwell, Toby Davies, Jack Ellis,

Linda Kerr-Scott, Robyn Moore, Alyson Spiro, Graham Walters, Ingrid Wells

1988: *Sept–Oct:* **Oliver!** (as Bill Sikes)
Theatre Royal, York
Directed by: Jonathan Petherbridge
Music & Lyrics by: Lionel Bart
Cast: Linda Dobell, Ted Richards, John Fleming, Angela Vale, Julian Bleach, Simon Clark, Nick Murchie, James Tomlinson

1988: *Nov–Dec:* **Macbeth** (as Porter/Sergeant/Caithness)
Royal Exchange Theatre, Manchester
Directed by: Braham Murray
Written by: William Shakespeare
Cast: David Threlfall, Frances Barber, John Hannah, John Watts, Ian Hastings, Wyllie Longmore, Tilly Tremayne, Peter Rumney, Stephen Lind, James Clyde, Dan Maxwell, Richard Henders, Sandy McDade

1989: *May:* **The Fireflies of the Boulevard present: The Revels of Gargantua in Exile** (role not known)
Hampstead Theatre, London
Written by: Martin Duncan
Cast: Chris Blades, Jim Broadbent, Tom Cairns, Stephen Daldry, Buffy Davis, Linda Dobell, John Dove, Martin Duncan, Jane Gurnett, Sue Holland, Darlene Johnson, Philip Joseph, Julie Peasgood, Steven Pimlott, Brian Protheroe, John Ramm, Alex Renton, Clare Venables

(The performance was staged in aid of the Theatre's building fund)

1989: *Sept–Oct:* **The Increased Difficulty of Concentration** (role not known)

> *Old Red Lion Theatre, London*
> Directed by: Tasmin Oglesby
> Written by: Václav Havel
> Cast: Roland Curram, Julie Righton, Sally Mortemore, Saskia Wickham, Caroline O'Neill, Adam Ray, Bill Radmall

1989: *Dec–Feb 1990:* **She Stoops to Conquer** (as Tony Lumpkin)

> *Royal Exchange Theatre, Manchester*
> Directed by: James Maxwell
> Written by: Oliver Goldsmith
> Cast: Una Stubbs, Lorraine Ashbourne, Graham Colclough, David Crellin, Karen Drury, Peter Faulkner, Ewan Hooper, Annie Lethbridge, Peter Lindford, Thomas Lockyer, John Southworth, Damian Wild
> *(In February and March 1990, the production embarked on a national tour, taking in theatres in Nottingham, Bradford, Cambridge, Basildon, Edinburgh and Belfast.)*

1990: *June–Sept:* **The Threepenny Opera** (as Macheath)

> *Bubble Theatre Tent, London*
> Directed by: Jonathan Petherbridge
> Written by: Kurt Weill and Bertolt Brecht

Cast: Fiona Bruce, Chris Larner, Caroline England, Hal Fowler, Philip Wright
(Each week, the production played in a different park in and around London: in Blackheath, Sutton, Redbridge, Bexley, Richmond Green, Newham, Walthamstow, Peckham Rye and Mitcham)

1990: *Dec–Jan 1991: Sugar* (as Jerry/Daphne)
West Yorkshire Playhouse, Leeds
Directed by: Martin Connor
Written by: Bob Merrill, Peter Stone and Jule Styne
Cast: Stephen Mann, Sarah Payne, Brian Greene, Wendi Peters, Daniel Ryan

1991: *Mar–Apr: Your Home in the West* (as Sean Grogan)
Royal Exchange Theatre, Manchester
Directed by: Braham Murray
Written by: Rod Wooden
Cast: David Threlfall, Lorraine Ashbourne, Gillian Kearney, Margo Gunn, Derek Walmsley, Dale Gregson, Dilys Hamlett

1991: *Jul–Aug: Doctor Heart* (as Doctor Jan Heart)
Royal Exchange Theatre, Manchester
Directed by: Braham Murray
Book by: Peter Muller, James Brody and Laszlo Tolcsvay
English version and Lyrics: Trevor Peacock
Cast: Lee Montague, Frances Tomelty, Ian

Bartholomew, Lorraine Ashbourne, John Branwell, Clive Hayward, Christopher Bramwell, Perry Douglin, Cliff Howells, Carol Noakes, Anthony Psaila

1991: *Sept–Oct: Decadence* (as Steve/Les)
Octagon Theatre, Bolton
Directed by: Ian Hastings
Written by: Steven Berkoff
Cast: Lorraine Ashbourne

1992: *Feb–Mar: The Revenger's Tragedy* (as Hippolito)
Quarry Theatre, West Yorkshire Playhouse, Leeds
Directed by: Jude Kelly
Written by: Cyril Tourneur
Cast: Reece Dinsdale, Tom Mannion, Dermot Walsh, Ann Penfold, Zara Turner, David Crellin, Ian Mercer, Ella Wilder, Trevor Laird, Hepburn Graham Jr., Michael Buffong, Dennis Edwards, Joe Spare, Jeffrey Robert

1992: *June: Cabaret* (as MC)
Crucible Theatre, Sheffield
Directed by: Roger Haines
Book by: Joe Masteroff
Music by: John Kander; lyrics by: Fred Ebb
Cast: Sally Ann Triplett, Simon Burke, Ursula Smith, John Levitt

1992: *Aug–Sept:Hush* (as Dogboy)
      Royal Court Theatre, London
      Directed by: Max Stafford-Clark
      Written by: April de Angelis
      Cast: Marion Bailey, Stephen Dillane, Debra Gillet, Dervla Kirwan

1993: *Jan–Mar:King Lear* (as Fool)
      Royal Court Theatre, London
      Directed by: Max Stafford-Clark
      Written by: William Shakespeare
      Cast: Tom Wilkinson, Hugh Ross, Philip Jackson, Iain Glen, Adrian Dunbar, Nigel Lindsay, Lia Williams, Saskia Reeves, Cara Kelly, Peter Hugo-Daly

1993: *Dec–Jan 1994:* **Punchbag** (as Peter)
      Hampstead Theatre, London
      Directed by: Glen Walford, fight director William Hobbs
      Written by: Robert Llewellyn
      Choreography: Danny John-Jules
      Cast: Eamonn Walker, Sophie Heyman, Buffy Davis

1994: *Oct–Nov:* **The Rover** (as Willmore)
      Jacob Street Studios, London
      Directed by: Jules Wright
      Written by: Aphra Behn
      Music by: Nitin Sawhney

Cast: Cecilia Noble, Maya Krishna Rao, Vicky Licorish

1995: *May–June:* **Unidentified Human Remains and the True Nature of Love** (as David)
        Royal Exchange Theatre, Manchester
        Directed by: Braham Murray
        Written by: Brad Fraser
        Cast: Patrick O'Kane, Marie Francis, Gary Oliver, Laurissa Kalinowski, Gary Whittaker, Amy Marston

1995: *Jul–Aug:* **Mojo** (as Potts)
        Royal Court Theatre, London
        Directed by: Ian Rickson
        Written by: Jez Butterworth
        Cast: Tom Hollander, Aidan Gillen, Hans Matheson, David Westhead, Matt Bardock

1997: *Mar–Apr:* **Hurlyburly** (as Phil)
        Old Vic, London
        Directed by: Wilson Milam
        Written by: David Rabe
        Cast: Rupert Graves, Daniel Craig, Elizabeth McGovern, Susannah Doyle, Kelly Macdonald, Stephen Dillane

1997: *June:* **This is a Chair** (various roles)
        Royal Court Downstairs, London
        Directed by: Stephen Daldry
        Written by: Caryl Churchill

Cast: Timothy Spall, Lennie James, Desmond Barrit, Linus Roache, Amanda Plummer, Sam Kelly, Ewen Bremner

1997: *Aug–Nov:* ***Hurlyburly*** (as Phil)
Queen's Theatre, Shaftesbury Avenue, London
Directed by: Wilson Milam
Written by: David Rabe
Cast: Rupert Graves, David Tennant, Jenny Seagrove, Mark Benton, Stephen Dillane, Susannah Doyle, Jessica Watson

2001: *Jun–Sept:* ***A Lie of the Mind*** (as Jake)
Donmar Warehouse, London
Directed by: Wilson Milam
Written by: Sam Shepard
Cast: Sinead Cusack, Catherine McCormack, Anna Calder-Marshall, Peter McDonald, Emma Rydal, Keith Bartlett, Andrew Tiernan

2002: *Sept–Nov:* ***Othello*** (as Iago)
Royal Exchange Theatre, Manchester
Directed by: Braham Murray
Written by: William Shakespeare
Cast: Paterson Joseph, Lorraine Ashbourne, John Branwell, John Cording, Emma Darwell-Smith, Katherine Kelly, Richard Metcalfe, Joseph Murray, Sam Spruell, Will Tracey, Ben Toye
(For his performance as Iago, Serkis won the award for Best Actor in a Supporting Role in

the September 2003 Theatrical Management Awards.)

2003: *Sep–Oct: The Double Bass* (Director and Designer)
Southwark Playhouse, London
Written by: Patrick Susskind, translated by
Michael Hofmann
Cast: Bev Willis

TELEVISION

1989: *29 Jan–5 Feb:The New Statesman* (as Peter Moran)
Yorkshire Television/ITV
(Featured in two episodes: '**The Wapping Conspiracy**' and '**The Haltemprice Bunker**')
Directed by: Geoffrey Sax; Produced by: Tony Charles
Written by: Laurence Marks and Maurice Gran
Cast: Rik Mayall, Michael Troughton, Marsha Fitzalan

1989: *8 Apr–13 May:* ***Morris Minor's Marvellous Motors***
(as Sparky Plugg)
Noel Gay/BBC North West/BBC1
(Featured in all six episodes of the series)
Directed by: Juliet May; Produced by: Nick Symons
Written by: Tony Hawks and Neil Mullarkey
Cast: Tony Hawks, Timothy Bateson, Camille

Coduri, Carl Gorham, Tony Haase, Una Stubbs

1989: *20 June: **Made in Spain*** (as Hooligan)
Central Television/ITV
Directed by: Herbert Wise; Produced by: Nicholas Palmer
Written by: Tony Grounds
Cast: Lill Roughley, Camille Coduri, Jill Benedict, Ella Wilder, Vincenzo Nicoli, Roger Lloyd Pack, Breffni McKenna

1989: *Sept–Jun 1992: **Streetwise*** (3 series) (as Owen)
Childsplay Productions/TVS/ITV
Series 1: 25 Sep–18 Dec 1989
Series 2: 11 Apr–13 Jun 1991
Series 3 (*Streetwise: Double Take*): 19 May–9 Jun 1992
Directors include: Ian Emes, Peter Tabern, Andrew Body, Bob Carlton, Simon Cellan-Jones
Producers: Peter Tabern, Valerie Farron
Writers include: Peter Tabern, Jon Hardy, Simon Moss, Al Ashton, Brendan J. Cassin, Matthew Graham
Cast: Stephen McGann (series 1 & 3), Suzanna Hamilton (series 1 & 2), Sara Sugarman, Garry Roost, Paterson Joseph, Sorcha McMahon (series 1 & 2), Nicola Cowper, Joanne Ridley (series 2 & 3), Gerry Cowper (series 3), Ken Campbell (series 3), Kieran O'Brien (series 3), Matt Bradley (series 3)

1989: *30 Sep: **Saracen*** (as Dudin)
Central Independent Television/ITV
(Featured in the episode '**Into Africa**')
Directed by: Tom Clegg; Produced by: Deirdre Keir
Written by: Ted Childs and Chris Kelly
Cast: Christian Burgess, Patrick James Clarke, Michael Byrne, John Bennett, Ingrid Lacey

1990: *27 Mar:* ***The Bill*** (as Dean Platt)
Thames Television/ITV
(Featured in the episode '**One of the Boys**')
Directed by: Alan Wareing; Produced by: Michael Simpson
Written by: Jonathan Rich
Cast: Eric Richard, Nula Conwell, Christopher Ellison, Jon Iles, Mark Wingett, Kevin Lloyd, Trudie Goodwin, Lynne Miller, Larry Dann, Nicola Wright, Matt Bradley

1992: *26 Dec:* ***The Darling Buds of May*** (as Greville)
Yorkshire Television/ITV
(Featured in the episode '**Le Grand Weekend**')
Directed by: Gareth Davies; Produced by: Simon Lewis
Written by: Stephen Bill, adapted from original work by H. E. Bates
Cast: David Jason, Pam Ferris, Philip Franks, Catherine Zeta Jones, Abigail Rokison, Isla Blair, John Harding

1993: *27 Apr:* **The Bill** (as Alex Rackin)
    Thames Television/ITV
    (Featured in the episode '**Return to Sender**')
    Directed by: Jeremy Silberston
    Written by: Michael Jenner
    Cast: Kevin Lloyd, Eric Richard, Kerry Peers, Mark Wingett, Trudie Goodwin, Andrew Paul, Christopher Ellison, Tony O'Callaghan, Joseph Kpobie, Vivienne Martin, Helen Rimmer, Janet Steel

1994: *21 Jan:* **The Chief** (as Jacko Dolan)
    Anglia Television/ITV
    (Featured in **Series 4, Episode 3**)
    Directed by: Roger Gartland; Produced by: Ruth Boswell
    Written by: Ray Jenkins
    Cast: Martin Shaw, T. P. McKenna, Karen Archer, Tom Mannion

1994: *24 Mar–7 Apr:* **Grushko** (as Pyotr)
    Mark Forstater Productions/Europool/BBC1
    (Featured in all three episodes)
    Directed by: Tony Smith; Produced by: Nicky Lund
    Written by: Philip Kerr
    Cast: Brian Cox, Paul Brennen, Eve Matheson, Jack Klaff, Stephen McGann, Amanda Mealing, Robert Llewellyn, Dave Duffy

1994: *24 Apr: **Pie in the Sky** (as Maxwell)*
Witzend Productions/BBC1
(Featured in the episode **'Passion Fruit Fool'**)
Directed by: George Case; Producers: Jacky Stoller, David Wimbury
Written by: Paul Hines
Cast: Richard Griffiths, Maggie Steed, Joe Duttine, Alison McKenna, Angela Clarke, Jim Carter, Patrick O'Kane

1994: *17 Nov–22 Dec: **Finney** (as Tom)*
Zenith/Tyne Tees Television/ITV
(Featured in all six episodes)
Directed by: David Hayman; Produced by: Nigel Stafford-Clark
Written by: David Kane
Cast: David Morrissey, Melanie Hill, Clive Russell, Pooky Quesnel, John Woodvine, David Hayman, Christopher Fairbank, Mark Benton

1996: *11 Mar: **Kavanagh QC** (as O'Brien)*
Central/Carlton UK Productions/ITV
(Featured in the episode **'The Burning Deck'**)
Directed by: Charles Beeson; Produced by: Chris Kelly
Written by: Russell Lewis
Cast: John Thaw, Geraldine James, Sean Chapman, Rupert Penry-Jones, Lisa Harrow, Ray Winstone, Anna Chancellor

1997: *23 Dec:* **Agatha Christie's The Pale Horse** (as Sgt Corrigan)

United Film & Television/Anglia Television/ITV
Directed by: Charles Beeson; Produced by: Adrian Bate
Written by: Alma Cullen, adapted from the novel by Agatha Christie
Cast: Colin Buchanan, Jayne Ashbourne, Hermione Norris, Leslie Phillips, Michael Byrne, Jean Marsh, Ruth Madoc

1998: *6–27 Sept:* **The Jump** (as Steven Brunos)
Warner Sisters/Central/ITV
(Featured in all four parts)
Directed by: Richard Standeven; Produced by: Lavinia Warner
Written by: Adrian Hodges, based on the novel by Martina Cole
Cast: Adrian Dunbar, Jonathan Cake, Susan Vidler, Sue Johnston, Michael Angelis, John Light, Mark Benton

1999: *17 Jan:* **Shooting the Past** (as Styeman)
TalkBack Productions/BBC2
(Featured in **Part 2** only of this three-part drama)
Written and Directed by: Stephen Poliakoff; Produced by: John Chapman
Cast: Lindsay Duncan, Timothy Spall, Liam Cunningham, Billie Whitelaw, Emilia Fox, Arj Barker

1999: *16–23 May:* ***Touching Evil*** (as Michael Lawler)
United Film & Television/Anglia Television/ITV
(Featured in both parts of the story **'Innocent'**)
Directed by: Bill Eagles; Produced by: Philip Leach
Written by: Tony Etchells
Cast: Robson Green, Nicola Walker, Michael Feast, Shaun Dingwall, Tara Moran

1999: *5–19 Dec:* ***Oliver Twist*** (as Bill Sikes)
Diplomat Films/United Productions/WGBH (Boston)/HTV/ITV
(Featured in **Parts 2–4** of the four-part adaptation)
Directed by: Renny Rye; Produced by: Keith Thompson
Written by: Alan Bleasdale, adapted from the work by Charles Dickens
Cast: Julie Walters, Robert Lindsay, Emily Woof, David Ross, Michael Kitchen, Lindsay Duncan, Desmond Barrit, Roger Lloyd Pack, Sam Smith, Alex Crowley

2000: *30 Apr–1 May:* ***Arabian Nights*** (as Kasim)
Hallmark Entertainment
Directed by: Steve Barron; Produced by: Dyson Lovell
Dramatised by: Peter Barnes
Cast: Mili Avital, Alan Bates, James Frain, Tcheky Karyo, John Leguizamo, Hugh Quarshie,

Jason Scott Lee, Dougray Scott, Vanessa Mae, Rufus Sewell, Jim Carter, Alexei Sayle
(The broadcast dates here refer to the two-part film's terrestrial premiere in the UK – on BBC1 on consecutive nights.)

2003: *27 Apr (USA):* **The Simpsons** (as guest voice of Cleanie)
Gracie Films/20th Century Fox Television/Fox Network
(Featured as guest voice in the episode **'Dude, Where's My Ranch?'**)
Directed by: Chris Clements
Written by: Ian Maxtone-Graham
Voice cast: Dan Castalleneta, Julie Kavner, Nancy Cartwright, Yeardley Smith, Hank Azaria, Harry Shearer
Guest voice cast: Jonathan Taylor Thomas, David Byrne
(This episode was first transmitted in the UK on Sky One on 16 August 2003.)

2004: *27 Nov:* **Spooks** (as Riff)
Kudos/BBC3/BBC1
(Featured in the episode **'Celebrity'***)
Directed by: Bill Anderson; Produced by: Andrew Woodhead
Written by: Howard Brenton
Cast: Peter Firth, David Oyelowo, Hugh Simon, Rupert Penry-Jones, Shauna Macdonald, Rory MacGregor, Nicola Walker, Olga Sosnovska,

Raza Jaffrey, Rebecca Palmer, Tim McInnerny, Arabella Weir

(The series was broadcast in some countries – including the USA and France – under the title MI-5)

*This episode was first broadcast on BBC3. Its terrestrial premiere occurred on 29 Nov 2004 on BBC1.

2006: *26 Oct: **Longford*** (as Ian Brady)
Granada Film/HBO/Channel 4
Directed by: Tom Hooper
Produced by: Catherine Wearing, David Boulton, Helen Flint
Written by: Peter Morgan
Cast: Jim Broadbent, Samantha Morton, Lindsay Duncan, Anton Rodgers, Robert Pugh, Sarah Crowden

2006: *24 Nov: **Simon Schama's The Power of Art*** (as Vincent Van Gogh)
BBC2
Directed and Produced by: David Belton
Presented by: Simon Schama

2007: *18 Mar: **Arena: Underground*** (as Voice of the Driver)
Lone Star Productions/BBC4
Directed by: Zimena Percival
Shown as part of a themed evening of programmes called 'Tube Night'.

2007: *13–31 Aug:* * *Monkey Life* (Narrator)
Primate Planet/Five
(Narration for all 14 episodes)
Directed & Produced by: Claudia Riccio, Natalie Wilkinson
**No episode was broadcast on 27 Aug 2007.*

2008: *26 Oct–11 Dec:* **Little Dorrit** (as Rigaud/Blandois)
BBC/WGBH (Boston)/BBC1
Directed by: Dearbhla Walsh; Produced by: Lisa Osborne
Written by: Andrew Davies, adapted from the work by Charles Dickens
Cast: Matthew Macfadyen, Claire Foy, Tom Courtenay, Sue Johnston, Freema Agyeman, Maxine Peake, Bill Paterson, James Fleet, Emma Pierson, Rosie Cavaliero, Alun Armstrong

2008: *22 Nov:* **Einstein and Eddington** (as Albert Einstein)
Company Pictures/HBO Films/Pioneer Pictures/BBC2
Directed by: Philip Martin; Produced by: Mark Pybus
Written by: Peter Moffat
Cast: David Tennant, John Bowe, Rebecca Hall, Lucy Cohu, Patrick Kennedy, Jim Broadbent, Anton Lesser

2010: *30 Nov:* **Imagine: The Weird Adventures of Eadweard Muybridge** (as Muybridge)
BBC1

Directed and Produced by: Jill Nicholls
Presenter and Series Editor: Alan Yentob

2010: *6 Dec:Accused* (as Liam Black)
RSJ Films/BBC1
(Featured in the episode **'Liam's Story'**)
Directed by: Richard Laxton; Produced by: Sita Williams
Written by: Daniel Brocklehurst and Jimmy McGovern
Cast: Jodie Whittaker, Neve McIntosh, Tom Ellis, Mia Smith

2010: *27 Dec:* **Andy Serkis – Playing Screwtape** (as Screwtape)
Doherty Associates/Sky Arts 1
Directed by: Pete Doherty; Produced by: Philip Glassborow
Also featuring: Geoffrey Palmer, Douglas Gresham
*(Documentary about the making of the radio drama **Screwtape**)*

2011: *10 Aug:* **Natural World: Empire of the Desert Ants** (Narrator)
BBC2
Producer: Ian Gray; Series Editor: Steve Greenwood

FILM

1994: *Prince of Jutland* (as Torsten)
Directed by: Gabriel Axel
Cast: Gabriel Byrne, Helen Mirren, Christian Bale,
Tony Haygarth, Steven Waddington, Ewen Bremner,
Freddie Jones, Brian Cox, Kate Beckinsale
*(The film was released in North America under the
title 'Royal Deceit')*

1995: *The Near Room* (as Bunny)
Directed by: David Hayman
Cast: Adrian Dunbar, David O'Hara, David Hayman,
Julie Graham, Emma Faulkner, James McAvoy

1996: *Stella Does Tricks* (as Fitz)
Directed by: Coky Giedroyc
Cast: Kelly Macdonald, James Bolam, Hans
Matheson, Ewan Stewart, Paul Chahidi, Lindsay
Henderson

1997: *Career Girls* (as Mr Evans)
Directed by: Mike Leigh
Cast: Katrin Cartlidge, Lynda Steadman, Kate Byers, Mark Benton

1997: *Loop* (as Bill)
Directed by: Allan Niblo
Cast: Emer McCourt, Alisa Bosschaert, Tony Selby, Susannah York

1997: *Mojo* (as Sid)
Directed by: Jez Butterworth
Cast: Ian Hart, Ewen Bremner, Hans Matheson, Aidan Gillen, Martin Gwynn Jones, Harold Pinter, Ricky Tomlinson

1998: *Among Giants* (as Bob)
Directed by: Sam Miller
Cast: Pete Postlethwaite, Rachel Griffiths, James Thornton, Lennie James, Rob Jarvis, Alan Williams

1998: *The Tale of Sweety Barrett* (as Leo King)
Directed by: Stephen Bradley
Cast: Brendan Gleeson, Brendan O'Carroll, Tony Rohr, Lynda Steadman, Dylan Murphy, Liam Cunningham

1999: *Topsy-Turvy* (as John D'Auban)
Directed by: Mike Leigh
Cast: Jim Broadbent, Allan Corduner, Timothy Spall, Lesley Manville, Ron Cook

2000: *Five Seconds to Spare* (as Chester)
Directed by: Tom Connolly
Cast: Max Beesley, Ray Winstone, Gary Condes, Ronny Jhutti, Kris Marshall, Sarah-Jane Potts, Lee Ross, Rachel Weisz, John Peel

2000: *The Jolly Boys' Last Stand* (as Anthony 'Spider' Dale)
Directed by: Christopher Payne
Cast: Milo Twomey, Rebecca Craig, Anton Saunders, Edward Woodall, Matt Wilkinson, Rupam Maxwell, Sacha Baron Cohen, Mark Frost, Sean Graham, Jo Martin

2000: *Pandaemonium* (as John Thelwall)
Directed by: Julien Temple
Cast: Linus Roache, John Hannah, Samantha Morton, Emily Woof, Emma Fielding, Samuel West, Guy Lankester, Dexter Fletcher

2000: *Shiner* (as Mel)
Directed by: John Irvin
Cast: Michael Caine, Martin Landau, Frances Barber, Frank Harper, Matthew Marsden, Kenneth Cranham, Danny Webb, Nicola Walker

2001: *The Lord of the Rings: The Fellowship of the Ring* (as Gollum/voice of Witch-King)
Directed by: Peter Jackson
Cast: Elijah Wood, Ian McKellen, Orlando Bloom, Sean Astin, Sean Bean, Cate Blanchett, Ian Holm, Christopher Lee, Dominic Monaghan, Viggo

Mortensen, John Rhys-Davies, Liv Tyler, Hugo Weaving

2002: *24 Hour Party People* (as Martin Hannett)
Directed by: Michael Winterbottom
Cast: Steve Coogan, Lennie James, Paddy Considine, Danny Cunningham, John Simm, Ralf Little, Shirley Henderson

2002: *Deathwatch* (as Pvt Thomas Quinn)
Directed by: Michael J. Bassett
Cast: Jamie Bell, Ruaidhri Conroy, Mike Downey, Laurence Fox, Dean Lennox Kelly, Torben Liebrecht, Kris Marshall, Hans Matheson, Hugh O'Conor, Matthew Rhys, Hugo Speer

2002: *The Escapist* (as Ricky Barnes)
Directed by: Gilles Mackinnon
Cast: Jonny Lee Miller, Gary Lewis, Jodhi May, Paloma Baeza, Vas Blackwood, Philip Barantini

2002: *The Lord of the Rings: The Two Towers* (as Gollum)
Directed by: Peter Jackson
Cast: Elijah Wood, Ian McKellen, Orlando Bloom, Sean Astin, Cate Blanchett, Bernard Hill, Christopher Lee, Liv Tyler, Dominic Monaghan, Viggo Mortensen, Miranda Otto, John Rhys-Davies, Hugo Weaving, David Wenham

2003: *The Lord of the Rings: The Return of the King* (as Gollum)

Directed by: Peter Jackson
Cast: Elijah Wood, Ian McKellen, Orlando Bloom, Sean Astin, Viggo Mortensen, Cate Blanchett, Liv Tyler, Billy Boyd, Bernard Hill, Ian Holm, Dominic Monaghan, Miranda Otto, John Rhys-Davies, Hugo Weaving, David Wenham

2004: *Blessed* (as Father Carlo)
Directed by: Simon Fellows
Cast: Heather Graham, James Purefoy, Fionnula Flanagan, Alan McKenna, David Hemmings

2004: *13 Going On 30* (as Richard Kneeland)
Directed by: Gary Winick
Cast: Jennifer Garner, Mark Ruffalo, Judy Greer, Kathy Baker, Phil Reeves

2005: *King Kong* (as Kong/Lumpy)
Directed by: Peter Jackson
Cast: Naomi Watts, Jack Black, Adrien Brody, Thomas Kretschmann, Colin Hanks, Evan Parke, Jamie Bell

2006: *Alex Rider: Stormbreaker* (as Mr Grin)
Directed by: Geoffrey Sax
Cast: Alex Pettyfer, Mickey Rourke, Sophie Okonedo, Ewan McGregor, Bill Nighy, Damian Lewis, Stephen Fry, Alicia Silverstone, Ashley Walters, Robbie Coltrane

2006: *The Prestige* (as Alley)
Directed by: Christopher Nolan

Cast: Hugh Jackman, Christian Bale, Michael Caine, Rebecca Hall, Scarlett Johansson, David Bowie

2006: *Flushed Away* (as voice of Spike)
Directed by: David Bowers, Sam Fell
Voice cast: Hugh Jackman, Kate Winslet, Ian McKellen, Bill Nighy, Jean Reno, Shane Richie

2007: *Extraordinary Rendition* (as Maro, the Interrogator)
Directed by: Jim Threapleton
Cast: Omar Berdouni, Ania Sowinski, Jimmy Yuill, Hugh Ross

2007: *Sugarhouse* (as Hoodwink)
Directed by: Gary Love
Cast: Steven Mackintosh, Ashley Walters, Ted Nygh, Adam Deacon, Tracy Whitwell

2008: *The Cottage* (as David)
Directed by: Paul Andrew Williams
Cast: Reece Shearsmith, Jennifer Ellison, Steven O'Donnell, David Legeno

2008: *Inkheart* (as Capricorn)
Directed by: Iain Softley
Cast: Brendan Fraser, Paul Bettany, Helen Mirren, Jim Broadbent, Eliza Hope Bennett, Jamie Foreman, John Thomson

2010: *Sex & Drugs & Rock & Roll* (as Ian Dury; also Executive Producer)

Directed by: Mat Whitecross
Cast: Naomie Harris, Olivia Williams, Mackenzie Crook, Bill Milner, Ray Winstone, Toby Jones, Wesley Nelson, Tom Hughes

2010: *Brighton Rock* (as Mr Colleoni)
Directed by: Rowan Joffe
Cast: Sam Riley, Andrea Riseborough, Helen Mirren, John Hurt

2010: *Burke and Hare* (as William Hare)
Directed by: John Landis
Cast: Simon Pegg, Tom Wilkinson, Isla Fisher, Tim Curry, David Hayman, Christopher Lee, Jessica Hynes, Ronnie Corbett, Reece Shearsmith

2010: *Animals United* (as voice of Charles)
Directed by: Reinhard Klooss, Holger Tappe
Voice cast: Jim Broadbent, Stephen Fry, Omid Djalili, Dawn French, Joanna Lumley

2011: *Rise of the Planet of the Apes* (as Caesar)
Directed by: Rupert Wyatt
Cast: James Franco, Freida Pinto, Tom Felton, Brian Cox, John Lithgow

2011: *Death of a Superhero* (as Dr Adrian King)
Directed by: Ian Fitzgibbon
Cast: Thomas Sangster, Sharon Horgan, Jane Brennan, Aisling Loftus, Ned Dennehy, Michael McElhatton

2011: *The Adventures of Tintin: Secret of the Unicorn* (as Captain Haddock)
Directed by: Steven Spielberg
Cast: Jamie Bell, Daniel Craig, Nick Frost, Simon Pegg, Mackenzie Crook

2011: *Arthur Christmas* (as voice of Lead Elf)
Directed by: Sarah Smith, Barry Cook
Voice cast: James McAvoy, Hugh Laurie, Bill Nighy, Jim Broadbent, Imelda Staunton, Ashley Jensen, Michael Palin, Robbie Coltrane, Joan Cusack, Sanjeev Bhaskar, Jane Horrocks

2011: *Wild Bill* (as Glen)
Directed by: Dexter Fletcher
Cast: Charlie Creed-Miles, Liz White, Will Poulter

2012: *The Hobbit: An Unexpected Journey* (as Gollum; also 2nd Unit Director)
Directed by: Peter Jackson
Cast: Martin Freeman, Ian McKellen, Richard Armitage, Luke Evans, Elijah Wood, Orlando Bloom, Cate Blanchett, Evangeline Lilly, Hugo Weaving, Ian Holm, Billy Connolly, Barry Humphries, James Nesbitt, Bret McKenzie, Christopher Lee

2013: *The Hobbit: There and Back Again* (as Gollum; also 2nd Unit Director)
Directed by: Peter Jackson
Cast: Martin Freeman, Ian McKellen, Elijah Wood, Orlando Bloom, Cate Blanchett, Evangeline Lilly,

Hugo Weaving, Benedict Cumberbatch, Luke Evans, Richard Armitage, Christopher Lee, Stephen Fry, Barry Humphries, James Nesbitt

FORTHCOMING / IN DEVELOPMENT
(at time of writing):

Freezing Time (as Erickson; also Director)
The Spider (as Everett)
Directed by: Robert Sigl
Cast: Malcolm McDowell, Eleanor Tomlinson

VIDEOS/SHORT FILMS

1996: *Neneh Cherry: Woman* (promotional video)
Directed by: Jamie Thraves

1998: *Insomnia* (as Harry)
Directed by: Andrew Gunn
Cast: Melanie Comerford, Steven O'Donnell, Anne Orwin, Susan Vidler
*(The film was broadcast by Channel 4 on 26 Jan 1999, as part of its late-night slot for short films, **The Shooting Gallery**.)*

1998: *Clueless* (as Dave)
Directed by: Jonathan Karlsen
Cast: Jason Flemyng, Susan Vidler, Matt Bardock

2000: *Jump* (as Shaun)
Directed by: Simon Fellows

Cast: John Thomson, Freddie Davies, Lee Ross, Lorraine Ashbourne

2001: *Snake* (Director)
Cast: Rupert Graves, Bev Willis, Lorraine Ashbourne

2003: *The Long and the Short of It* (Assistant Location Manager)
Directed by: Sean Astin
Cast: Andrew Lesnie, Praphaphorn 'Fon' Chansantor, Paul Randall, Peter Jackson

2003: *Greenpeace UK: Save the Forests* (appearance)
Also featuring: David Attenborough, Ewan McGregor

2003: *The Ancient Forests* (appearance)
Directed by: Julien Temple
Also featuring: Emma Fielding

2004: *Standing Room Only* (as Granny/Rastafarian/Hunter Jackson)
Directed and written by: Deborra-Lee Furness
Cast: William Ash, Nicholas Audsley, Sophie Dahl, Maureen Lipman, Joanna Lumley, Mary Elizabeth Mastrantonio, Michael Gambon, Hugh Jackman
*(The 12-minute film premiered at the Melbourne International Film Festival, Australia, on 26 July 2003. It also made up a segment of **Stories of Lost Souls**, released in 2005.)*

2006: *Stingray* (as voice of Stingray)
Directed by: Neil Chordia
Cast: Dominic West, Mathew Horne, Lucy Punch
(The 13-minute film premiered at the Palm Springs Short Films Festival in August 2006.)

2009: *Suicide Man* (as voice of Taxi Despatch)
Directed by: Craig Pickles
Cast: Claire Cathcart, Ralph Ineson, Lesley Manville, David Westhead
(25-minute film.)

AUDIO

RADIO/AUDIOBOOKS

1996: *27 Oct:* **Talking to Mars** (as Dimi)
BBC Radio 3
Directed by: Hilary Norrish
Written by: David Edgar
Cast: Henry Goodman, Dorothy Tutin, Selina Cadell, Kate Fenwick
(*This play was broadcast as part of a season of productions called* **Drama Now.**)

2008: *23 Aug–15 Nov:* **The Brightonomicon** (as Count Otto Black)
Hokus Bloke Productions/Ladbroke Radio/BBC Audio Books.
(Featured in all 13 episodes)
Written by: Robert Rankin with Elliott Stein
Cast: David Warner, Jason Isaacs, Rupert Degas,

Michael Fenton-Stevens, Mark Wing-Davey, Ben Miller, Martin Jarvis, Kerry Shale, Sarah Douglas, Kevin Eldon, Patrick Barlow, Brian Murphy, Jonathan Cecil, Katherine Parkinson, Rich Fulcher
(Although broadcast as a radio serial on the BBC digital station BBC7, it was previously issued as an audiobook on 14 Feb 2008.)

2009: *15 Oct:* **C.S. Lewis's The Screwtape Letters** (as Screwtape)
(released) *Focus on the Family Radio Theatre/Tyndale*
Directed by: Paul McCusker
Cast: Bertie Carvel, Geoffrey Palmer, Philip Bird, Roger Hammond, Laura Michelle Kelly, Douglas Gresham
(The package contains four CDs and one DVD. It has not, at the time of writing, been serialised on British radio, although it has aired on some American stations.)

2010: *27 Mar:* **Reasons to Be Cheerful: The Ian Dury Story** (Narrator)
BBC Radio 2
Producer: Neil Cowling
(This documentary about Dury's life and career had previously been broadcast in January 2010 on the BBC digital station 6Music.)

2011: *16 Feb:* **Song Stories: Mack the Knife** (Narrator)
BBC Northern Ireland/BBC Radio 2
Producer: Owen McFadden

ADVERTISING VOICEOVERS

2006: *Vodafone*

Date Unknown: *NatWest Bank*

GAMES

2005: *Peter Jackson's King Kong: The Official Game of the Movie* (as voice of Lumpy)
Directed by: Michel Ancel
Voice cast: Jack Black, Adrien Brody, Colin Hanks, Thomas Kretschmann, Naomi Watts

2006: *Lord of the Rings: Battle for Middle Earth II – Rise of the Witch King* (as voice of Gollum)
Directed by: Jill Donald
Voice cast: Elijah Wood, Sean Astin, Billy Boyd, Christopher Lee, Ian McKellen, Dominic Monaghan, John Rhys-Davies, Jason Carter, Hugo Weaving

2007: *Heavenly Sword* (as voice of King Bohan; also Dramatic Director)
Directed by: Ben Hibon, Nina Kristensen
Voice cast: Anna Torv, Ewan Stewart, Lydia Baksh, Race Davies, Steven Berkoff, Richard Ridings, Stuart Adcock

2009: *Risen* (as voice of The Inquisitor; also Dramatic Director)
Directed by: Andrew S. Walsh
Voice cast: John Rhys-Davies, Lena Headey, Gus Gallagher, Adrian Bower, Brendan Coyle

2010: *Enslaved: Odyssey to the West* (as voices of Monkey/Pyramid; also Motion Capture Director)
Directed by: Nina Kristensen
Voice cast: Lindsey Shaw, Richard Ridings

FURTHER READING

Andy Serkis's own memoir about his experience working on *The Lord of the Rings* trilogy – *Gollum: How We Made Movie Magic* (Collins/HarperCollins, 2003; with contributions from Gary Russell) was an extremely useful resource, as was Brian Sibley's *The Lord of the Rings: Official Movie Guide* (Collins/HarperCollins, 2001). Serkis's own website at www.serkis.com is regularly updated with plenty of news and information about his ongoing career.

INDEX